CW01665684

Laboratory of Immediate Architectural Intervention

intravention
durations
effects

Umeå School of Architecture

The Deutsche Nationalbibliothek lists this publication
in the Deutsche Nationalbibliografie;
detailed bibliographic information is available
on the internet at http://dnb.d-nb.de

Cover Images:
Front Cover, A Relational Mesh, 2013 © Alberto Altés Arlandis
Back Cover, CMYK 0 100 100 20 Red UMA, 2013 © Alberto Altés Arlandis

Alberto Altés Arlandis and Oren Lieberman, Editors
Intravention, Durations, Effects
Notes of Expansive Sites and Relational Architectures

© Copyright 2013 by Authors/Editors and Spurbuchverlag, Am Eichenhügel 4, 96148 Baunach, Germany
All rights reserved.

Publication © by Spurbuchverlag
1. print run 2013

No part of the work must in any mode (print, photocopy, microfilm, CD or any other process) be reproduced nor – by application of electronic systems – processed, manifolded nor broadcast without approval of the copyright holder.

AADR – Art, Architecture and Design Research publishes research with an emphasis on the relationship between critical theory and creative practice.
AADR series editor: Rochus Urban Hinkel
Production: pth-mediaberatung GmbH, Würzburg
Cover design and book layout: Alberto Altés

Typeset
Helvetica Neue

Paper
Multi Art Silk 130 gr/m2

This book presents research and work of the Laboratory of Immediate Architectural Intervention at Umeå School of Architecture, Umeå University (Sweden) and has received the generous support of the Swedish Research Council *Formas* through the Strong Research Environment "*Architecture in Effect*".

ISBN 978-3-88778-393-8

For further information on Spurbuchverlag and AADR visit our website www.spurbuch.de.

Laboratory of Immediate Architectural Intervention

intravention durations effects

Edited by
Alberto Altés Arlandis and Oren Lieberman

Contributions by

Roemer van Toorn
Hélène Frichot
Peter Kjaer
Per Nilsson
Susan Kelly
Karin Berggren
Javier Rodrigo Montero
Aida Sánchez de Serdio
Francesco Apuzzo and Axel Timm

Umeå School of Architecture

contents

intravention, durations, effects

acknowledgements

acknowledgements

First of all, this book would have never been possible had I not been hired by Peter Kjaer to join the faculty team at Umeå School of Architecture. My gratitude goes to him for that opportunity and for many things shared and learnt these years at UMA. Second of all, and most importantly, this book is only possible thanks to an incredibly productive and ongoing collaboration with Oren Lieberman with whom I co-direct the "*Laboratory of Immediate Architectural Intervention*" (LiAi) at Umeå School of Architecture. Only a very small fraction of what I have learnt through him and in our discussions is reflected in the book. I hope this is only the first of many joint publications and projects together.

I got to know about Umeå School of Architecture through Sten Gromark, who was my supervisor during a research stay at Chalmers School of Architecture and connected me as an external researcher to the *"Architecture in Effect"* Strong Research Environment. I want to thank him for his support and help. It was also him who introduced me to Ana Betancour and Carl-Johan Westerlund, with whom I have later shared very interesting conversations, discussions and reviews. Very special thanks to them also.

I am indebted to my colleagues in "*Architecture in Effect*" who have helped me develop parts of this work through their insights, comments and suggestions in the seminars we have had together as well as during the "*Rethinking the Social*" symposium that took place at UMA in February 2013. I am particularly thankful to Katja Grillner for her availability and the support she has granted to this book.

I cannot skip a warm thank you to Roemer van Toorn, whose inspiring work has in many ways also brought me to UMA, and whose help and insights have been invaluable during these years of development of the LiAi.

I also want to thank all my colleagues at UMA for making possible-and-real an inspiring, challenging and motivating intellectual environment to which I am happy and proud to belong. Special thanks among them to Walter Unterrainer, Sepideh Karami and Thomas Olofsson who have been and continue being especially supportive, as well as militant partners in our everyday learning-quest. Thank you Per Nilsson for your mind-opening observations and constant fight against illegitimate power.

A very warm thanks to all our guests and contributors to this book, for their energy, commitment and insights, and for their patience throughout the process of making it. It has been a pleasure and a privilege to work with you all. In particular, I want to thank Hélène Frichot for her generous effort to write an excellent foreword, she is not only extraordinarily sharp but also very kind.

And of course, thanks to all the students who have participated in and contributed to the creation of the LiAi and with whom I have shared so many intense moments. Thanks to Erika, Anna, Audingas, Olga, Maria, Martin, Christina, Febe, Tobias, Veronica, Kirstine, Paula, Sofia, Kimberley and Johan.

Thanks also to Antonio Millán Gómez who is still, in the distance, a generous PhD supervisor.

And very special thanks to Karin Berggren for her inspiration, help and support.

alberto altés, Umeå, August 2013

introduction

introduction

Intravention, Durations, Effects: Notes of Expansive Sites and Relational Architecture(s)

This book is a carefully edited collection of work and research produced at the *Laboratory of Immediate Architectural Intervention*, Umeå School of Architecture, Umeå (Sweden), from July 2011 to July 2013. It includes short texts, architectural manifestos, research papers, interviews, conversations, and a reflective journey through the work produced at the laboratory. It is also a compilation of fragile and hesitant voices and experiments, tests and discussions, in and around what one could provisionally call, in lack of a better name, relational architecture. And as you will see later, I believe that fragility and hesitation are necessary *qualities* of our work and our relentless moving and wayfaring.

It is organized in three parts: in the first one, after the foreword, the laboratory and some of its actions, reflections and proposals are presented and discussed from our point of view, from the inside. In addition to our own texts, this section includes reflections by Peter Kjaer and Roemer van Toorn, as well as an interview with Francesco Apuzzo and Axel Timm from 'raumlabor berlin' with whom we have developed a very interesting and fruitful relationship. The second part, '*sites, agencies, matters of concern*', offers an overview of the work produced at the laboratory through graphic material (pictures and drawings) accompanied by a reflective discussion of the work and its relationships with what we have called, after Latour, our matters of concern. The third part shifts outwards and gathers contributions by some of the external guests whose committed participation we have had the pleasure of enjoying at some point during these years. Although related to our interests and positions, these contributions are those of 'outsiders' and therefore capable of enriching and expanding our range of questions and discussions in diverse and unexpected ways. This part includes texts by Susan Kelly, Javier Rodrigo, Antonio Collados, Aida Sánchez de Serdio and Per Nilsson.

The book ends with a text on the notions of 'sharing, displacing and caring', that initiates an exploration of what I think is a much needed - and anarchic - ethics of encounter and contribution, while sketching some of the questions, fields and lines along which I hope to continue moving forward in discussion, research and action.

alberto altés, Umeå, August 2013

foreword - hélène frichot

foreword
hélène frichot

A woman sits in her living room, the TV magazine held open in her lap as she thinks of the daughter who has not called her in months. Outside the sky is crepuscular dull, it's a northern autumn day. Suddenly in her window a face looms up and smiles where it does not belong, she starts back in fright. She stands up suddenly, steps backwards and then forwards, uncertain what to do next. Finally she approaches the window, and when she opens it a cold gust of air enters and with it an enquiring voice.

Before it is possible to speak of the power and necessary immediacy of architectural *intraventions* we must be able to imagine the event of an encounter that enables a fledgling relation to emerge. Perhaps the woman wants nothing to do with the architecture student who has ascended up an improbable mobile structure to peer enquiringly into her window, or else, perhaps this will be the beginning of a longer conversation, and even the promise of a more enduring relation that will lead to future encounters. Where architecture desires to *intravene* in its immanent milieu – to act from the midst of things, to explore a creative resistance to the present that enables us to imagine the world otherwise – first it must slow down enough to respect the radical contingency of an encounter, however small. It's worth slowing down and taking notice of the small things and their relations. For instance: Take a mobile structure, half float, half stairway, form a processional, and progress merrily down the street, produce an urban action that stirs up our daily habits, and modes of inhabitation.

I have been tasked here with offering a foreword to a collection of essays that argues for the importance of architectural *intraventions* as a more appropriate means of acting with a socio-political occasion than mere architectural form-making. The editors, Alberto Altés Arlandis and Oren Lieberman who with their students constructed such a relational object as the one I have briefly described above, talk about the end of the reign of architecture as an 'it', or as some discrete, well-designed, over-determined object sitting neatly in a circumscribed field. Although they have many worthy comrades working alongside them toward this rethinking of what architecture can do, not to mention trail-blazing precursors some of whom I will mention below, they have a long battle ahead of them. Inventing the means by which architecture can again find a way to believe in this complex, messy world, and make a valid contribution by way of enduring relations is an exhausting endeavour.

It must have been some time around 2007 when I was first introduced to the French curator Nicolas Bourriaud's book *Relational Aesthetics*. My neighbour Steve, in Brunswick, Melbourne, recommended it to me. Steve is the kind of artist who produces a work every seven years and then chooses not to show it. He works slowly, happy to disrespect the Capitalist mantra that time is money. In retrospect I also remember hearing about the remarkable event of *Utopia Station* at the Venice Biennale of 2003, which I could have attended, but did not: a missed opportunity. *Utopia Station*, curated by Molly Nesbitt, Hans Ulrich Obrist, and Rirkrit Tiravanija, featured work by many of the artists that Bourriaud had regularly curated, specifically Tiravanija, well-known for his noodle kitchen gatherings, also Liam Gillick. These experiments, drawing loosely on the happenings of the 1970's, placed the emphasis on collective formations of a briefly convened socius, and the near redundancy of aesthetic props. Aesthetic objects and infrastructures would only be proffered as the means of securing some encounter, producing a provisional relation, however fleeting.

What had been especially interesting to me in my first reading of *Relational Aesthetics* was the fact that Bourriaud was drawing heavily on Félix Guattari's ethico-aesthetic paradigm, which I was also trying to work with. I was attempting to find some passage between aesthetic expression and a means of making oneself worthy of one's encounters, of coping ethically within architecture. Obviously I'm a slow learner: all my art friends had known about this kind of 'relational aesthetic' work for a long while. At the time I asked myself whether architecture was doing something that could also be called 'relational aesthetics', and if so, how might it be recognised, according to what methods, materials, and compositions? In architecture a term that is more commonly used for works that are relational is 'participation', as made explicit in Doina Petrescu, Jeremy Till, and Peter Blundell Jones' important edited collection *Architecture and Participation* (2005), which neatly organises the topic according to politics, histories and practices of participation in architecture. More recently, Nishat Awan, Tatjana Schneider, and Jeremy Till's edited collection *Spatial Agency: Other Ways of Doing Architecture* (2011), surveys what I would call the minoritarian works of a large number of design practices concerned with enabling social and political change through spatial, material and relational means.

What is recovered for architecture in such publications and the design practices they map and make visible, is a socio-political project that promises the means of thinking outside the conceit of disciplinary autonomy where architecture gets fixed on its form-finding fascinations. Architecture, after all, can still take on a transformative role in society, and might even help us imagine new peoples and new worlds, even though, as Deleuze and Guattari suggest "*the artist or the philosopher is quite incapable of creating a people, each can only summon it with all his strength.*"[1] In a business such as architecture it is strength and persistence, and importantly, an ethics of care that is required in all our encounters.

In 2011 Rochus Urban Hinkel and I curated the *Relational Participation* roundtables at ADIP TU Berlin with the support of Architecture+Philosophy and the Design Research Institute, RMIT University, Melbourne, Australia. We had the aim of throwing out provisional bridges between what was happening in art practice and in architecture practice; we wanted to see what would happen when you conjoin relational aesthetics with participatory architectures. The roundtables included presentations by: Mario Asef, Susanne Hofman, Julia Martin, Alex Martinis Roe, Ulrich Beckefeld, Brandon LaBelle, Marianne Eigenheer, Christian Teckert, Kathrin Böhm, Doina Petrescu and Constantin Petcou (founders of AAA, Paris), Andreas Rumpfhuber, Gabi Shilling, Mathias Heyden. Jeremy Till and Jane Rendell were invited, but could not make it, and we should have invited Meike Schalk too, certainly her name had come up several times as an important participatory spatial agent. We organised the three days according to: relations between people and things; people and people; and people and places, and this ended up working out rather well because it helped us to collectively think through different kinds of relationality.

I want to insist that these moments of slowing down and taking the time to think together also open up forms of ethical experimentation. Some of the concerns we collectively discovered included: how much waste we still produce with our relational design experiments despite our best intentions; that to speak of relational participation is really a tautology, and the only thing that distinguishes us is our claimed disciplinary points of view, I'm an artist, you are a philosopher, and she is an architect, but we can all agree that our practices hold to many of the same matters of concern; and finally we lamented how difficult it is to resist the steam-rolling, all-consuming logic of integrating world Capitalism.

In July 2012, Doina Petrescu recommended we visit the Re·Architecture show at the Pavilion de l'Arsenal in Paris, including the further subthemes of RE·cycle, RE·use, RE·invent, RE·build. The exhibition gathered work from fifteen practices, including Raumlabor (Berlin); muf art/architecture (London); Atelier d'Architecture Autogérée (AAA) (Paris); Assemble (London); Rotor (Brussels), and so on.[2] Somewhat like *Spatial Agency*, the exhibition presented a selection of projects that every architecture student *and* architect should be introduced to in order to understand that there are other ways of doing architecture, other ways of *intravening* in the present. The pedagogical and design research efforts of the *Laboratory of Immediate Architectural*

Intervention can be included in such company. What's more, something of a family resemblance is emerging with a shared ethico-aesthetics, which is a positive development because undertaking relational or participatory architecture is not about discarding our expertise as designers. Some of the shared methods and materials that can be observed include: asset mapping of local community knowledge; the curation of temporary events and installations; a sustainable attention to the use and re-use of materials; quick and dirty detailing when required; off-the-shelf inventiveness and subversion of products; and crucially, an indispensable ethics of the encounter acknowledged with every occasion.

What I have attempted to sketch above is an idiosyncratic map with some of the sign-posts that have allowed me to recognise the kind of work that is being forwarded in this collection of essays. Another witness may well elaborate another itinerary, and other precursors, for example, a coterminous groundswell of feminist design practices should also be noted here. The important thing is that something is shifting in the architectural firmament, other, alternative ways of practicing architecture are being ventured, now with an emphasis on the relations we hope to secure in our present milieu.

We do not yet know what architecture can do. The capacity of architecture to reinvent its methods and modes of practice, to rethink its materials and compositions, revise its matters of concern, and recognise that an aesthetics should not be separated out from an ethics is something we need to persistently struggle with. An *intravention* does not come in from the outside, but accepts an always already located positionality, that it must act in the here and now from the midst of things and resist the present where it is most repressive. We cannot give up too soon, despite the fact that our methods and means of communication are so rapidly co-opted by Capitalist interests, by ideas men and women selling their merchandise, by property developers keen to integrate alternative aesthetics and even participatory encounters into their entrepreneurial projects. Immanent modes of experimental spatial existence must be exhaustively explored, and we need to reserve sufficient critical-creative strength to diagnose what has manifested as a more positive architectural composition, and what has instead decreased our affective powers of existence. //

1 Deleuze, Gilles and F. Guattari (1994) *What is Philosophy?* New York: Columbia University Press, p. 110.

2 See: http://www.pavillon-arsenal.com/en/expositions/DPUSDEF.pdf Accessed 31 July 2013.

B 0902 WL

immediate architectural interventions?

peter kjaer

The role of the architect is changing but only a few architects seem to take notice. It is changing because society has changed and the demands towards architecture have developed. The profession is thus also changing and some are even talking about a change in paradigm.

Looking at the western countries it is true that the market as such is changing; and not because of the financial crisis. Experiences from the US market show that business in architecture is becoming more complex. Many of the 'old businesses' disappear, but new areas are to be developed. Consulting might be a big part of the new business but also completely new types of practices are starting to emerge and must be developed: those that address architecture fundamentally as an aesthetic practice, much more than as the production of buildings. Moving towards the basics of practice.

Traditionally, the architect would meet the customer, get an assignment from him/her, and then start the work. This idea of architectural design is to be changed. The architect is a specialist in design of course, but as true as that is, the concept of architecture has not changed since the modernist movement and functionalism, in the beginning of the 20th century, even if society has indeed changed a lot.

One of the real achievements of the modern movement was to make architecture common, to improve living conditions and aesthetic conditions for everybody while developing our built environment. In that respect, it was a success: architects had visions and comprehensive theories on society; visions and theories on how to build cities and how to create landscapes were competences architects built on and related to, and the architectural practice was "to give design" to these theories and visions. Such a paradigm is still basic for architectural practices and educations in the western world, as if society and economies were still the same as 100 years ago.

We all know this is not the case, of course, even if we do not know what to put in place instead. And this is where we as architects are.

It seems as if trying to develop one theory would be an impossible task: the conditions are simply too different depending on whether the work is to be developed in Europe, Africa, Asia, India, Middle East, South or North America or Oceania. The local and regional, cultural, political and economical conditions will be important parameters in every architectural intervention aiming to contribute to the development of the societies or communities in which it happens. But this indicates that architecture needs to reflect and establish a theoretical approach project by project, case by case. And even if anthropological and economic methods are important, they alone are not sufficient as architectural solutions. As architects we are obliged to integrate these aspects in the aesthetic proposals we always produce.

For these reasons, Umeå School of Architecture (UMA), has defined itself as a laboratory of architecture: to explore and examine new forms of architectural practice. The most urgent issue is to examine, describe and test new criteria and conditions for architecture, addressing the relation between people and architecture, between architecture and the social, political and ethical reality of our world.

Architectural projects and aesthetic interventions conceived at UMA aim at examining, involving and testing. They are interventions in the sense that there are always consequences, and aesthetic since they, through their presence, are capable of producing meaning.

The context does represent an important condition depending on whether the work and projects are related, for instance, to the development of informal settlements in places like Dharavi in Mumbai, or the rebuilding of Port au Prince in Haiti, or the retrofitting of the Swedish suburban settlements from the 1960's and 1970's. Before carrying out these very concrete architectural interventions, methods are rehearsed, theories and built works are examined and tested, and people in the communities/cities are involved.

Aesthetics is a philosophical discipline and architecture is an aesthetic practice. Architecture can be regarded as an embodied philosophy, which by its very physicality is capable of producing meaning. This is one of the key issues for UMA: to recognize, as the main aim of architectural practice, the production of meaning. //

Where are the options?
What is at stake?
Are there really options?
How should we choose?[1]

questioning strong discourses: the liai

alberto altés arlandis and oren lieberman

The notion that there is any singular definition of the architectural profession, is, at least on the margins, continuously questioned. But the 'middle' is strong, and the very fact that a multiplicity of 'other' agendas and their attendant methodologies are marginalised attests this strength.

1 Mol, Annamarie. Ontological Politics. A Word and Some Questions, The Sociological Review Volume 46, Issue S, pages 74–89, December 1998.

Perhaps, however, being outside what might be seen as conventional practice, one that is all too often complicit with neoliberal agendas isn't such a bad position to be in. But: is one ever really 'outside'? As many have pointed out, including Pierre Bourdieu, neoliberalism is a "*...'strong discourse'. It is so strong and so hard to combat only because it has on its side all of the forces of a world of relations of forces, a world that it contributes to making what it is.*"[2]

There is, as Mol says, much at stake here. Too numerous to list are the inequalities, tragedies, and oppressive regimes which are engendered by this 'strong discourse'. Architecture, with its wide purview of spatial, social, cultural, political, economic, technological and ethical concerns, cannot sit on the side as a bystander. But what, indeed are the options in the face of our knowing and unknowing implication in the biopolitics of power over lives?

At the Laboratory of Immediate Architectural Intervention, we believe that our only option is to understand, critique, intervene in, and devise the various apparatuses which are enmeshed in our enactments of the world in order to qualitatively transform it. Agamben understands the apparatus as anything which can "*capture, orient, determine, intercept, model, control, or secure the gestures, behaviors, opinions, or discourses of living beings*".[3]

He not only includes Foucault's "*prisons, madhouses, the panopticon, schools, ... factories, disciplines, judicial measures*" but also "*... the pen, writing, literature, philosophy, agriculture, cigarettes, navigation, computers, cellular telephones and--why not--language itself ...".*[3]

Apparatuses co-determine our enactments of the world.

Our work questions one of architecture's apparatuses – the oft-persistent mirroring and representation of spaces of neoliberal agendas – and develops transversal, diffractive methodologies that produce effects in exchange with, and which transform, sites.

The Laboratory interrogates an expanded notion of site, one which is physical, social, topographical, emotional, phenomenological, biographi-

---

2 Bourdieu, Pierre. (Utopia of endless exploitation: The essence of neoliberalism, Le Monde Diplomatique archive Dec. 1998, http://mondediplo.com/1998/12/08bourdieu accessed 28.08.11)

3 Agamben, Giorgio. What is an Apparatus?" in What is an Apparatus? And Other Essays. Stanford: Stanford University Press, 2009: p. 14

cal, institutional, dialogical, negotiable, discursive, gendered, colonised. So sites include spatial elements and issues of various sorts (geographical, local, physical, regional, national, global); individuals; specific groups and organizations; political and economic components and interests (e.g., the state, NGOs, local or regional regimes, political parties, etc.), time (history, the seasons, duration, etc.); technologies; material infrastructures; specialized knowledge/expertise; 'things' of all sorts; 'sociological' dimensions (e.g., religion, race, sexuality, gender, ethnicity, nationality); moral/ethical dimensions; and situation-specific discourses.

Sites, as apparatuses, are made, not 'given'.

In the Laboratory, sites are excavated and made through their discourses of issues and their methodologies of events. Real local, regional, national, and global issues transverse the laboratory's practices of performative, immediate intervention in, and transformation of, space in 'real time and place'.

The Laboratory broadens the architect's range of activities, and empowers its community through its members' ability to actually make a difference. This making a difference entangles us ethically and politically in the world.

Just as Umeå School of Architecture was conceived of as a critical laboratory of architecture - one in which the discussion about architecture and architectural education and their roles in the transformation of society is permanently installed - so too, the LiAi is developed to be committed to research in its broadest sense, a research that is focused on practice as much as it is on theory, or rather, on an intense entanglement of the two.

The LiAi is becoming what it is precisely on the basis of intense and productive discussions among us - its coordinators- and our guests, our students and other members of the faculty at the Umeå School of Architecture and the rest of the Art Campus in Umeå.

As for what we mean with 'intervention', or what are the possible understandings of 'immediate', these remain fundamentally open questions that make the laboratory a laboratory. Nevertheless, we try to explore and discuss them throughout this book, advancing a number of provisional answers, whilst unfolding a multitude of other questions.

The LiAi is structured around the idea

of architectural intervention, interrogated in relationship to its duration and effects, in and around the community where it takes place - indeed, in its potential to create community. Whilst the approach of the laboratory can be related to certain artistic practices, it is rooted in an understanding of spatial conceptualization and production as the architect's most important skills.

Very differently from those who have revisited the idea of a 'light theory', advocated by those who label themselves as 'post-critical' and urge us to stop thinking in order to "*[...] aim wildly at getting something going. Anything. Bigger pictures, funnier punch lines, larger stakes*"[4], we believe that it is not enough to just do 'something, anything', but that we need to carefully discuss and assess, among other things, the duration of that 'something' and the effects that 'something' has on its surroundings, on the world (things, people, spaces, places, discourses, events, ...) and of course, also, the duration of those effects.

Our practices and interventions are entangled with our thoughts, in a seamless thinking/making that makes the world as the world makes us and our thinking/making.

The Laboratory encourages interventions that engage actively in and with the public realm (here understood as broadly and openly as possible). We want our interventions to do 'things' to the public sphere, to produce space and to do 'things' to other things, and to other bodies and to other discourses. Sometimes these interventions will just happen, sometimes they will 'stand and wait', sometimes they will 'ask' to be carried elsewhere, or initiate their own dialogues with other people and things and institutions. More generally, they will help us investigate, test and explore the ability of architecture to interfere with, make sense of and participate in the often inexplicable and inarticulate making of the city and the world.

Often starting from direct involvement, being-there, observation and situational analysis - understanding the role of architectures within the meshwork of relations they are part of instead of looking at them as autonomous and isolated (closed) objects - the laboratory explores the possibilities of architectural practices that conceive and artic-

---

4 These were the words of the "hi-jackers" (as they introduced themselves) of number 5 of the well known journal of architectural theory "Log". Somol, Robert E. and Sarah Whiting, 2005, Log 5, Any Corporation, New York

ulate diverse processes of community development and transformation.

As we already mentioned above, the “sites” of these interventions in the public sphere are made, not given, and their ‘construction’ includes involvement with other institutions, governmental agencies and other actors. Sites might include asylum homes for unaccompanied refugees (minors), displaced houses, backyards, institutions, a network of connected spaces, parts of the hinterland in Norrland, dance scenes in Västerbotten, a suburb, a salad-factory, the Russian community in Umeå, a walk along the river, the Art Campus in Umeå, or all the fast-food restaurants in the city, to name a few...

In some cases these interventions will be just tools in the process of testing and researching, maybe helpful to collect information, to start a dialogue or to create a platform for other interventions to come. Almost always they try to raise and give some answers to questions such as: how is the city being transformed and produced? How can we participate in the making of the city? How can we make that ‘making’ a public matter again? How do we articulate our co-existence? How and for whom do we architect the city? //

immediate architectural interventions, duration and effects: apparatuses, things and people in the making of the city and the world

alberto altés arlandis and oren lieberman

Inside a quiet cafe, in a well-known European city, a group of master's students in architecture sit around a table while they wait for a guest to arrive. Everyone is a bit excited since the guest is a famous figure of architectural theory that will probably throw some light onto their ongoing discussions about something called 'relational architecture'. They have invited the guest for an encounter/interview/ conversation. But the guest is quite late.

Students and teachers start a discussion partly initiated by some lines read from a transcription of an interview with the absent guest:

- "*Speculative theories are the basis to develop projective matter*" reads someone aloud.
- "Yes, but aren't we talking all the time about being concrete?" reacts someone immediately.

- "Wait, there's something even more interesting here, listen: "*[...] more and more designers embrace pluralism and the endless relations that an intelligent system can generate. The danger is that their search for difference or the stimulation of the unpredictable is elevated to an absolute law, and the possibility of difference is fetishized*" says the reader again.

- "What does he mean by fetishizing difference?" asks someone else.

- "Hmm... I think that would be if you start focusing exclusively on producing 'difference', no matter how small or unimportant that difference is, and that takes over everything else" replies one of them. "As if for instance the fact that I am moving this sugar dispenser now..." and he takes the sugar dispenser in his right hand and moves it to another position on the table while he goes on... "was understood as changing the world".

- "Well.... but in fact, it is changing the world, isn't it?" says someone else from the far end of the table.

- "Not really!" says another one that had been quiet until now.

- "I think it does change the world to some extent" adds one of them.

- "I am not sure that is true" says another.

- ...[1]

---

1 The sections quoted (recited) in the dialogue are by Markus Miessen and Roemer van Toorn, respectively, as found in Van Toorn, Roemer, 2009, "Architecture as Political Practice: Roemer van Toorn in Conversation with Markus Miessen" in Conditions: Independent Scandinavian Magazine on Architecture and Urbanism, #1, Strategy for Evolution. Oslo, Norway.)

"Bringing things back to life [...] to switch our perspective from the endless shuttling back and forth from image to object and from object to image, that is such a pronounced feature of academic writing in the fields of anthropology, archaeology, art and architecture, to the material flows and currents of sensory awareness in which images and objects reciprocally take shape."

Tim Ingold[2]

"[...] Guardians of the history of emancipation in an intervallic period, historical riots point to the urgency of a reformulated ideological proposal, a powerful idea, a pivotal hypothesis, so that the energy they release and the individuals they engage can give rise, in and beyond the mass movement and the reawakening of History it signals, to a new figure of organization and hence of politics."

Alain Badiou[3]

We begin setting out our thoughts on immediate architectural interventions with a couple of considerations. One of them addresses the architectural profession's progressive disconnection from the social, from the political, from history, from the local, from ethics, from the body, from the 'discipline' itself. A whole generation of architects has abandoned the design of coexistence - undoubtedly one of the main tasks of architecture – in order to embrace, on the one hand, the serial fabrication of what we see as anti-architectures that repeat types, materials and structural systems on the basis of a pragmatic and productive juxtaposition of normative restrictions and the interests of bankers, investors, and developers; and on the other hand, the production of 'stunning' unique prototypes of image-architecture that satisfy the ill, self-worshipping yearnings of architects mired in the ceaseless luxury of formal exploration for the sake of form. We are critical of what is being embraced and of the practices that perpetuate disconnection from lived lives.

---

2 Ingold, Tim (Forthcoming) "Making: Anthropology, Archaeology, Art and Architecture", (London: Routledge).

3 Badiou, Alain (2012), "The rebirth of history: Times of Riots and Uprisings", (London ; New York: Verso) 120.

Although setting up the 'other' as, in a sense, the unmarked term to talk about difference can be problematic, it may be helpful to speak about the differences in approaches to architectural production.

To generalize for a moment: offices like Hadid's, or Foster's, or many others of smaller sizes and turnover, have a different ontological and ontogenic position than ours. That is, they understand how a building comes into being, its processes and practices of development, in a particular way: how one procures work, how one organizes an office, how one communicates to different audiences along the way of building, etc. And, again, with the risk of overgeneralizing, they believe that the building is the center around which all else revolves. They perhaps understand that it will produce effects in both its immediate physical and social contexts; however, these potential effects are not often considered seriously to be part of the building itself. There is a formalist tendency in much of the work, which may or may not produce beautiful objects, and may or may not produce positive effects. The buildings produced might be seen as interventions, but are they transversal? Or diffractive? They are certainly not *intraventions* in the way we will define them below.

Underlying our critique is a position that architecture is not an autonomous entity that is devised in the architect's studio on the basis of his/her capacities as 'genius' and through some kind of obscure, almost magical process and then deployed on a pre-existing piece of land. Rather, it is a complex and relational practice that comes about in various 'fields', and takes place in collaboration with things and people, and is always material as well as cultural *and* political *and* technological *and* artistic *and, and...* It is a practiced practice, involving many different actors, people, institutions and apparatuses.

Interventions

Our desire to intervene reflects this awareness and critique of these conditions of disconnection and distancing between people and the social, as well as between people and 'bodies' – their own or those of materials, technologies, and indeed discourses. Our desire to intervene is a desire to affect the world, and resonates with the given that, as Antonio Machado says, *'we lay down the path while walking'*. We believe in the need to be 'inside', intervening here and now, close to where we are and with the tools we have at hand, with borrowed methodologies, and invented methods. We want *'to architect'*.

The 'tool' of intervention is indeed a powerful one. First of all it presupposes a place/time in which to intervene, that is, it takes, and makes, a position. But if we also believe that the very nature of being (and therefore, space) is understood to be always in the coming-into-being – laying down the path – how do we then contemplate something – anything – being 'there' in any sort of 'stable' way before our interactions with it? Well, we are not relativists, and we can and do establish contours that delineate particular conditions of architecture (for instance, its disconnection to the social, its abandonment of coexistence as a motivator, its production of elitist image-making, topographies, weather, …). This is understandable and necessary, because we need to start somewhere, even if we say we are starting 'in the middle' …

We need to have an awareness of 'history' (and understand whose historiography we happen to be entangled with), in the sense that it is difficult to speak or act from a position, even to conceive of a position, if nothing was there before we 'arrived' and any such negation of the 'before' amounts to almost the same as a negation of history. In that sense we would claim that there are certainly many 'things' already there when we arrive, from some shared understanding of the material characteristics of the space, to the acquired memories recorded in those things and spaces throughout time, through the field conditions that determine, to a certain extent, those spaces and those things and, most importantly, our own embodied 'skills', acquired through time in a process of growth and development that enables us to act.[4] A radical negation of the existence of anything prior to our interactions with things entails an additional risk: that of extreme individualism. Other people and other things were there before, and have been interacting with each other and with other things and people in turn, and the results of all those previous interactions will affect our here-and-now interactions in fundamental ways.[5]

The idea that there is a history, an 'already there', a site which we might say preexists *this* moment, this just *now*,

---

4 For a more detailed account of the implications of attentiveness and "developmentally acquired responsiveness" i.e. embodied skilled practice, for the relationships between the concept of agency and the complexity of living organisms as opposed to inert matter, please check "When ANT Meets SPIDER: Social Theory for Arthropods" in Ingold, Tim (2011), Being alive : essays on movement, knowledge and description, (London ; New York: Routledge) xviii, 270.

5 It will be at this point obvious to the reader that we are also thinking of concepts such as *habitus* or *dispositions*, as developed by Pierre Bourdieu. See: Bourdieu, Pierre (1990), The logic of practice, (Stanford, Calif.: Stanford University Press) 333, pp. 55-56

is substantiated by our *attention* to it, an attention which makes (us part of) that site. And it is through a notion of expanded site – rather than a notion of scale with its predilections of hierarchy and nestedness – that we understand the extent of the intervention, i.e., the materials, institutions, social groupings, etc. of which we are involved and are 'bracketing in' to our considered purview. Through both the expansion of site into various concerns, and the simultaneous considered selection (the bracketing out, and in) of various actants, agendas, antagonisms and histories, we ethically and politically mark out and are entangled in the world. Where we want to intervene becomes a crucial question, in what site, how, for/with whom? So sites and the interventions that make them afford us the possibility to talk about judgments and political intentions as well as to measure effects. Do we want to enable a particular conversation? Do we want to challenge neoliberal worlds? Do we want to do both?

Intraventions

This notion of attention finds resonance in Karen Barad's work, where we find a focus on intra-actions rather than inter-actions. She posits not a world that is somehow unstable due to our inability to define moments and spaces, but proffers a world that is full of very precise phenomena produced through enacted intra-actions between things (including people, objects, animals, plants, etc.). Such an enactment – what she calls an 'agential cut' – locates quite precisely "*... a local causal structure among 'components' of a phenomenon in the marking of the 'measuring agencies' (effect) by the 'measured object' (cause).*"[6]

So for us interventions both measure and make, existing as both separate entities (of a city, a street, an institution, a landscape) as well as effects. It follows that we could define interventions as apparatuses, enacting them, firstly, not as passive objects but as things which do things to spaces and times, and secondly, as carrying political 'power' through their desires and agendas.

Here again we are defining architecture not as an 'it' but as a process, or perhaps an apparatus. Again: architecture is a verb, i.e. *to architect*. Supporting this active stance, we focus on the transformational nature of the interven-

6 Barad, Karen (2003), 'Posthumanist Performativity: Toward an Understanding of How Matter Comes to Matter', Signs, 28 (3), 801-31.

tions that are performed in real times and places, and work through the concept of the performative (in relation to the speculative *projective* practices of most architectural production). Our focus on the performative in practice means that our bodies are explicitly entangled in our work, and underline our view that we are, in an ecological and expanded 'cognitive' sense, both 'distributed' through things and places and other people and discourses as well as somehow 'bounded'. So in relation to our matters of concern, we are interested in what we can 'do' with architectural interventions and understand them to be performative not only with respect to their transformative power but also to their ability to establish identities, which may be in agonistic conflict with others.

We posit a new concept to further our work in these 'conditions': ***intra***vention, a word about which we are quite enthusiastic. Although it is only a matter of a couple of letters, intra's focus on the 'within' clearly establishes *intraventions* as already a part of the space and times in which they are 'intravening'; quite a different focus than the 'inter'. It is indeed a very productive notion which defines the (makeshift) limits of a specific situation with which we might interrogate/engage, and helps us deal with the apparently endless expandability of the relational meshwork of material and sensory flows, therefore allowing us to start 'doing/making' immediately. When we *intravene*, we 'cut' (in Barad's sense) to both locate and make a site we inhabit. This is not a negation of transversality, but an embrace of it.

It also speaks about intentionality: one 'decides' what the *intravention* includes or excludes. It is of course therefore an intensely political act, as well as an aesthetic one. Barad's notion of the 'cut' as a defining, parameter-setting tool is useful; at the Laboratory of Immediate Architectural Intervention (LiAi) we cut in various ways, not the least of which is through the use of our 'matters of concern'. As cuts, these are in themselves quite performative: the juxtaposition of particular terms immediately generates various and interesting interplays that in turn start setting the parameters of our discussions while at the same time they interrogate and help us judge the relevance of our intraventions.

Our matters of concern are our 'terms of engagement', the ways in which we deal with the task of 'architecting' as a function, i.e. a process that is contingent on other processes and other 'things'. If Badiou would say that architecture is a function of the generic procedure 'art' and the scientific category 'geography', we might well say that we see 'architecting' as a function of, or an amphibian stand[7] between, philosophy and art, aiming at the transformation of our conditions of coexistence and at the articulation of spaces for being and living together. This speaks indeed of a need to question architecture's position within the realm of technology or technique, as well as epistemologies that conceive it as a discipline or body of knowledge within art or science.[8]

Again, the performative nature of our matters of concern, and an understanding of architecture as a function, makes it part of the realm of the political, of choosing what and for whom we function, of taking responsibility, and of negotiating the implications of such choices.

The terms of our engagements are multiple, and the relationships among their components diverse and certainly not one of dialectical opposition but of productive entanglement: body/apparatus, critical/projective/relational, agency/structure/ANT, the other/difference, the other/coexistence, transversals/micropolitics, aesthetics/politics, affordance/gift, diffraction/representation, discourse/event, and documentation/judgment.

We investigate and encourage working with our oft-neglected body as an experiencing, a knowing, and a difference-making entity in the production of space. Heightening or consciously orchestrating our everyday 'techniques of the body' – that is, the ways our body negotiates and is implicated in our material and cultural apparatuses to create meaningful social interaction – can result in performative methods for *intravention*, questioning, and change.

Being close to the sites of our actions foregrounds our bodies' roles in the making of the world. And if the body itself can be seen as an apparatus, it exists always intra-acting with other things that co-determine effects. And this is no less true for the apparatus of the state than for a particular way of documenting.

---

7 For a very interesting account of what such an amphibian position might be and its implications for research in the Arts, check: Nilsson, Per (2009), "The Amphibian Stand: An Philosophical Essay Concerning Research Processes in Fine Art", H:ström Text & Kultur.

8 These reflections about architecture as a function and its relationship to the political have only been possible thanks to the interesting and sharp comments of our Spanish colleague, philosopher and architect Israel Casanovas, to whom we remain, as always, grateful.

We explore the possibilities of a relational approach to architecture that expands the critical vs. the projective debates that have been installed within the field for so long. We believe, with Teddy Cruz, that the future of urbanization will no longer be led by the production of new buildings, but will instead require a fundamental reorganization of socioeconomic relations, which is also a design challenge in which we must take active part.

Even if the complex and relational nature of the world cannot be disputed, it is often ignored, or at least relegated to a position at the bottom of the architect's list of things to interrogate and integrate. The relationships in any complex meshwork of people, places and things constitute the structure of durable practices, territories and fields. Various cultural, social, political and economic practices are maintained and sustained through these relationships.

The discussion of the interplays and reciprocal entanglement between our ability to act and to choose how to act and for whom, i.e. agency, and the existing *habitus* of practices and conditions that co-determine and define the limits of such ability, i.e. structure, is enriched and becomes more relevant in the light of recent advancements in the fields of science studies and what is known as actor-network theory. An understanding and exploration of architecture in those terms turns out to be very productive.

We address the notion of 'the other' through several dimensions. One relates to a kind of bottom line ethics of respect, and care for difference, for a multiplicity of actors and their beliefs; a basic understanding that others shouldn't be harmed. Another, related dimension for us can be highlighted in the difference between a belief that there is one truth, on and about which we can have our own perspective, and the belief that there are many worlds which of course can communicate and share things, but are in fact different. Yet another dimension would speak of the interplays between that notion of the other and the one of coexistence, to rethink the role of architecture in the production of spaces for being and living together.

Our engagement with transversality and micropolitics, touched upon here and there throughout this paper, is not a minor one: the interlocking of, for instance, immigration policies in Europe, and Sweden, the arrival and presence of unaccompanied minors in homeland territories, the relationship between urban planning and the distribution of the population in space, discourses of integration and the presence of a certain number of asylum homes in a particular peripheral, urban enclave of Sweden's Norrland, appears to be also cut by discourses and practices of biopolitics, the position, shape and nature of a particular set of furniture, the size of a room and the configuration of a particular domestic space in which those minors live their lives, which might be only accessible through some initial conversations with those kids and their 'guardians'.

Architecture operates through making, and through making things visible; it produces and reproduces new and old spatial and aesthetic apparatuses. As we have said, it is not an autonomous practice but contingent and relational, it has to negotiate its position, it is, therefore, political. It is political also because it plays an important role in our distribution in space: it sets us together or apart. Architecture, as we will see, is in that sense a function, and participates in the complex interplays of the state and politics, as well as in other social and political discussions.

Another of our engagements starts through our attention to architecture's ability to afford us 'things' and conditions of possibility, as well as the relationship of the above-mentioned ethics of respect and care with affordability. These reflections make also possible to conceive of architecture as a gift, and to imagine the potential of architecture to be an embodied critique of building-as-consumable-object as well as to produce 'uncertainties', contingent relationships and unexpected effects which can help define more positive value systems.

The notion of diffraction helps us think of different things coming into contact with each other and producing effects through their mixing in each other's medium. In terms of waves (light, sound, etc.), it is clearly different from that of reflection, which has waves bent back away from an encounter, remaining in their own medium. A focus on reflection then might be more about a typical understanding of representation's mirror, rather than on diffraction's transformation of the world, our ability to make a difference rather than displacing the same elsewhere.

The reliance of architectural production in representational techniques and approaches has distanced it from itself and its powers, lately in more than worrying fashion: architectural images today, by the hand of new representation and construction technologies, and thanks to the enormous accumulation of political and economic capital, forget the inherent limitations of representation and dilute the difference between what is represented and what is built, restricting, almost eliminating the possibility of interpretation, as if aiming to neutralize or control the interplays of the real and the fake. The most fantastic and impossible drawings ever imagined are literally built, suddenly appearing in the middle of the desert; complete islands are conceived, materialized and urbanized in a few months or years. The rhetorics of void and wrapping are camouflaged underneath surfaces and skins, and articulated through fantasy, deception and magic.

The city can be seen instead as mixtures of immediate, singular, specific, enacted, practiced, diffractive, performative, interactive, transformational, improvisational, embodied, political, ethical, transversal, intervenient events, i.e., things that happen; and discourses of various sorts: histories, interpretations, commentaries, theories, disputations, categorisations and orderings.

We will engage with and produce in 'real time' singular events, as well as the discourse that participates in the performance of those singularities. If the power of the event speaks, as Badiou tells us at the beginning, of a latent urgency and a memorable energy, such energy has to be combined with a shared demand and the working of, by means of discursive articulation, the problem of politics par excellence, namely, organization.

Methodologies of events, discourses of issues, *intraventions* and their effects must be made public in order to both enhance those effects and share the knowledge derived of their enactment. Documenting what happens is paramount and can't be left for a final, retrospective analysis or account. Since elements of judgment are involved already in the very first steps that lead to the invention of these sites, events, issues and interventions... so must be the stories and their methods devised and put-to-work in 'real-time' to explain the complex meshworks, including processes, implementations, outcomes and intentions.

Our matters of concern are indeed tools for cutting, for establishing the (shifting) limits of our expanded sites. They are full of intention, just as the terms themselves are in tension, setting up dialogues and arguments and different worlds that together make things common and common things. Intentionality is an index of the architect's position and aims. Like our matters of concern, the intention of the performer who *intravenes* informs the *intravention* and determines the (initial) limits of the ambit in which the *intravention* takes place. It initiates the definition of the *intravention*, even though these limits will necessarily change or evolve as we go. And, we shouldn't forget that this intentionality arises out of un/non-conscious aspects of our being, as well as out of 'affect-ual', bodily, and discursive, awareness.

We see *intraventions* as heuristic devices, as apparatuses that are imbued with a will to transform. The *intravention* is not autonomous but contingent and relational and dependent on many other things. The *intravention* is made as it happens, and it makes us at the same time. It takes place or happens in a situated field (the site), not on an endless/infinite meshwork, but as part of the relationships and co-existences between the elements comprised within that 'constructed' site. Again: things, people, institutions, apparatuses, histories, events and discourses that we start to define through an initial 'cut'.

If an *inter*vention is an addition to what is an impossible condition of a pre-existing situation or event and therefore something that exists also before and 'outside' the situation/field/place where it happens, then an *intra*vention is born through that situation, it becomes. It is a becoming, it is unfolded as it happens within and part of the site, it is interior to that site (we don't break in: as always, we are already there).

If Barad's intra-action is defined through an agential cut in the on-going life of the world - everything is intra-action for her - our *intra-vention* happens, to a certain extent, out of a willingness to engage in transforming/disturbing that life. It has the ability to produce change by transforming the site we are considering from within.

Criteria of ***Intraventions***

Paramount in the assessment of the *intravention* is its relationship with time. We can think on the one hand of its 'duration', as literally the time it lasts, regarding both the materiality of the objects that make it and that of the meshwork in which the objects are entwined. In this first 'side' of temporal criteria we can also include the duration of the effects (for how long is the *intravention* affecting/transforming the world?). On the other hand, if we think of it as a 'thing', we can speak of its 'durability', as its inherent ability to both dwell within the assemblages, clusters and meshworks in which it takes part, as well as to coordinate and curate those assemblages.

The duration of our *intraventions* and their effects, which are crucial, are multiple. It might be, of course, that if something is around longer it has more impact … but not always. Let's take an example. We intervene with something a very short lifespan (for instance, we build something which remains for 24 hours and then is removed). Though physically present for a mere day, the things that this *intravention* sets in motion, that is, the effects it has, might be significant. People of course remember it, but it might also be that people theorize it, that people begin to repeat aspects of it (e.g., an event which happened within it gets staged again in another setting), etc. And their duration and effects are evident in the ability of *intraventions* to trigger and afford dreams, generating something that didn't previously exist. A common hope, an imaginary.

Another aspect of our *intraventions* is immediacy, a concern which transverses complex meshworks. We can do things that occur quite quickly, and quite closely. However, to understand quick only according to the clock would negate the various 'timings' of the world; to understand close only as physical distance would disregard emotional bonds, as well as social media's always now, always here. Because we see architecture as relational and connected to all those other 'things', we prefer to work in close proximity as our aim is to affect the world around us, to make a difference, and therefore the immediate, the here-and-now become important.

The *intraventions* that we are interested in,

- … ask questions of their effects and their duration, producing effects that matter.

- … endure, either through their effects - in the cases in which they are themselves short - or through their own lasting existence, that continues to effect a pressure in their surroundings and therefore transforms the world in meaningful ways.

- … ask questions of our complicity in others' agendas.

- … challenge the order of things, confronting the status quo with the inadmissible, that, as Rancière puts it, *"reconfigure[s] the distribution of the sensible"*.[9] In that sense we are inter-

9 Rancière, Jacques. (2006), The politics of aesthetics : the distribution of the sensible, (Pbk. ed. edn., London ; New York: Continuum) 116.

ested in *intraventions* that ask questions of both consensus and dissensus.

- ... take the other into account. The various others. *Intraventions* treat these others seriously and emerge from a fundamental ethical drive that transpires in our encounters with them.

- ... create situations of freedom, revealing ideologies and generating spaces for a freer existence through coexistence.

So we are interested in *intraventions* that produce effects that matter. It follows that we need some criteria to assess the effects and to decide what it means to matter, for what and for whom. We might say we need to 'assess', or, rather, judge an *intravention*, reflecting on what makes one more or less successful than another.

As we have said, an essential criterion of the *intravention* is its transformative power: its effects will matter inasmuch as they manage to transform the world in a meaningful way. In order to do so, we believe that *intraventions* must on the one hand oppose particular strong discourses and on the other hand involve and engage a multiplicity of other actors/people/things.

The extent to which the *intraventio*n is explicitly enmeshed in both the material flows and the currents of sensory awareness that make life as it happens will also be an important measure, and reflects our focus on the performative.

Our *intraventions* should be as fully integrated and entangled as possible, and must address public matters, that is, issues of public concern. Their singularity must be used to critique and question the multiple/the plural through/with the polemical.

They must confront the conditions of 'the many' in/through potentially destabilizing, i.e. inadmissible, actions.

Such radical *intraventions*, must aim at *"making more room in the world for new political forms [...and] new excitations of power"*.[10] They must test, and experiment with, unexpected forms of 'effective togetherness' that ask questions about the definition of the commons and what is public and what

10 Thrift, N. J (2008), Non-representational theory: space, politics, affect, (International library of sociology; London: Routledge) x, 325, pp. 22

these definitions exclude, searching for forms of 'grouping' and/or 'organization'.[11]

If these *intraventions* address 'the public', they must also have the power to involve 'publics', in the sense of managing to engage multiple and various actors. Often, this engaging of various actors is initiated/afforded by an ability to connect through aesthetics. Intraventions can operate not only through agonism or dissensus, but also by being friendly and 'cool'.

The various collective and distributed ingredients of the *intravention* should also lead to collaborative ownerships that are emergent rather than claimed. Such 'self-distributing' forms of ownership are both the result of and an active part in the establishment of alternative communities of practice.

We can then ask a series of questions: How are the changes generated by our *intraventions* establishing connections amongst the city's inhabitants? How are our *intraventions* questioning 'official' discourses of public space in the city? How is the city 'rewired' through such *intraventions*? How are the proposed and effected transformations able to generate previously inexistent possibilities or ideas? How do they foster new 'dreams' about public, or rather, shared space? How could our *intraventions* guarantee the functional and discursive integrity/durability of such new public spaces? How would our *intraventions* incorporate, and further enable collaborative ownership and communities of practice?

These are some of the questions which keep us busy as we try 'to architect' our part in the making of the city and the world through immediate architectural interventions. The minimally different event is not enough. An Event needs an Organization and an Idea. To architect is a function and it is therefore political. Intraventions help us articulate those terms towards *architecting politically.* //

---

11 Thrift puts it this way: "How is it possible, in other words, to group around states that are neither dependent on lasting objects nor on fixed locations?", in Thrift, N. J (2008), pp. 22

from berlin to the polar circle: a conversation with raumlabor - karin berggren and alberto al

from berlin to the polar circle: a conversation with axel timm and francesco apuzzo from raumlabor

karin berggren and alberto altés arlandis

raumlabor, or 'space laboratory', is a collective of 8 trained architects based in Berlin (Germany), that work in the intersection of architecture, city planning, art and urban intervention. They have been exploring alternative and playful modes of architectural production since 1999 when they started working together, usually proposing temporary projects that transform the urban landscape through what they call 'urban prototypes'. Their works include the temporary transformation of the metro station *Eichbaum* (Essen/Mülheim, Germany) into an opera house, the temporary Officina Roma entirely built out of trash for the RE-cycle exhibition at the MAXXI museum, and the mobile building laboratory 'The Generator' that welcomes the public to interact around the construction of modular furniture.

During the autumn semester of the 2011-2012 academic year, we invited Axel and Francesco from raumlabor to come to the Laboratory of Immediate Architectural Intervention for a week to develop a collaborative workshop aimed at designing and building "something" that could be placed in public space as an intervention.

KB+AA: Hej Axel, Hej Francesco! We were very happy to have you with us at UMA last year and we are now very glad to be able to have this 'conversation' with you. As you know, your participation had quite a number of 'effects' and it has afforded us many productive discussions with our students. (We are already planning a strategy to make you come again to the polar circle soon, maybe by moving the invitation to the spring when everything flowers in Sweden…) But our aim here is to share some of the reflections, thoughts and discussions inspired by your visit and its products with you, in order to keep them alive and evolving. We believe that this conversation can be interesting for our research and teaching within the Laboratory of Immediate Architectural Intervention, but also in a much broader sense, as a reflection on the ways in which we (can) participate in the making of our cities and the world.

On the one hand we are interested in talking to you as raumlabor and exploring the approaches that you as a group or network (or as you say a 'collective of architects') have been rehearsing in different places for a number of years now; but on the other hand we are also very interested in talking to you as Axel and Francesco, (this was one of the reasons why we invited you in the first place to come to Umeå School of Architecture). We mean that we think you have a particular way of understanding what an intervention in the city can be and also a particular way of working, which does not meet some kind of global idea or internal policy of 'raumlabor', but follows your desires, intuitions and feelings, as much as the preference you two have to work together.

In the raumlabor webpage, you describe your work as "*deeply rooted in the local condition*", what were your initial reactions to our proposal to invite you to construct/perform an intervention in a place like Umeå, an environment in the far north to which you had no prior connection?

FA: To work in cities that are different to the central European in terms of culture, social conditions and geographic environment for us always implicate an improvement to our methods. We often don't plan a lot beforehand but react on site to the specific situation.

AT: Our approach to the workshop with students in Umeå was to collectively create a tool for the students to find out more about the local conditions.

KB+AA: Normally your work is based on your own ideas and intuitions, what were your feelings towards coming to Umeå with a sort of pre-designed 'assignment' through which we were asking you to allow the ideas to emerge collectively during the workshop with the students, and already setting the condition of having some kind of 'built' outcome that had to be completed within the week?

AT: A collective approach is very common to us in our studio work as well as in several participatory projects outside our studio. We have also been working in educational environments, teaching and setting workshops with students.

FA: The most intense moments in these kind of activities are when, after hours of discussion and tries, accompanied by uncertainties, at one point an idea comes up with the feeling that it has to be the path to follow during the remaining time, joining the energies to come to tangible results at the end. The time is for sure a parameter with a strong influence on the process.

KB+AA: What was your experience of working in this particular collaboration, close together with the students of the LiAi, and how did you see your own role in this collaboration?

AT: Sometimes, and particularly in the workshop with the LiAi, there is a bit of a pressure to create outcomes in a quite short period of time. When trying to achieve something collectively it can happen that discussions and designs go back and forth for a long time until decisions are made on themes, processes and forms, but after some days there is still no 'materialization'. With the students of LiAi it happened to be in a way that with the impact of everybody in the group, a satisfying projection of the collective process was quite quickly achieved, and we could start with the production right away...

FA: Approaching a workshop, as a process of collaboration, it is not so easy to be just a teacher, especially acting in a catalytic way, not allowing your own imagination to overcome that of the students. At the LiAi this worked really

well, the students were autonomous and dedicated.

KB+AA: LiAi stands for "*Laboratory of Immediate Architectural Intervention*", and one of the main tasks of the laboratory is to explore the possible meanings of terms like 'Intervention', and even 'Architecture'; to reflect around what an 'intervention' is and what an 'architectural intervention' can be. How do you see these words and what do they mean to you?

AT: The expression 'intervention' and 'architectural intervention' is very fuzzy, as you can even call the construction of real estate an intervention. When we were still studying at TU Berlin, Oren Lieberman, our teacher at that time, invented the term 'impenditure'. None of the students could really tell what that meant but there was some relation to it. So maybe that is what I think 'intervention' means to me; something that you install, that you 'give in' to a spatial and social situation in order to observe the change…

FA: The common use of the word intervention, referring to medical, military or political issues, is related to an operation of a limited duration, performed with the aim to solve an urgent problem. An architectural intervention can maybe not solve problems in a short

time, but it can help to make phenomena visible in a social space, to question habits and prejudice and bring people together in different ways.

KB+AA: What parameters do you use to assess and judge the "success" of your interventions, and what do you consider to be the key elements in constructing a successful intervention?

AT: Hmm, this is a really difficult question to answer in general. I can just say that there have been interventions of ours where there was an exchange and interaction happening, between people that I had not expected to come together, and discussing topics that (I think) they usually do not even think of. So that would be a success for me. From what I know of the life of the 'flyttblock', I judge it as successful that the students continued experimenting with it and really used it as a tool for exploring the public space in Umeå.

FA: Involving the local actors, considering them to be the real experts, is often a fundamental point for us. If something, not only physically, remains with the people after we leave, we have the sense of a bit of success.

KB+AA: You often stress the importance of providing 'open' and 'collective' spaces for social interaction. In

the description of one of your interventions involving public furniture you talk about 'built-in interaction', do you see your task as architects as limited to the making of the physical space in which interaction can take place, or are there also other possibilities of inducing or generating discussions or interactions through architectural intervention? Is it enough to produce the space/tools necessary for interaction, or is something else needed? And what do you mean by 'interaction' exactly?

AT: In our GENERATOR projects we defined (workshop) space/tools as hardware and the design ideas/proposals as software that can be implemented depending on task/environment/constraints, and that is also flexible for development. But the experience shows that the 'performance' is also crucial. Within this performance there is communication, and negotiation on spatial and other questions is triggered.

FA: For the project "crossing path superbench" in Milan we just installed a large amount of typical public benches with an untypical colour in a 'walk through' urban green area. In this case we were not present on site with a

building workshop; the interaction between people was generated as a reaction to the surprising and somehow dysfunctional configuration of normal benches at this site, without special qualities but still really present in their everyday routine.

Our building workshops, based on the construction of furniture on the street, together with locals who just drop by as well as other participants that specifically come to join the experience, are intended as a vehicle. Moments of interaction on a first level, due to the physical work on an object, are followed by interaction in terms of communication, and consequently the creation of relationships.

KB+AA: Regarding this communication that you aim to 'provoke' or induce; if we look at your project "The Crunch", which is a temporary public 'building' made of thrown-away every-day objects such as furniture and household appliances, you say that it provides a "*forum for conflicts and discussions*". How do you see the nature of these 'conflicts and discussions', and how do they emerge besides being given a physical space?

AT: To take "*the crunch*" as an example one can say that there is also the performative aspect (the sound installation) part of the project and the strong image of the everyday - thrown away as a wave rolling towards you. In most of our work we experience that the provided space and design is not enough for initiating a process of development.

The '*oak tree opera*' project seems to me like a good example with both a spatial intervention and the construction of the social space within it over a longer period of time. So depending on the 'found' and the way of interaction and interweaving with users, local institutions, the implementation of a variety of scenarios and program is very often crucial as well.

FA: Some of our projects in the public space begin by introducing a moment of surprise and/or perturbation. For the project "*white spots*" we worked in a residential area of Munich nearby a prison where we literally occupied parking lots with thirty-three cars of the same colour, just through legal parking with a special floating choreography. Starting with an initial irritation, this action created a situation of conflict and the consciousness about the everyday presence of cars in the public space of a street.

KB+AA: How do you see the role of this creation of spaces and opportunities for social interaction, in the process of city transformation? Somewhere you have expressed your opposition to utopian ideas and a lack of interest in addressing the big questions regarding the city, but aren't you aiming at having a certain impact in the city when you intervene and initiate or steer the processes you engage with? Don't you believe that another, different and better city is possible?

AT: Actually there isn't a lack of interest neither in addressing the big questions nor to utopian ideas. And we strongly believe that a better city is possible. (We wouldn´t work on that if not) We just do not believe that the better future is only connected to technological progress. That raises the question (C.Price) "*if technology is the answer, what was the question?*" Many of the utopian projects of the past are connected to technological innovation in the near or far away future. So if we say "*bye bye utopia*" there is a criticism of the belief that technology can solve our problems but also a reflection on the loss of utopias...

FA: In order to make our cities better it is necessary for citizens to begin to experience the space outside their private space as their own, which means

that local energies and desires should play a role in the transformation of the environments.

Often, the top-down measures of embellishment that municipalities install in the public space of problematic neighbourhoods become subject to vandalism. I don't remember that any of our interventions built together with local residents in similar situations was ever vandalised. What we experience on this scale could be a model for processes on a larger scale.

KB+AA: Your work is known as playful and generous; you create a good atmosphere and make people smile. You refer to your work as a 'game' of instant urbanism, but how do you think of 'time' beyond that instant, of what can be done with the momentum generated by a party or the playful atmosphere of an event that entertains? Why do you choose these strategies, and how do you turn these innocent and harmless events into powerful transformative interventions that last and resonate?

Do you ever find it problematic to manage the balance between intervention and party, engaging and entertaining?

FA: I don't think we do it according to a chosen strategy, it depends strongly on our own personalities. When we work in a playful way we do it being really serious, like children when they play.

AT: It makes it much easier to address and interest people if we play the game joyfully and generously. In many cases it lowers the threshold for a variety of people to become part of a process. But it can also become a problem as there is sometimes a perception of non-seriousness or lack of content, as if something playful cannot also be serious…

The same applies to instant/temporary and longer term/evolutionary and to bottom-up and top-down. For me there is not a contradiction in working with both and all the in-betweens. Actually we try to stress the idea of combining the top-down planning approach with immediate interventionist action. That way experimental instant action can enrich a longer term planning process.

KB+AA: Yes, we wanted to ask you precisely about this relation between short term and long term activism; you label your work 'instant urbanism', just like we at the LiAi have chosen to use the term '*immediate architectural intervention*', what are according to you the main qualities in these ideas of immediacy and instancy?

AT: The 'immediate' is a quality in itself for me; you have to take a risk, expose yourself and your ideas and get direct responses to that. That way a direct communication on the matters can be implanted and developed.

FA: Planning and building architecture goes hand in hand with a tedious and obscure process for everyone who is not professionally involved in it. For instance, for all the people that will later live in an environment conceived from the outside, a process often strongly determined by economical parameters.

With our projects we propose a direct and intimate approach to the object in the public space, to architecture, through concrete activities. Our aim is that people reclaim the public space, trusting in it and activating imagination and perspective for a social life besides the restrictive rules and habits of a commercially oriented society.

KB+AA: At the LiAi we are reflecting on how our actions can help 'create community'. You often mention that

from berlin to the polar circle: a conversation with raumlabor - karin berggren and alberto altés

you want to encourage alternative and unexpected use of public space, and that you aim to involve citizens in the transformation of the urban environment. Do you see it as your main task to raise questions and encourage reflection, or do you also aim to produce certain effects, to push development in a specific direction?

FA: Coming as we do from the outside, you immediately see things that a local might not notice or has forgotten due to certain habits. So an obvious first intention of our activities is making visible, and encouraging reflection on, specific circumstances. From there onwards however, our work rarely limits itself to offering a distanced commentary, but instead tries to involve people in prospectively long-term processes of transformation.

AT: For me most of the times it is most interesting to construct processes that are open and not clearly defined (designed) to produce specific effects or results. Yet there are always some prognoses that the things happening are assessed against. So the main task would be to find the balance between pushing in a specific direction and openness. For the involvement of citizens you have to be very aware of this and very specific in how you do it.

FA: Each intervention is an experiment but of course we act using a certain vocabulary of tools. Some of them are obviously ephemeral, like a dinner, others aim to leave something physical, such as a shelter, which can be used or transformed by the locals.

KB+AA: And how do you see such structures, or physical remnants, once you lift your hands from the project? Are they still part of 'your' intervention? If we look at the case of the '*flyttblock*' project here in Umeå, what kind of relationship did you develop with these structures while you were in Umeå? And how has that relationship disappeared or developed afterwards?

AT: You might call it a 'warm' relationship (mine to the *flyttblock*), that developed during our time in Umeå mostly because of the unique experience of collective achievement. I was really happy about the motivation of the student group (that didn't know much of each other at that time) and the desire to make something together, stretching the limit of what is possible.

After working on it daytime and night time it really seemed that everybody wanted to experiment with the objects in the city right away even though it was freezing cold and raining cats and dogs.

KB+AA: Since they were initially built, they have been transformed by the students and appropriated by different publics, they have spread and moved through the city, they have reproduced and constituted sites for movie screenings and round table discussions, they have been inside public buildings and outside in squares and other public spaces, they have been used as supporting structures for numerous other activities, and they have even engendered a smaller, more manageable 'cousin'... Did you foresee or expect the different uses and shapes that the different '*flyttblock*' have taken? Were these effects/side-effects ever part of the 'plan', and how do you feel about them in retrospect? Was there ever a plan at all? Did you have any feeling of responsibility towards the '*flyttblock*' and their effects and do you have it now?

AT: We have only had some sporadic reports on what happened afterwards, but what you describe sounds really nice to me. There was for sure a 'plan' but a very open one, so I don´t feel 'responsible' of the further process that has been designed and organized by the students but happy that it developed that way.

FA: The flyttblock were conceived as instruments that have to be activated; in that sense the imagination of some possible use and constellations was an integral part of the process of developing them. After the week of intense work, on the last day, when the flyttblock had their first appearance in the city and different kinds of use in different spots in Umeå were organised, we experienced a moment of failure: because of the rain, the wooden wheels swelled up so much that they locked into the shafts and we were only able to push them together to the river having something like a party. Maybe this experience of failure was important to raise the will of the students to improve and make them look ahead for other possibilities. I'm also very happy about the new development; this is the best thing that could happen to a project. And the fact that we don't have to feel responsible in the future for something we did because someone else adopted it is also a bit of success. But, please, keep us informed about the evolution.

KB+AA: We will absolutely keep you updated! We have one final question for you: At the LiAi we talk a lot about how we can intervene in and interact with the urban environment, and how this can play a part in city transformation and development.

Questions about 'duration' and 'effects' are often raised; what does the intervention do, for how long does it do it, what are the side-effects of the intervention, and are any of these effects and side-effects still present once the initial event is over? Architectural interventions are often staged as 'happenings'; temporary and transitory in their nature, how do you see the possibilities of your interventions having an effect that lasts beyond the duration of the event itself, and do you think that these long-term effects are something that should be aimed for?

AT: There are some theatre pieces I saw 20 years ago that lasted for two hours that still have an effect on me. So I don't know if an effect depends on temporality.

FA: I agree. I think if we every time try to adjust the intervention according to a desired long-term effect, we would probably forget important parameters like improvisation, openness and taking risks. Back to the flyttblock and this moment of failure last year: as we were blocked on the street under the strong rain we asked people who stopped by to help us. With those who helped us push for 200 meters we started a conversation about our activities. I'm sure they still have a vivid memory of this episode. // Umeå-Berlin, September 2012

(KB+AA: At the time in which the book was finished and printed, Francesco and Axel had already been in Umeå again, developing with us another intervention in relationship to the LiAi's theme of "the other/coexistence". Their time with us was, again, a great experience: their ideas and proposals were extremely challenging, mind-opening and able to question the conditions in which the city is being made and the terms of our work as architects as well as the local conditions of Umeå's difficult, but inspiring climate. It obviously requires another conversation with them, soon.)

situated knowledge: the laboratory of immediate architectural intervention - roemer van toorn

"To know what one is speaking about, (...) requires that one knows who is speaking and from where: it is necessary to know that one always speaks from within a world from which comes the structure of consciousness of the one who is speaking and who, in order to know what he is saying, must know this world and this structuration at risk of otherwise remaining within an ideology"[1]

situated knowledge: the laboratory of immediate architectural intervention

roemer van toorn

A lot of researchers in the field of architecture speak from above and outside lived experiences. They lose sight of their conditional nature, take no risk in speculation, and circulate as members of a promotion campaign or form of administrative inquisition over the world paralyzing all practitioners with their critique, without any proposition on what could be done tomorrow.

---

1 Goldman, Lucien. (1977) *Lukács and Heidegger: Towards a New Philosophy*.

When Lucien Goldman spoke his words in Paris during the turbulent days of 1968 he referred to what Karl Marx and Friedrich Engels once said in "*The German ideology*"[2] that when someone speaks, one should always ask oneself "*Who is speaking and from where?*" Goldman targeted people such as the philosopher Jacques Derrida and others who where stepping in the footsteps of Martin Heidegger, dealing with the world from an ivory-tower; as if life could be determined far from a consciousness determined by life itself. It is remarkable says Terry Eagleton "*…that intellectual life for centuries was conducted on the tacit assumption that human beings had no genitals. Intellectuals also behaved as though men and women lacked stomachs.*"[3] Heidegger's rather abstract concept of 'Dasein' is indeed – as Emmanuel Levinas once said, a "*Dasein that does not eat*".

In the Laboratory of Immediate Architectural Intervention theory never speaks for itself, and neither does the lived experience; instead they inform each other in an interdependent manner. In their research approach, Oren Lieberman and Alberto Altés Arlandis seem to acknowledge that our human existence is at least as much about desire and fantasy as it is about truth, reason and power. Sociology, economy, anthropology, history, politics, philosophy, economics, art, film, dance, literature, design, the city, the everyday, photography, fashion, the experience of the thing, and other fields, all inform the laboratory's research to grasp what our live experience is about. The interdisciplinary weaving method of the studio shows that theory and practice cannot do without each other when you wish to understand the present and want to mobilize its liberating energies. Through their immediate interventions they unveil and discover reality and commit themselves to the present, they cannot but make their hands dirty while transforming a given reality to the better (at least that is what many of its students hope to establish).

Instead of assailing reality with a priori positions the immediate interventions lab analyses the facts, which apparatus is at stake, and, in the process of creation, make decisions capable of transforming a project in concrete and surprising ways. The architect tries to overrule his/her own prejudices by developing, in the process of intervention, where the information could lead

---

2 Marx, Karl. and Friedrich Engels, (1959) *Basic Writings on Politics and Philosophy*.

3 Eagleton, Terry. (2003) *After Theory.*

him or her in direct confrontation with the other. The distancing of critical theory is replaced by a curatorial attitude. When you practice – what I have once called a projective theory – you don't arrive at a project with a bag full of prior theory or design prejudice, but start to map the many (and potential) controversies within the co-existence of life. Lieberman and Altés are not telling us what is right or wrong, but prefer to analyze what society, its inhabitants, its users, politicians, architects, planners and alike enact; and help them to mobilize opportunities from within a given situation through their engaging interventions. Not the urban or architectural project in itself is celebrated, but the broader social, economical, cultural context and processes architects enact through their physical and spatial interventions are what count.

It is not about the autonomy of form but all about process. How through creative interventions scenarios and strategies, which deal with the many mutations in our urban landscape, alternative routes can be mobilized.

The Life of Things

Rather than considering an object as a fact or a value, dividing the world in the objective powers of the thing as in the natural sciences, or only look, as in social sciences, to the object to be used as a white screen onto which society projects it ideals, Lieberman and Altés work from a developed theoretical perspective that brings these two scientific cultures together. Research into either the 'hard' or 'soft' qualities of an object are naturally applied in practice, but how these two cultures function together in reality - forming a complex dynamic whole - goes often unnoticed, says Bruno Latour. This is remarkable to say the least because in reality we do not make a distinction into two cultures; quite the opposite, we assume hybrid and simultaneous relations all the time. For this reason, the researchers Michel Serres and Bruno Latour propose that we should cast the 'soft' or 'hard' object from our minds. It is better to talk of the quasi-object.

The quasi-object equips us to develop a new model of knowledge that goes beyond dividing an object into two cultures. Rather than considering an object as a fact or a value, to see it simply as a (stylistic) form or social function, we must begin to grasp the facts and values as intrinsically interdependent wholes. "*Quasi-objects are much more social*" says anthropologist and philosopher Bruno Latour, "*much more fabricated, much more collective than the 'hard' parts of nature, but they are in no way the arbitrary receptacles of a full-*

fledged society. On the other hand they are much more real, nonhuman and objective than those shapeless screens on which society – for unknown reasons – needed to be 'projected'."[4]

As Marian Fraser observed "*Matter does not 'exist in and of itself, outside or beyond discourse, but is rather repeatedly produced through performativity, which brings into being or enacts that which it names.*"[5] It is this situated knowledge of the quasi-object that Lieberman and Altés seem to be after with their immediate interventions.

When we focus on a coffee cup for instance, all kinds of relations set themselves into action. We can think of the entire history of Turkish coffee making, the people who harvest the coffee beans, the manufacturing process of the cup, how the distribution and marketing influenced the design, the memories and desires an Illy café can activate.

For Lieberman and Altés the real is full of circulating substance, innovation, interpretation and change. Instead of looking to form as something with a fixed and eternal meaning such as in classical architecture, their lab starts with the fact that matter is caught up in the flux of time rather than representation. In foregrounding time in urbanism and architecture the laboratory starts to deal with the encounter of perception (the program of life) and matter, that being and matter are never stable, that matter and movement are imbued with and inseparable from situated knowledge.

Open Systems and After

For Deleuze and Guattari thinking in terms of circulating substance, energies, flows, desiring machines and movement was not a goal in itself – not just to have a set of appropriate tools to better understand society in its full complexity – but foremost invented to subvert and break the bourgeois processes full of order and clichés. They believed that a kind of nomadic existence that allows for spontaneous groupings and organizations of people - or with a simple definition open systems, or multitudes - could free us from the suffocation of normality.

A similar approach can be found in the approach of Lieberman and Altés. Ac-

---

4 Latour, Bruno. (1993) *We Have Never Been Modern*, Harvard University Press, Cambridge, Massachusetts.

5 Fraser, Marian. (1999) "Classing Queer: Politics in Competition", in *Performativity and Belonging*, Vikki Bell ed. Theory, Culture & Society.

cording to me, and for instance Gillian Howie, Deleuze follows a too mystical romantic perspective that – although intended as a progressive route to walk – isn't able to go beyond the mechanism of advanced control we associate with neo-liberalism today. With our culture of sprawl we have entered an endless sea of sameness disguised as difference. Unfortunately neoliberalism has become Deleuzian. The Right acts big, while the Left is still engaged in a performative contradiction of continuing to dream of liberty in the face of a pessimistic skepticism about resistance and outdated forms of emancipation.

Instead of a negative critic which no longer believes that any future could be realized through the logic of practice in the middle of society, or a pessimism that in the words of Perry Anderson "*strafed meaning, over-ran truth, outflanked ethics and politics, and wiped out history*"[6] the Laboratory of Immediate Architectural Intervention has initiated a unique research method, which enables each student to mobilize the situated knowledge by intervening within the order of things, through their bodily presence and intellectual capacities as (future) architect.

If these actions create situations of freedom has been in most first year projects an open question. And that leads me to the question of whether the laboratory for immediate architectural intervention can indeed sustain to 'just' dive into the middle of fragmentation, surf the waves of late-capitalism from within by its immediate interventions alone. I look very much forward to seeing how the lab will challenge this question.

Something is definitely missing in today's capitalist realism. After all with the collapse of the banking system we stand at the beginning of a return to full-blown history. This return to history has not only led to a renewed interest in radical ideas and politics developed in the past, but also marks a new beginning in search of new forms of sociality (including developing a new kind of cartography to map the many controversies which the laboratory has started to develop). Rethinking the social in architecture is thus an actual and urgent issue to address that cannot be solved by means of immediate interventions alone. //

---

6 Anderson, Perry. (1983) *In the Tracks of Historical Materialism*.

sites, agencies, matters of concern

**this section of the book
presents a journey through some of the
research and interventions carried out at the
laboratory of immediate architectural intervention
at umeå school of architecture
during the academic years
2011-2012 and 2012-2013**

**the research and interventions were
made possible through the engagement,
motivation, dedication and skills of our students:**

**kimberley beauprez
veronica gerini
erika henriksson
maria hudl
paula idun
christina kousgaard
martin livian
johan marklund
anna misharina
olga oreshkina
febe roels
kirstine skyum
audingas sumskas
sofia sjölin
tobias westerlund**

body/apparatus
critical/projective/relational
agency/structure/ANT
the other/difference
the other/coexistence
transversals/micropolitics
aesthetics/politics
affordance/gift
diffraction/representation
discourse/event
documentation/judgment

Our matters of concern have evolved since we started establishing the LiAi. They certainly work… and in a very particular way.

Just as we define them both in terms of found texts and references and our own particular ontologies and epistemologies, so too the students: they are presented with these diptychs or triptychs of matters of concern and are asked to 'map' as well as to think through them. They do this with the knowledge that they are not quite sure of the meanings either… and yet, their mappings produce the meanings as they go, just as they are 'diagnostic' in the sense that they reveal certain predilections and preoccupations.

We have learned a tremendous amount from them about these matters of concern through their meanderings and uncertainties and their proclamations.

These matters of concern, as enacted in the mappings for instance, achieve specificity ... they no longer reside solely in the discourse of the 'about', but in the lines and colours of the visualisations on screen or printed out.

What is happening here is not an application of theory, but a making of tangible agendas and positions, i.e., a making of theory. The matters of concern enable this positioning and demarcation of areas of interest and... yes, concern. But the areas are not abstracted, they are very real and resonate with spaces and flesh and things and interactions...

These matters of concern are not only tools for 'mapping', or for exploring and delineating agendas and positions but are also very concrete instances of thought. Though as framing devices they indicate realms of perception, thought and action, they are as well open enough to allow the production of the unexpected, the exploration of the uncertain, and the joy of speculative play. And: they are damn serious. They are ways of approaching crucial questions, things that genuinely matter. And their openness makes them excellent learning apparatuses as we have to work our way(s) through them and with them, exploring, discussing, speculating, testing and learning in the process of proposing what they could be or what they are.

Learning is here not a transferring of a series of frozen definitions, but a process and a practice through which a situated concept 'becomes'. And it becomes in concert with things, spaces and discourses, in concert with worries, intuitions and fascinations, along the lines of our movements in the city, and around the sites of our interventions. These, our matters of concern, are tools for 'architecting' the world responsibly.

plastic bags/ - olga oreshkina

take an object for a walk - architectural intervention and cultural consequences - liai 7

We see in this section of the book several instances of student work emerging from an introductory exercise that we are quite fond of, something we call '*take an object for a walk*'. Students engage with a domestic object in a way in which the object dictates the terms of its own analysis and these terms are then transformed into a

olga oreshkina - /**plastic bags**

take an object for a walk - architectural intervention and cultural consequences - liai 7

'practicing' of the city, a moving through the city enacted in the form of walking and guided by the object. The city is then encountered otherwise: other gazes, other walks, other speeds, other rhythms, other aims, other values... emerge and are performed in these movements through the city. Students entangle themselves with

story-umeå-heart/ - olga oreshkina + anna misharina

draft prototypes - architectural intervention and cultural consequences - liai 7

another, previously unknown, city. Olga for instance was capable of establishing an interesting relationship with handsome teenagers and light poles in the city, through a plastic bag, which allowed her to draw people's dis-figured faces, measure the distance to things differently and feel the strength and speed of the wind blowing

olga oreshkina + anna misharina - **/story-umeå-heart**

draft prototypes - architectural intervention and cultural consequences - liai 7

in the streets. Her performative skills were liberated with surprising effects, and what has proven even more remarkable, her outstanding abilities to record and document emerged from the outset and continued to develop. (In different ways, the relative openness of the exercise allows students to engage in different situations using the

story-umeå-heart/ - olga oreshkina + anna misharina

construction process - architectural intervention and cultural consequences - liai 7

skills and tools they already have). We can see here how, from the very beginning, the interplay of matters of concern is present, so that fields of interest such as those marked by the sets 'body/apparatus', 'performative/things' and 'documentation/judgement', start taking on very real lives and meanings of their own, unfolding in the

olga oreshkina + anna misharina - **/story-umeå-heart**

a break in the construction process - architectural intervention and cultural consequences - liai 7

practiced practices brought into the streets of the city and in the conversations and encounters with different people.

These sets of notions are planned 'concerns' of very specific parts of our work in the laboratory; one by one, we use our 'matters of concern' to connect texts that

story-umeå-heart/ - olga oreshkina + anna misharina

collaborative workshop - architectural intervention and cultural consequences - liai 7

we read in dedicated seminars, and to frame discussions, urban explorations and design challenges throughout the different terms of the program; yet, they are presented and introduced together and all at once, and affect our student's work as a constellation from the very beginning.

olga oreshkina + anna misharina - **/story-umeå-heart**

collaborative workshop - architectural intervention and cultural consequences - liai 7

In the case of 'story-umeå-heart', in which Olga and Anna worked together, the work evolved in quite interesting ways. From an initial critique of the official design for the logo of the 2014 European Capital of Culture in Umeå - a red heart inspired by the well-known 'smileys' that appeals to the idea of an essential 'heart of the city', the

story-umeå-heart/ - olga oreshkina + anna misharina

collaborative workshop - architectural intervention and cultural consequences - liai 7

values of which have already been pre-programmed and set by the managers of this cultural project - to a very broad engagement with the city and its making. This included: the development of physical prototypes in different scales; the organization of collaborative workshops with different actors in the city; the building together of

olga oreshkina + anna misharina - **/story-umeå-heart**

the other heart - architectural intervention and cultural consequences - liai 7

an alternative heart that allowed for diverse discussions around the validity of the idea of 'a heart of the city' and about the actual 'content' or 'material' of that heart; the negotiation and management of the possibility of an intervention that would place the alternative heart and documentation of the whole process in a prominent public space

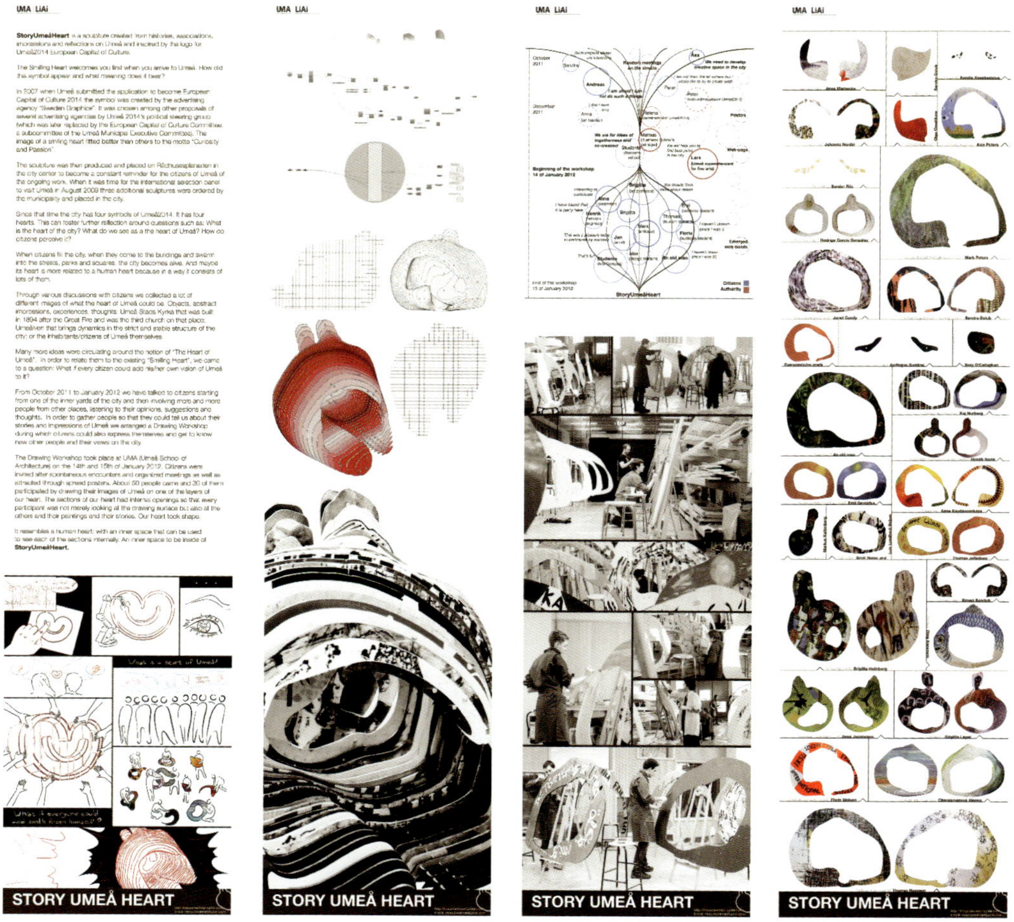

story-umeå-heart/ - olga oreshkina + anna misharina

exhibition panels - architectural intervention and cultural consequences - liai 7

of the city; and the actual documentation and carrying out of such an intervention. The students hoped that through the fragmentation of the heart into sections and in devising, colouring and making those sections, the various participants would contribute their part to a 'new' heart that could be seen as a 'truer' heart. But the process

olga oreshkina + anna misharina - **/story-umeå-heart**

story-umeå-heart at stadsbiblioteket - architectural intervention and cultural consequences - liai 7

is a powerful commentary on, and questioning of, the municipal campaign and the elements it imposes and takes for granted, when looked at as a whole. Moreover, if we look at it as a process with various and many parts and involving many different actors, what is foregrounded and takes on particular relevance is the dialogical spaces of ar-

in our own backyard - kirstine skyum holm and tobias westerlund

mobiles structures in umeå - urban explorations - liai 7

ticulation that emerged through and around the different 'actions' and things that happened. In these events people met, talked, discussed, thought about things they had not thought before and engaged in conversations about the city and its making. In the process, Olga and Anna not only rehearsed different techniques of material design and

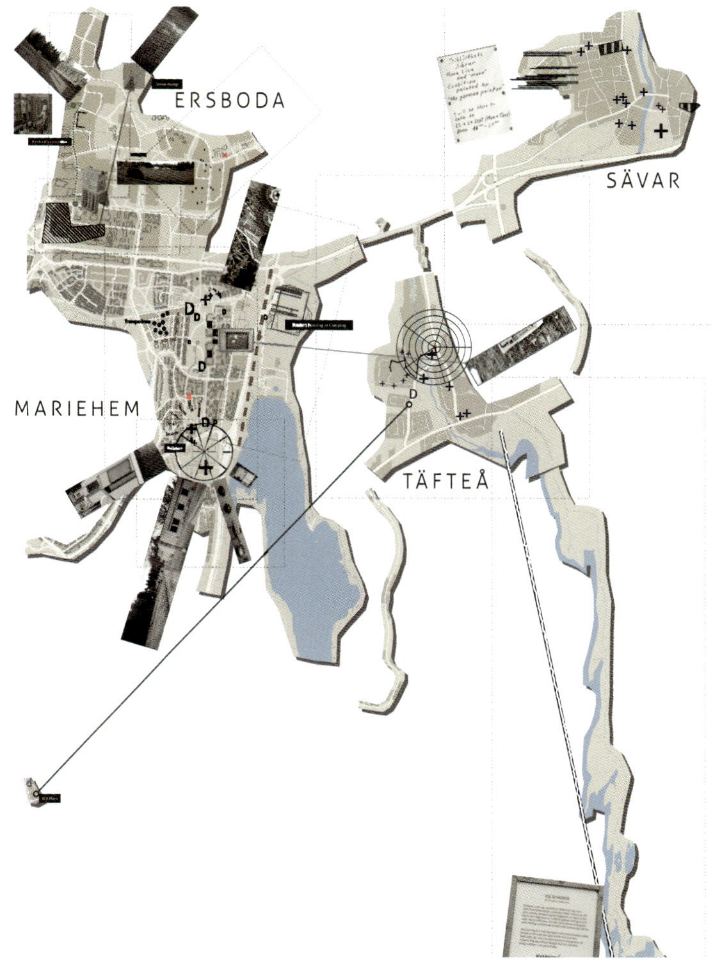

kirstine skyum holm and tobias westerlund **- in our own backyard**

mobiles structures in umeå - alternative cartographies - liai 7

construction, but learned and told us very interesting and important things and stories about the city. They were, right from the start, there: of the city.

The idiom '*In Our Own Backyard*' helps us further to 'inhabit' the city. It points both to ideas of proximity and familiarity - something that is close to us and that is basically

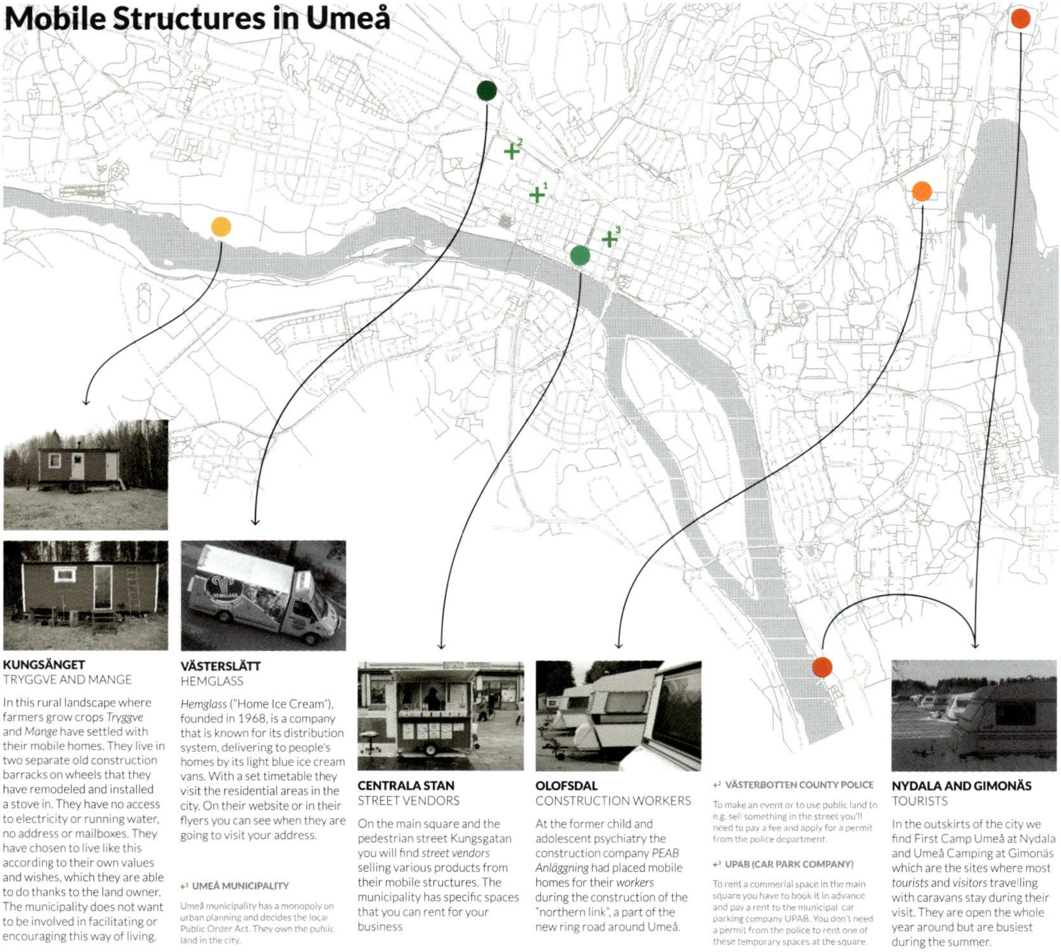

being mobile in umeå - tobias westerlund

mobiles structures - architectural intervention and cultural consequences - liai 7

attached to our homes - as well as to ideas of the hidden, the backside of things, that which is not on the surface, the obscure, dark and/or transgressive; that is, very real and present dimensions of our lives and very powerful forces in the making of the city and the world. We believe that exploring and inhabiting these backyards can be

tobias westerlund **- being mobile in umeå**

tryggve and mange live here - urban explorations - liai 7

a very productive way of engaging with a city we still don't know very well. For those who believe they are 'familiar' with that city - with its spaces, discourses and events - it can also be a tool for re-discovering what they have been taught to ignore of it.

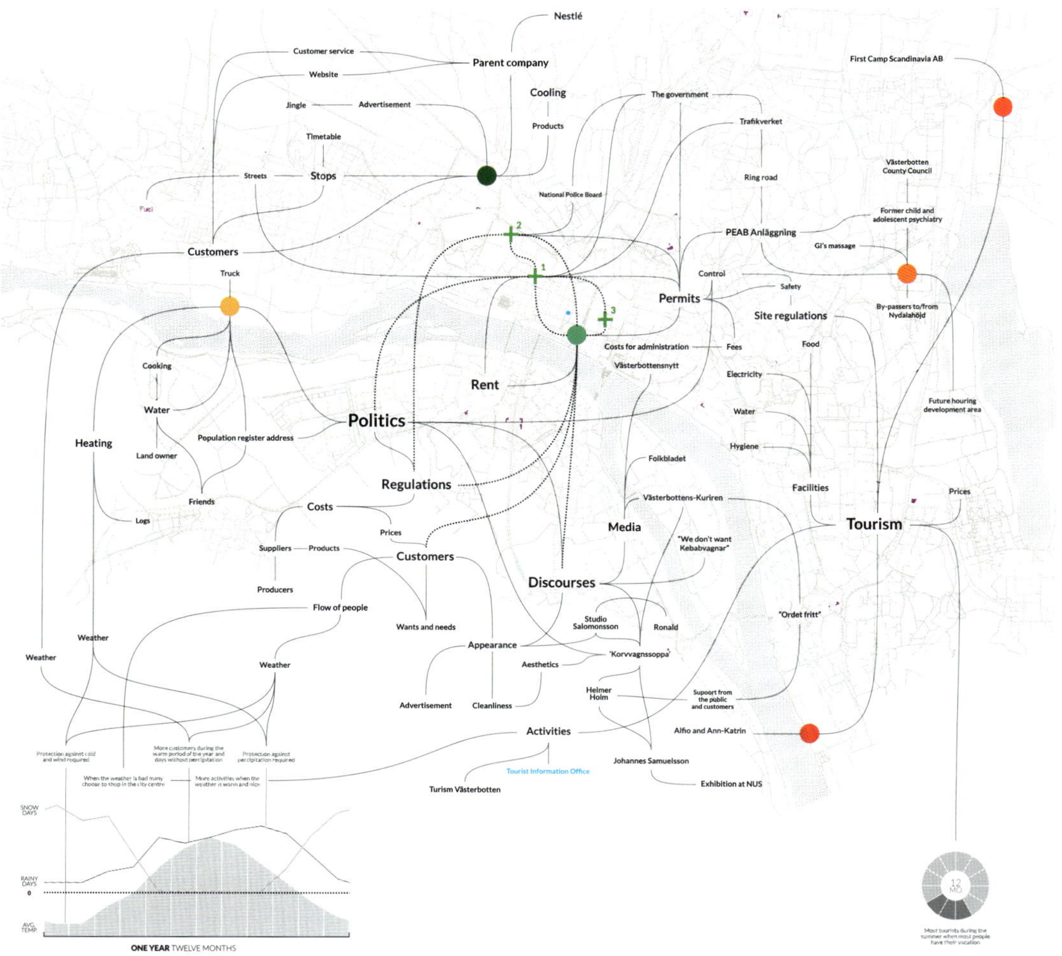

being mobile in umeå - tobias westerlund

sociogram - architectural intervention and cultural consequences - liai 7

In the case of Kirstine and Tobias, their explorations of several areas of Umeå such as Mariehem, Ersboda, Sävar and Täfteå allowed them to elaborate a very different alternative cartography based on their findings and experiences, but also, most importantly, brought them to a number of very real 'encounters' with for instance a thai

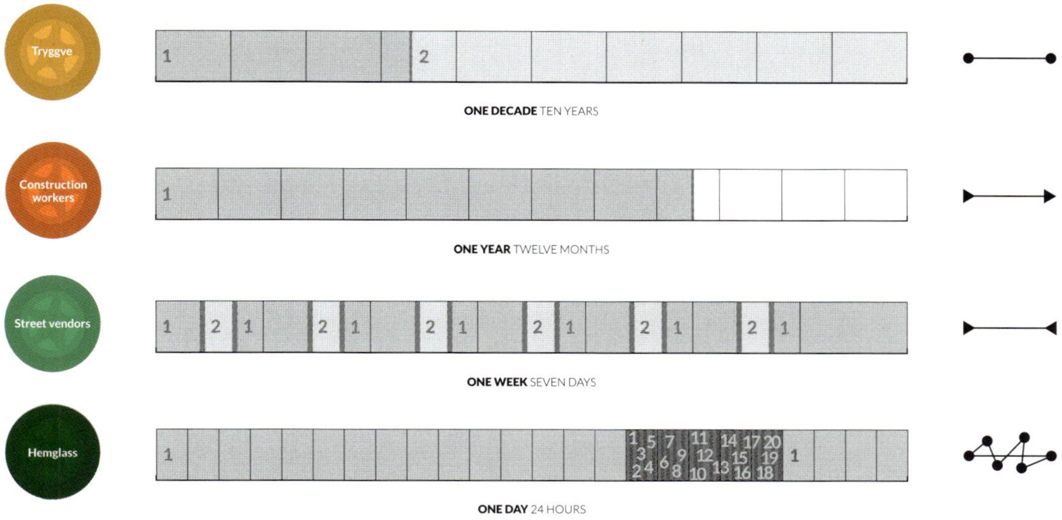

Timeline

How mobile are these actors in reality? The timelines show their movements over a specific time period. The numbers indicate different locations, a solid grey fill represents movement. The pictogram to the right gives an image of the pattern of the movement.

TRYGGVE
ONE DECADE

Seven years ago Tryggve had to move his trailer a few hundred meters to its current site. In order to move it he neede a truck since the trailer is heavy and the terrain is uneven. Though you would say that they live in a mobile home they are in fact not moving around with it a lot, only when there is a direct need for it.

CONSTRUCTION WORKERS
ONE YEAR

The construction workers occupied the site as long as the construction work lasted, then they moved away. It is a temporary solution to a temporary need of housing.

HEMGLASS
ONE DAY

The Hemglass truck moves around a lot between the different stops in the residential areas during a few hours each day. A timetable can be found in their webpage or in their flyers distributed by mail. You can even suggest new stops at their website.

STREET VENDORS
ONE WEEK

The vendors move with their structures between the storage (a garage or a carport) and the square where their business is, they always come back to the same spot.

tobias westerlund **- being mobile in umeå**

movements in time - notation systems - architectural intervention and cultural consequences - liai 7

woman inside a container in the forest, or a very curious collection of mobile homes parked together, that seemed to have been there for quite a while, perhaps 'immobile'. This led to a more thorough engagement with mobile structures in Umeå by Tobias, who looked for all kinds of mobile devices and structures in the city, including street

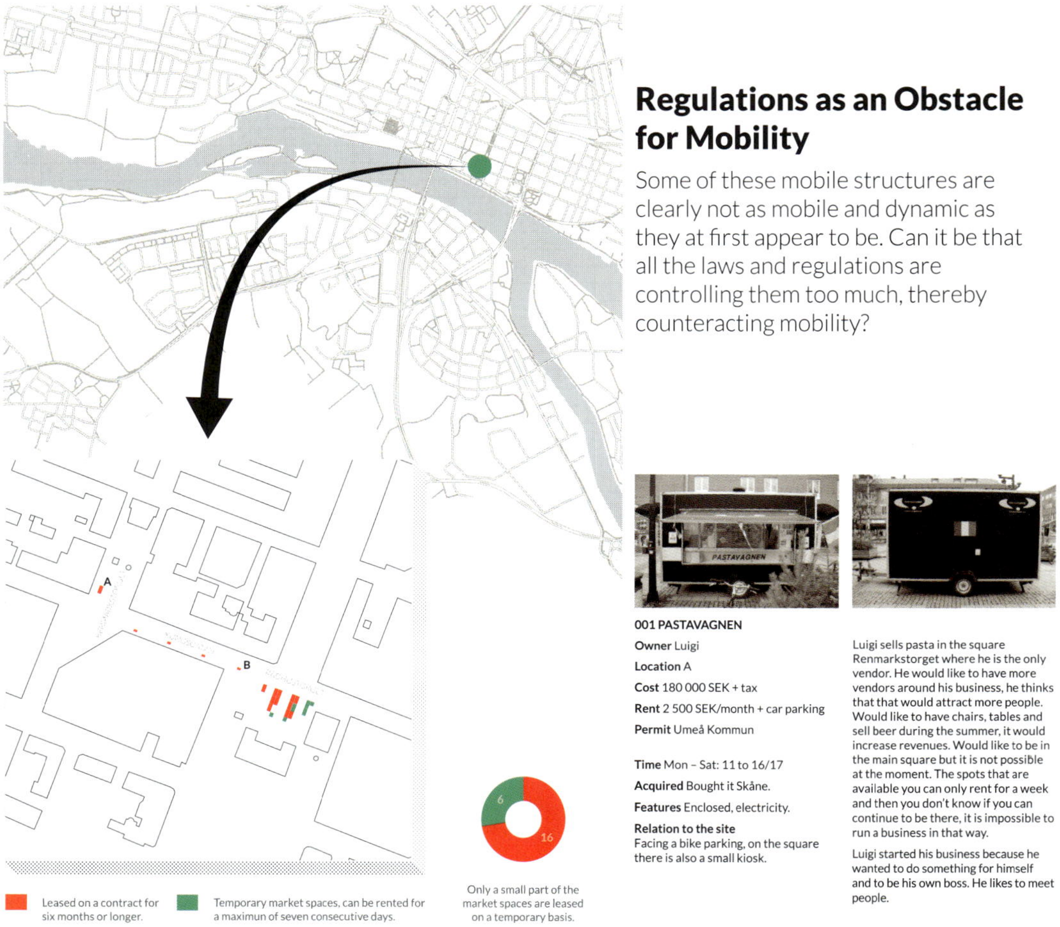

being mobile in umeå - tobias westerlund

mobility regulated - architectural intervention and cultural consequences - liai 7

vendors, market places, ice-cream vans, tourists, containers and floating homes, as well as regulations. He was able to map how things were not quite what they seemed, and most of these structures that 'were supposed' to be mobile, were in fact quite stationary. Tobias related this apparent immobility to the effects of quite strict

intravention, durations, effects

002 HELMERS KORVVAGN

Owner Helmer Holm

Location B

Time Mon – Sat: 11 to 16/17

Permit
Umeå Kommun. A permit for the location was included when he bought the trailer.

Acquired
Bought it from a man selling sausages at Renmarkstorget

Features
Enclosed/weather protected, approved for LPG (gas cylinder outside), roof for customers, electric light

Relation to the site
Turns the wagon from the wind to protect himself and customers.

Cost 31 000 SEK

Rent 1 546 SEK/month

Helmer sells sausages in the city because he likes to meet and talk to people. He is very satisfied with his korvvagn and would not like to change anything. He is dissatisfied with the market in the square. He have recently proposed to the organization Umeå C that the vendors should be arranged in a horseshoe/U-shape to give an overview.

When he is not working the trailer is stored in a carport in a residential area in Umeå.

005 TRYGGVE AND MANGE'S HOMES

Owner Tryggve and Mange

Location Kungsänget

Rent 0 SEK, they help the landowner with some practical work occasionally.

Permit Landowner

Time Year around

Acquired Found them in an advertisement in "Blänkarn" and "Blocket.se"

Features Enclosed, stove, the window can be covered with a curtain i felt to keep the heat longer.

Relation to the site
Positioned in a L-shape courtyard. View towards the river.

Tryggve and Mange have been in contact with the municipality a few times, discussion the situation with the mobile homes. The municipality has not shown a lot of interest to their questions.

They like the place where they have settled but would like to find a place closer to the city. It would also be nice if you could live like this in a "legal" and organised way.

They think that it would be great with places where you could put up mobile homes to then share a proper kitchen, toilet and shower with several others living in the same way.

If you make visits at the square and the pedestrian street over a longer period of time you will notice that it is always the same vendors occupying the spaces. You can question the municipality's writing that "...markets, street vendors and other events make the city more attractive by livelier trade and a more varied city life".

How the street vendors are arranged and can act in the city is strictly controlled by the municipality. There are a specific number of spaces that you can rent for your business (see map above). If you choose to do so you are allowed to be there between 9:00–21:00. The majority of the spaces are rented out for a minimum of six months at a time, while a smaller number of the spaces can be rented for up to seven days at a time, after that week you can only continue to rent that space if no one else wants to have it.

The municipality don't offer any other places in the city that street vendors can use or rent for their business.

The four spaces on Kungsgatan are the ones where you are obliged to have wagons with the new design that have been approved by the municipality. One of the vendors, Helmer Holm, has got an exemption from this rule for health reasons.

The planning, the rules and regulations are causing the static state of the situation. Of course we need regulations in order to avoid conflicts and to make sure that things don't get out of hand, but together with the centralization that is created here it has more resemblance with controlled environments like shopping malls than a varied city life.

tobias westerlund - **being mobile in umeå**
mobility in the main square - architectural intervention and cultural consequences - liai 7

regulations and control as obstacles to mobility. His work led him to the proposal of a (really) mobile structure that could act as a place for encounter and exchange, constantly moving through the city, people jumping in it and leaving or exchanging things, information and moments. The idea was discussed in relationship with the

being mobile in umeå - tobias westerlund

an exchange hub that moves - architectural intervention and cultural consequences - liai 7

lack of bakeries in the city and speculations about a system to make possible the distribution of home-baked bread that someone would collect from different homes and then transport to other people who may have expressed an interest previously. Again, many of our matters of concern are at work in this project, and things are

tobias westerlund **- being mobile in umeå**

an exchange hub that moves - architectural intervention and cultural consequences - liai 7

not only designed or devised but also built and put to work in the city. Things, apparatuses and spaces are interrelated through the actions of people, and the city emerges through their performances. But this is only possible in concert with ideas, thoughts, discourses, and theories that are also explored and produced through the inhabiting

a forest of berries: the informal economy of picking/ - kirstine skyum

waiting for the berries - urban exploration - in our own backyard - liai 7

and thinking of the city. On the other hand, the first encounter with the thai woman in the container allowed Kirstine to dive into a very complex exploration of the formal and informal worlds and economies that exist around berries, and that connect Umeå, Norrland, its forests and its industries, with the immigrants that come to Sweden to

kirstine skyum - **/a forest of berries: the informal economy of picking**

we buy berries - urban exploration - in our own backyard - liai 7

work as berry pickers, the law that regulates the use of the commons in Sweden, the politics of the rights to public access, as well as with various intermediary and final actors that transform the berries into diverse products and subproducts and send them to different places in Asia and then back to Sweden for commercial purposes.

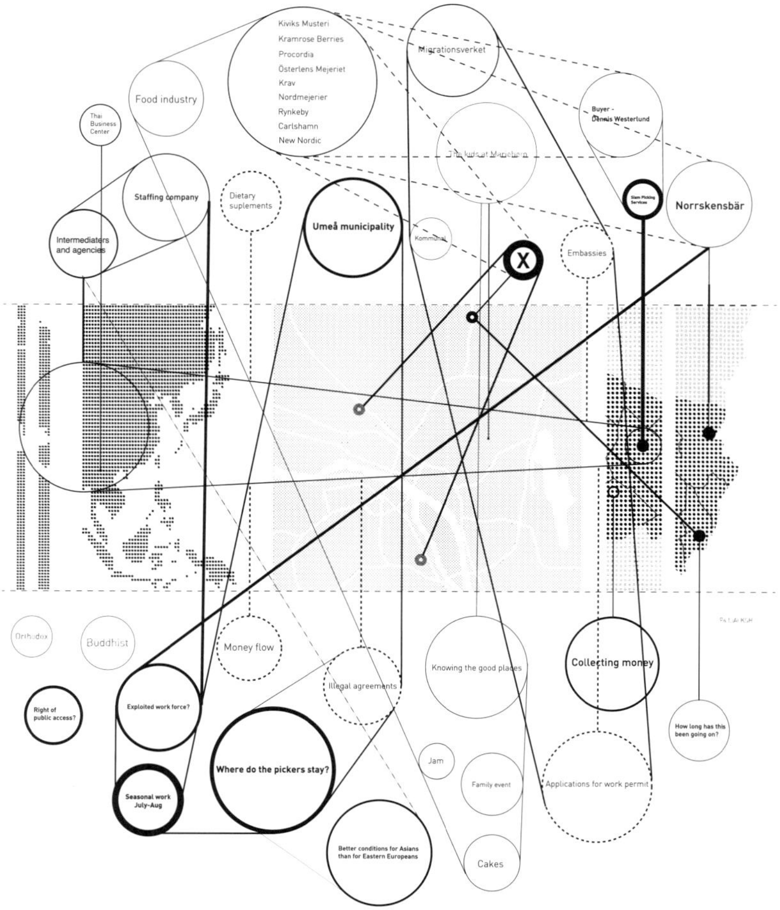

a forest of berries: the informal economy of picking/ - kirstine skyum

sociogram - in our own backyard - liai 7

However, her major interest remained close to Umeå: in the relationships with the berries and their picking, carried out by people in conditions that are, to the say the least, inadequate and unfair. Kirstine's becoming close to the berries paralleled her closeness to the berry pickers and their homes, or rather, to the absence of such homes,

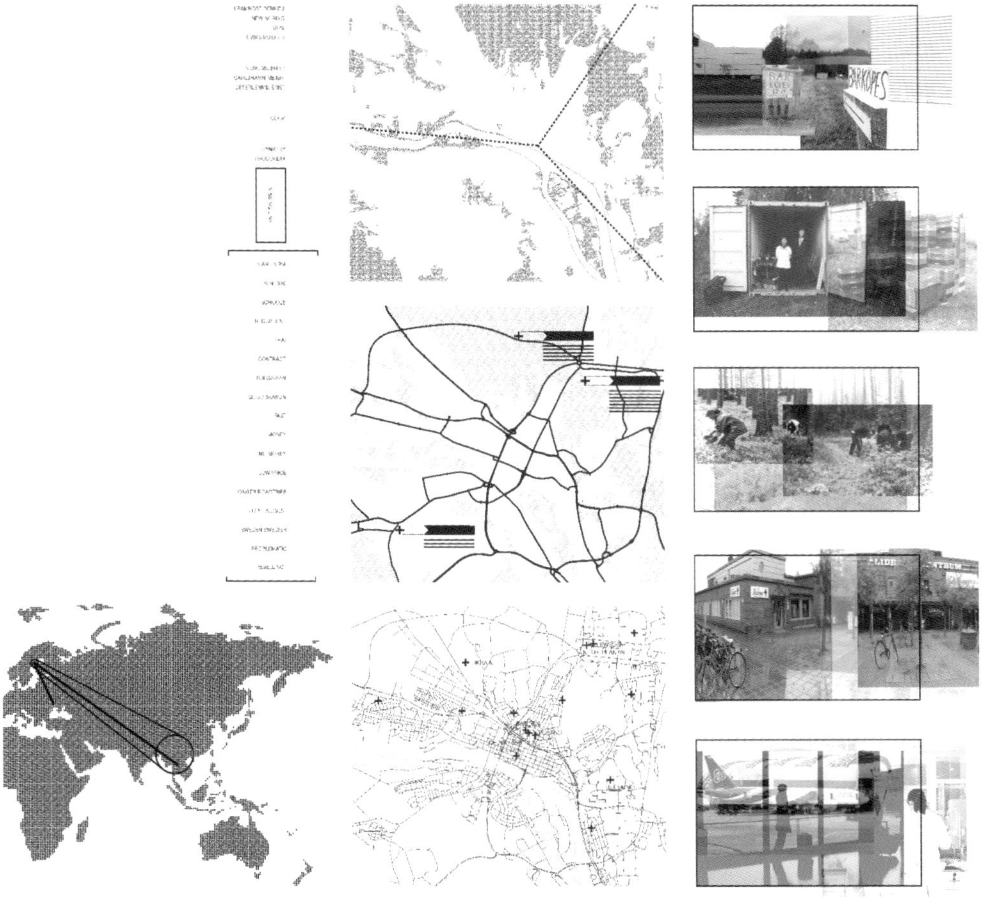

kirstine skyum - **/a forest of berries: the informal economy of picking**

urban exploration - in our own backyard - liai 7

and to the analysis of the conditions of their existence, tied in most cases to the forests and to diverse formats of 'the camp'.The ways in which this research and work ends up entangled with other inhabitants of the forest, the hunters, and understands them as privileged users of an otherwise 'privatized' resource (managed by the companies

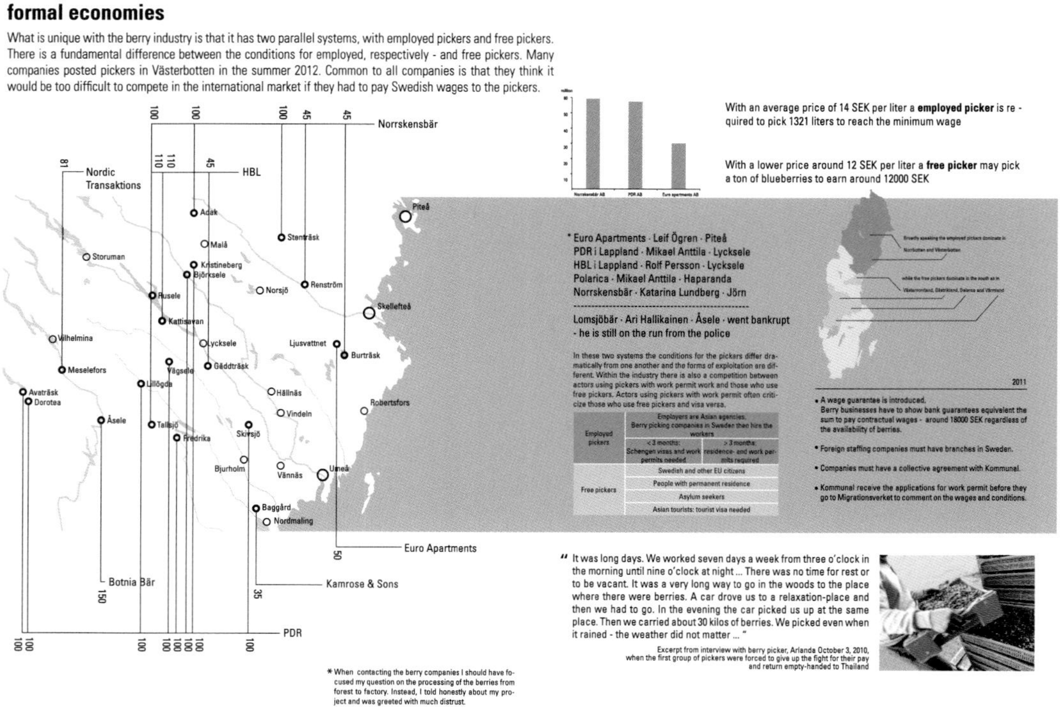

a forest of berries: the informal economy of picking/ - kirstine skyum

formal economies - in our own backyard - liai 7

that have been granted rights to exploit the timber) is incredibly transversal and diffractive. It acknowledges different logics and phenomena that coexist and coalesce in and on a 'forest of trees', and ends up re-articulating the possible meanings and uses of the towers that the hunters install and leave in the forest to aid them in their raids.

intervention / shelter

The intervention must be understood as a preliminary, small step towards a form of awareness of the kind of modern slavery that takes place every year in the Swedish forests. Adding shelters to existing hunting towers, the structure lends a bit of the hunters veto power and create an alternative working / living situation for free pickers. With a growing sector with labor from foreign staffing companies the risk increases that more people will be exploited.

In the summer of 2011 Migrationsverket came with new rules, the aim was to curb the incongruity that had existed in previous years. The number of pickers from Asian staffing companies halved to just about 2500. Instead came the so-called free pickers. Some statistics on the number does not exist, but it is guessed that it was about 1000. They came among others from Thailand, Bulgaria, Romania, the Baltic States and Poland. Many of these free pickers had been recruited by the company-like networks. These networks organized trips to Sweden, arranged places for tent camps, drove pickers by bus out in the forest - but without the pickers being employed. They were not insured or guaranteed salary, so therefore extremely vulnerable and deprived of rights. By connecting the pickers and the network of hunting towers /shelters it is the intention to provide an alternative to the primitive camps that are creating conflicts between the municipality and forest owners. The shelters are intended to be a base for pickers who want to break with unreliable employers and become independent and sell berries directly (in this context have to be an illustrated description of legislation in this area in the immediate context of shelter).

Both the hunter and the free berry picker want to be hidden, to live a discrete life in the forest. The shelter and the tower are both simple structures, consisting of only the most necessary and are aiming to blend in with the surroundings. The shelter is made so that it mimics the existing tower and at the same time act as an adaptive system - adaptive to the vegetation, area, etc. As the hunting towers, the location of the shelters are not caused by a master plan but from a knowledge of where to find berries/ where the elks move, it becomes a network for both hunters as well as pickers.

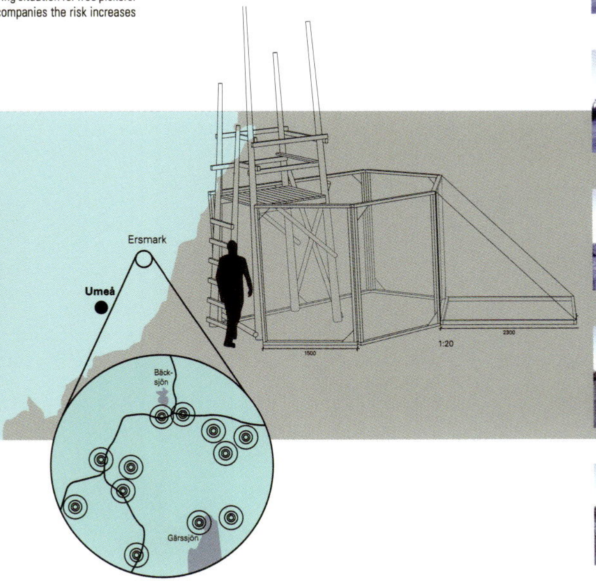

kirstine skyum - **/a forest of berries: the informal economy of picking**

intervention/shelter - in our own backyard - liai 7

The hunting towers are then explored and tested as inspiring and supporting structures for various interventions that can be read through an idea of shelter, but question at the same time the very presence of the berry pickers in the forest.

a forest of berries: the informal economy of picking/ - kirstine skyum

a local site for intervention - in our own backyard - liai 7

kirstine skyum - **/a forest of berries: the informal economy of picking**

a hunting tower - in our own backyard - liai 7

a forest of berries: the informal economy of picking/ - kirstine skyum
intervention/shelter attached to the hunting tower - in our own backyard - liai 7

kirstine skyum - **/a forest of berries: the informal economy of picking**
intervention/shelter attached to the hunting tower - in our own backyard - liai 7

street memories/ - olga oreshkina

gathering stories through letters - architectural intervention and cultural consequences - liai 7

In a completely different way, Olga carried out one of her explorations of the city through a careful process of re-collection of stories, which she asked different peo-

olga oreshkina - **/street memories**

prepared envelopes - architectural intervention and cultural consequences - liai 7

ple to share with her by means of writing them and either putting them inside several mailboxes that she left in strategic places or sending them by postal mail. She sent out many letters to very different people, asking them to write her back with stories about their city and about the streets in which they lived. She sent out notebooks

street memories/in our own backyard/ - olga oreshkina

gathering stories through notebooks - architectural intervention and cultural consequences - liai 7

that were ready to be filled with such stories and got a few back. One of the notebooks was particularly intense both in the way it was carried out and in relationship with the kinds of stories that it shared. The implication of the person that took the time to write, draw, paint and collect the pictures and media-cuts to illustrate the sto-

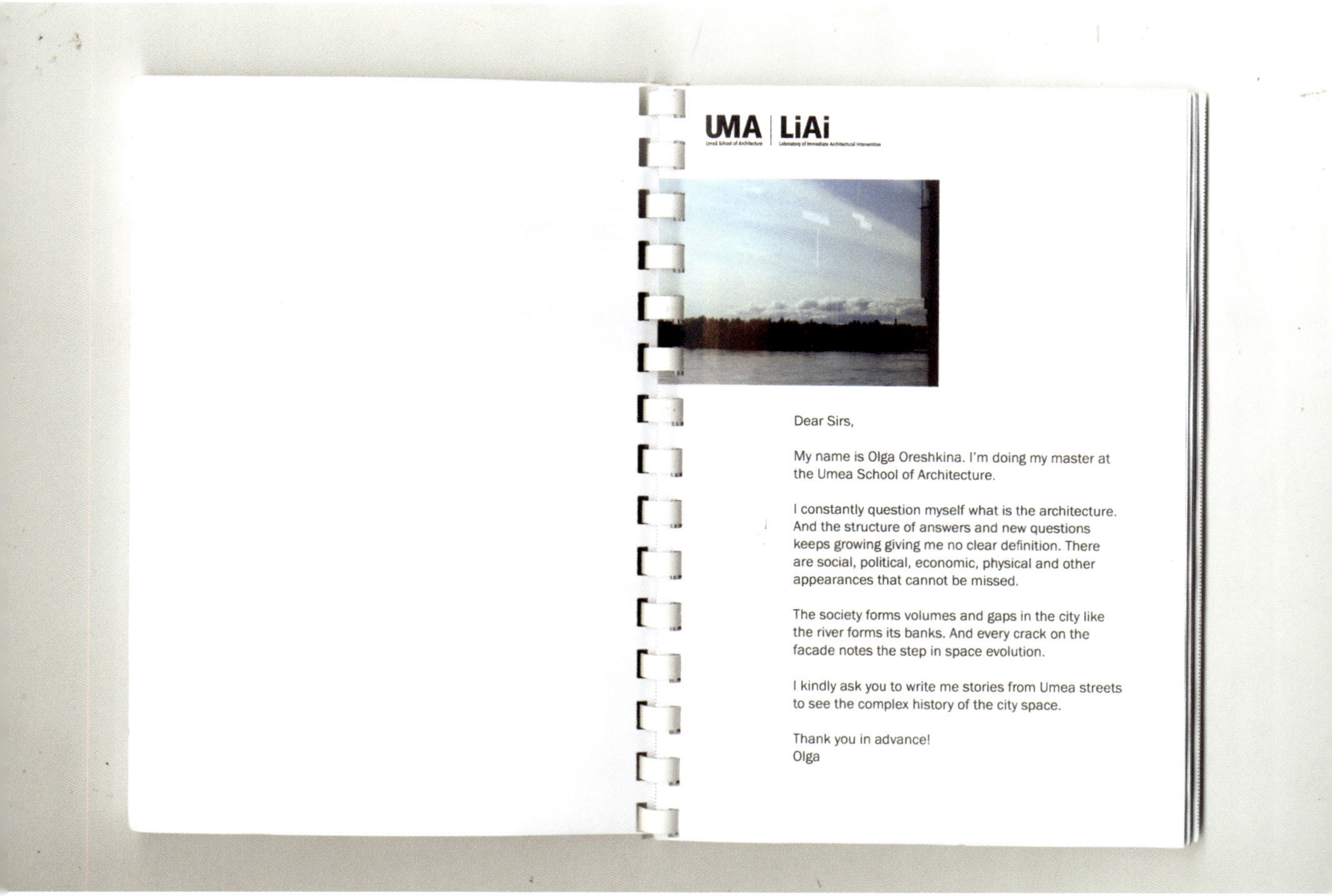

UMA | LiAi

Dear Sirs,

My name is Olga Oreshkina. I'm doing my master at the Umea School of Architecture.

I constantly question myself what is the architecture. And the structure of answers and new questions keeps growing giving me no clear definition. There are social, political, economic, physical and other appearances that cannot be missed.

The society forms volumes and gaps in the city like the river forms its banks. And every crack on the facade notes the step in space evolution.

I kindly ask you to write me stories from Umea streets to see the complex history of the city space.

Thank you in advance!
Olga

olga oreshkina - **/street memories/in our own backyard**

letter asking for stories - architectural intervention and cultural consequences - liai 7

ries was impressive and the intensity of the stories had very profound and lasting effects not only in Olga but in most of us at the Laboratory. The questions raised in the texts and illustrations managed to trigger interesting reflections and guided some of Olga's following steps in the laboratory. The notebook also provided very valuable

street memories/in our own backyard/ - olga oreshkina

pages from one of the collected notebooks - architectural intervention and cultural consequences -liai7

stories about the city, about Umeå, which have expanded the understanding we have of the city at the LiAi. The work around the material she obtained in the form of this notebook is not finished and some effects are still to come. This engagement with the stories of the city shows another way to approach urban exploration, and relates par-

olga oreshkina - **/street memories/in our own backyard**

pages from one of the collected notebooks - architectural intervention and cultural consequences -liai7

ticularly to matters of concern such as for instance 'discourse/event' or 'transversals/micropolitics': it pays attention and cares about the things thought and written about the city by otherwise unheard 'minds' and 'hands', it values undervalued discourses; but it does so in relationship with what is actually going on and happening in the

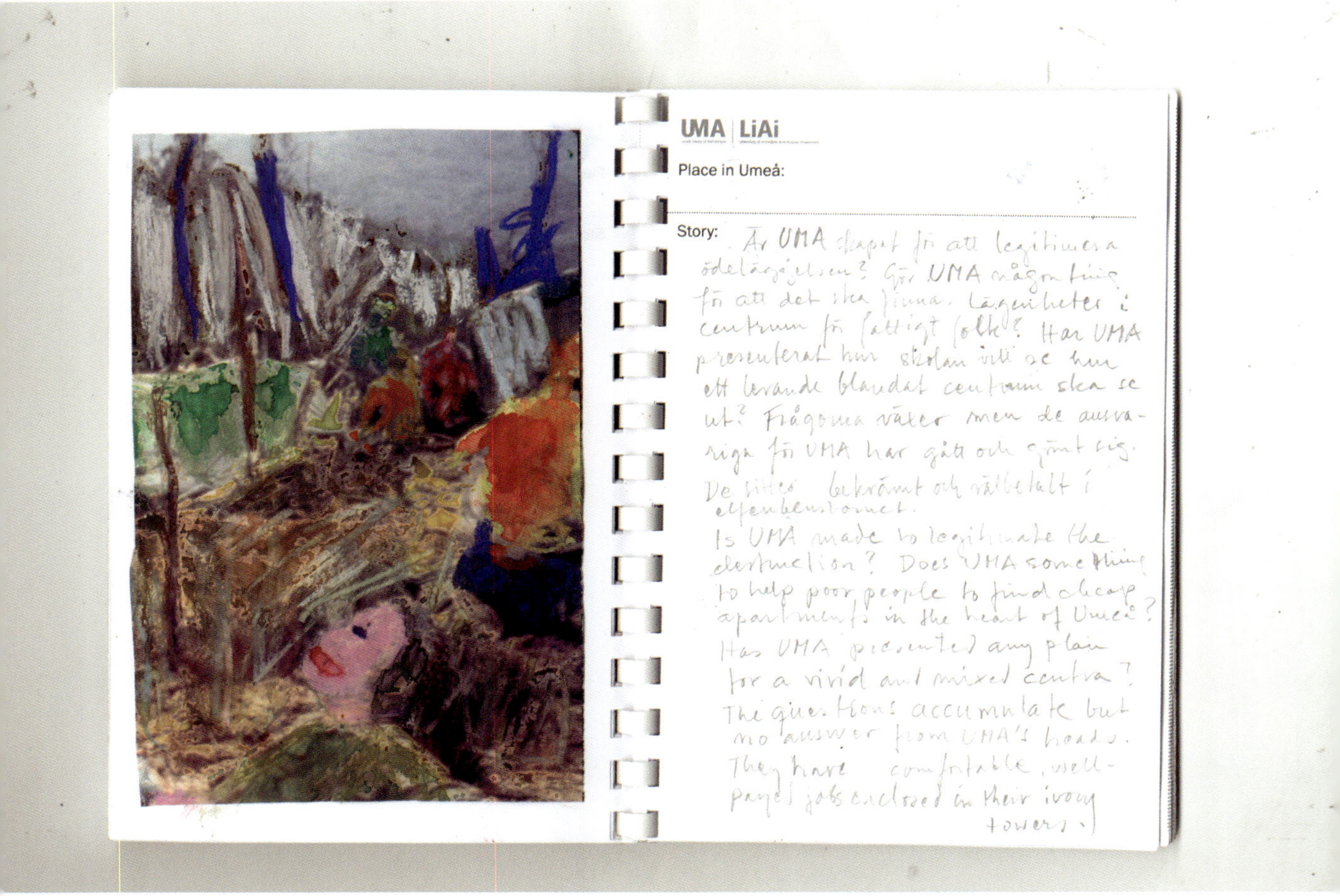

street memories/in our own backyard/ - olga oreshkina

pages from one of the collected notebooks - architectural intervention and cultural consequences -liai7

city, what has happened and the questions that emerge from these events and transformations. She works transversally, through mailboxes, notebooks and unspoken conversations with unknown others, establishing relations with 'foreigners', questioning the terms of what an urban exploration 'should be', questioning what the

olga oreshkina - **/street memories/in our own backyard**

pages from one of the collected notebooks - architectural intervention and cultural consequences -liai7

city is for an architect or an urban planner. Is the city made of stories?, one could ask. She inhabits the micropolitics of sharing through writing, reading and listening, the micropolitics of making mailboxes, printing notebooks and writing addresses, those of reading handwritten texts in a language she hardly knows and of looking at pictures

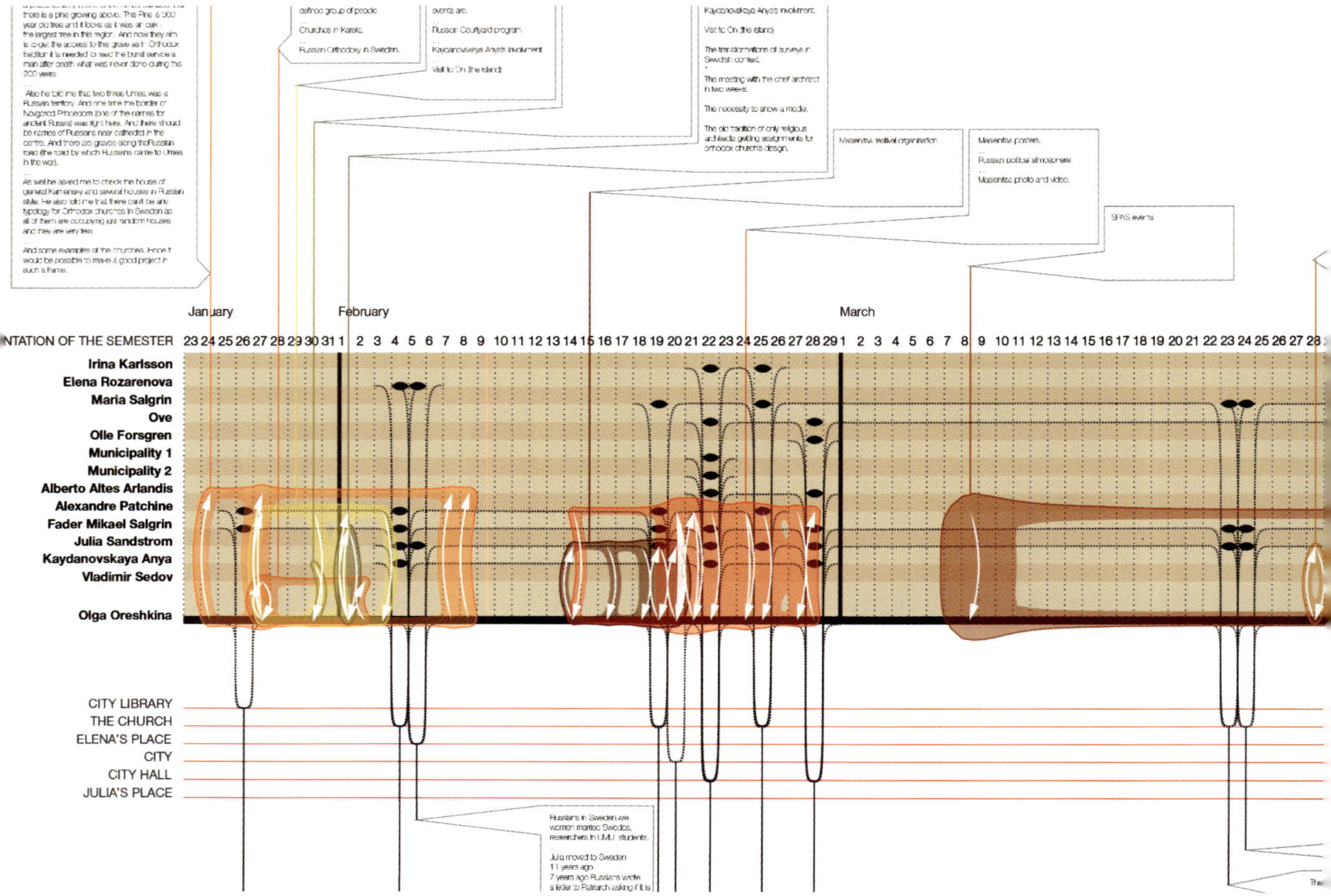

russian community center in umeå/ - olga oreshkina

performative mapping - diffraction - architecture as acupunctural strategy - liai 8

and drawings that make her uncomfortable as an architect but show her what a 'real' architect could do. This was an incredible piece of collaborative work.

Olga's work continued later in and around the Russian community in Umeå, exploring the possibilities that emerged from a crisis resulting from the need to relocate

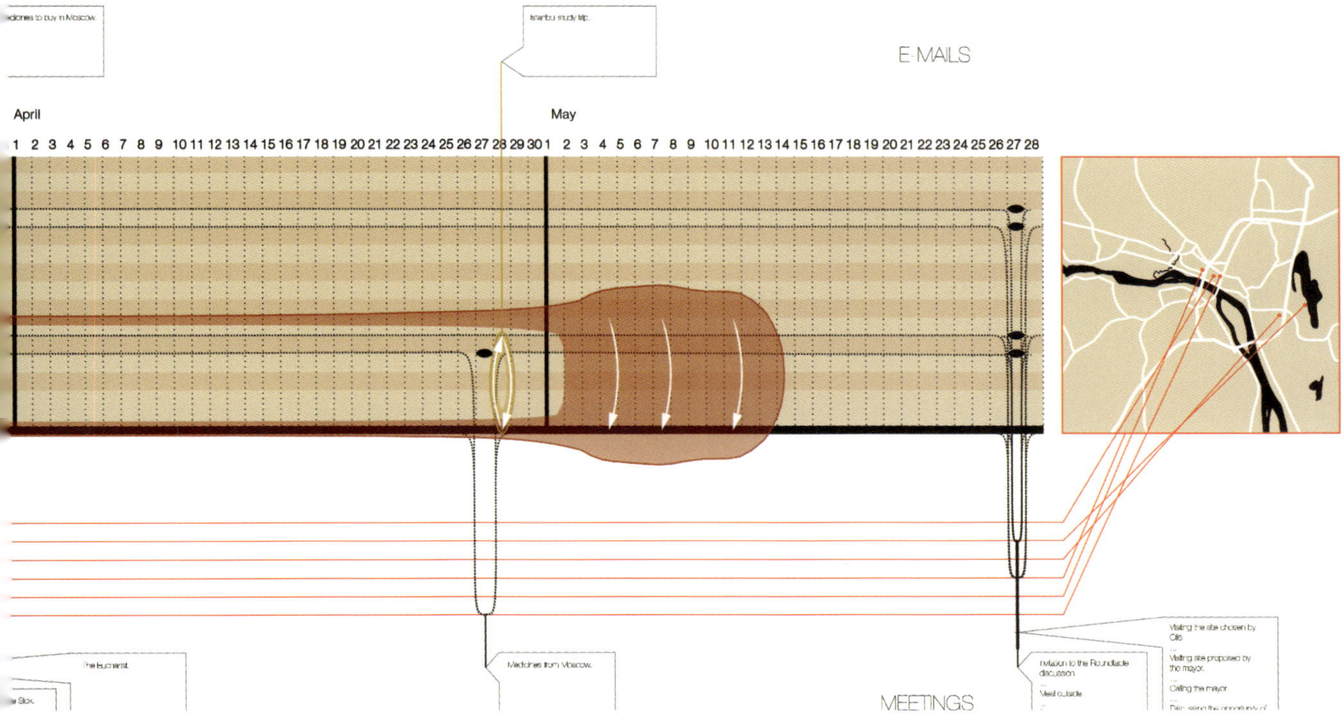

olga oreshkina - **/russian community center in umeå**

performative mapping - diffraction - architecture as acupunctural strategy - liai 8

their Church. They had to move from the building they were occupying to a new location still to be found that should be then made adequate. Her conversations with the members of the community and the leaders of the Church allowed her to understand their interest in the Church and their ideas about it: the Church was in fact a cultural

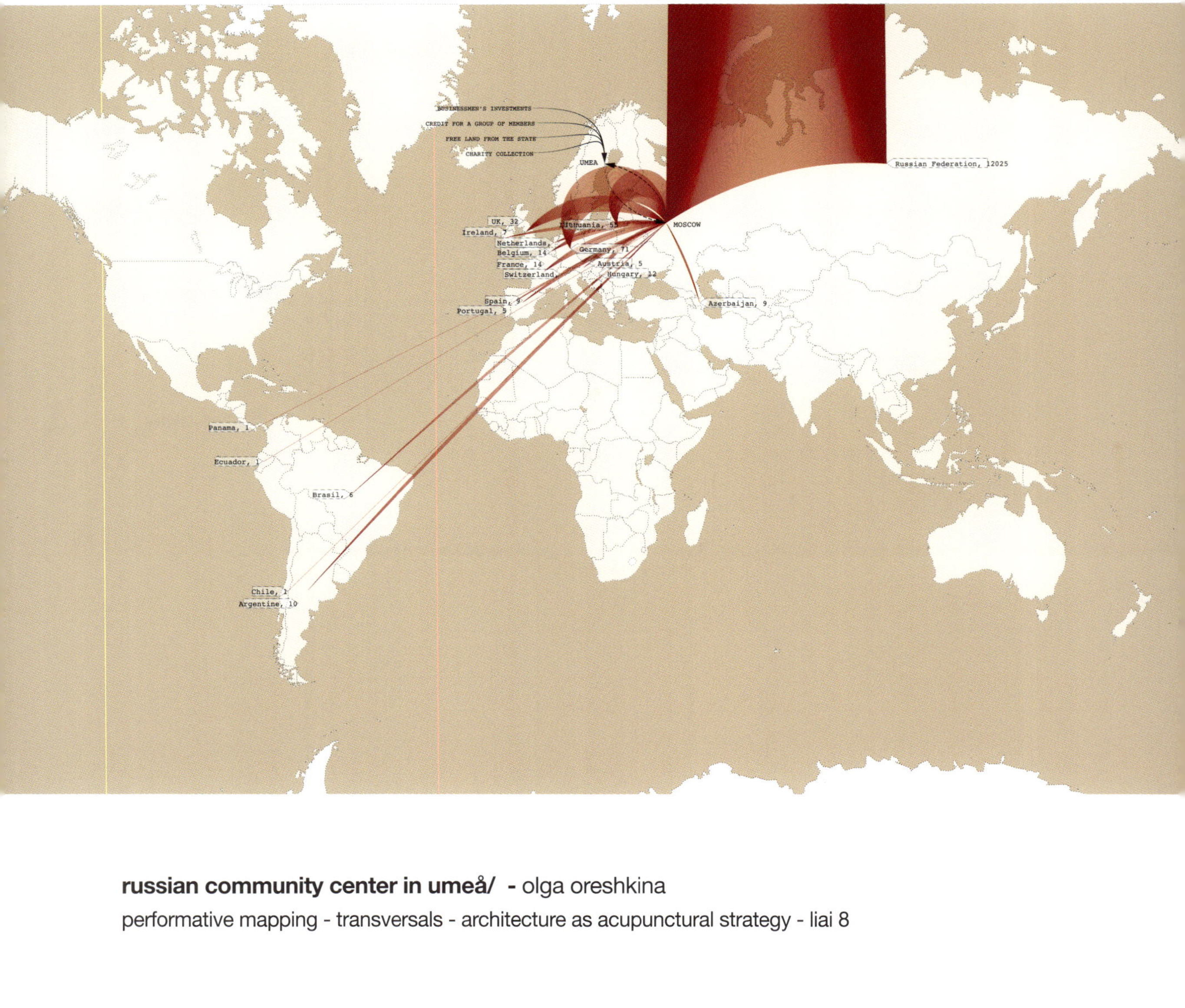

russian community center in umeå/ - olga oreshkina

performative mapping - transversals - architecture as acupunctural strategy - liai 8

community in and around which many different activities were organized, carried out and shared. The design for a new Church should therefore investigate such a condition even if it also had to understand and incorporate the tradition of Orthodox Russian church buildings and update it through the use of contemporary techniques, materials

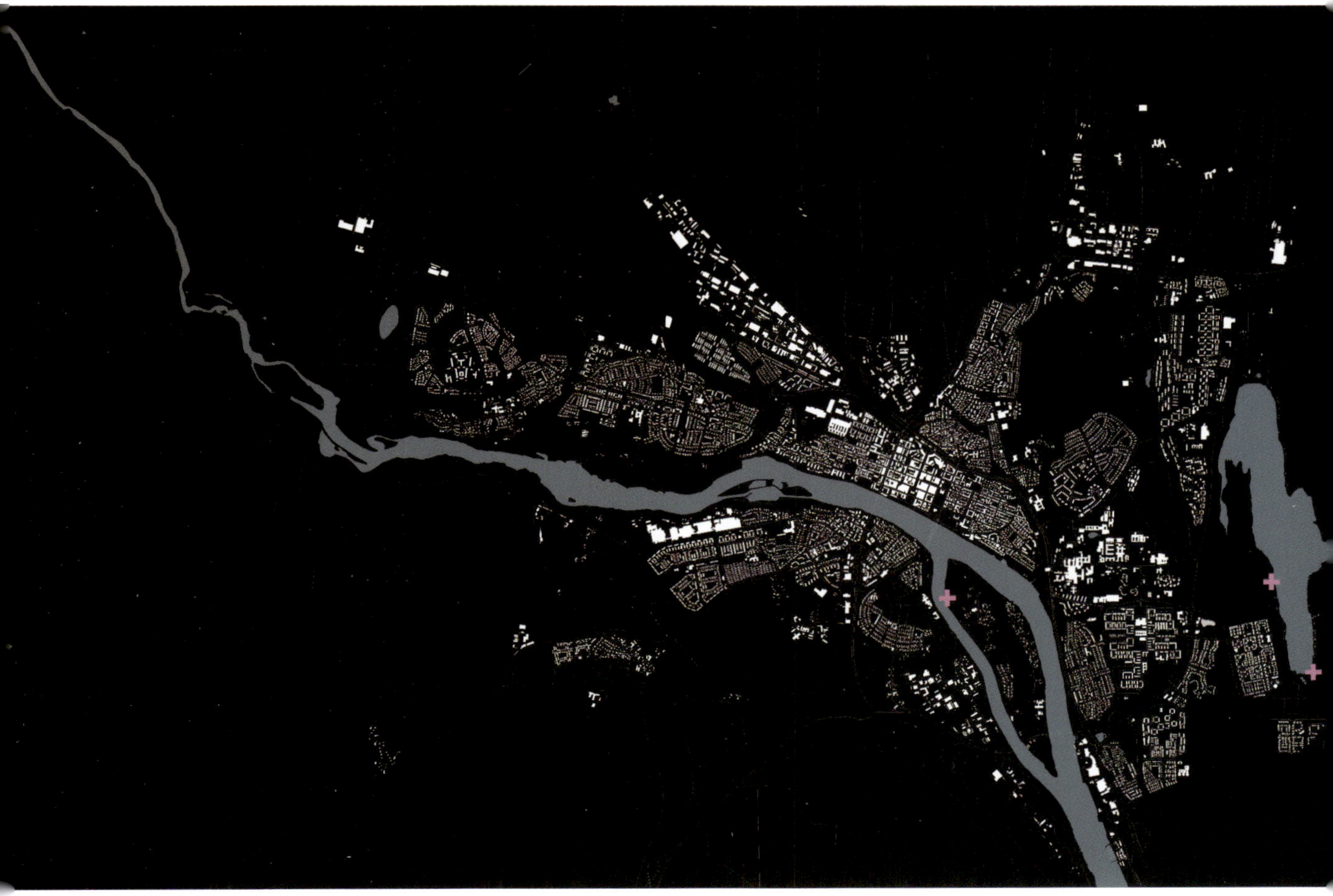

olga oreshkina - **/russian community center in umeå**
three sites - architecture as acupunctural strategy - liai 8

and sensibilities. Olga managed to produce very interesting and intense mappings of the micropolitics of her own engagement with the community, recording her actions, meeting, encounters, conversations and exchanges with all the actors involved in her project in one way or another. Together with another student, she organized several

b-sites/in our own backyard/ **-** maria hudl

a map of other places in umeå - architectural intervention and cultural consequences - liai 7

meetings in the municipality with the Head of the Building Department and later with the city-architect, during which they presented their work and research as well as their analysis of the possible locations. In these meetings, the leaders of the Church and some of the members of the Russian community were present and able to dis-

maria hudl - **/b-sites/in our own backyard**

a map of other places in umeå - architectural intervention and cultural consequences - liai 7

cuss their worries and needs through Olga's work and presentations which led to a relationship with them that is still alive today.

Maria Hudl focused her work during one of the terms on what she decided to call 'b-sites', elaborating a map of 'other places in umeå' that she identified as full-of-uncer-

exploring antagonism at the art campus/ - maria hudl and febe roels

antagonist practices in public space interventions - workshop - liai 7

tain-possibilities for different things to happen in/on/around them, as well as in some cases as locations to be kept as they were, full-of-nothingness.

In her joint work with Febe Roels, they chose to focus instead on the spaces of the Art Campus to which Umeå School of Architecture belongs, exploring the con-

maria hudl and febe roels - **/exploring antagonism at the art campus**

antagonist practices in public space interventions- workshop - liai 7

tradictions built into the notions of interconnectedness, proximity and collaboration that are used to promote and present the campus, and the actual uses that the inhabitants of the campus give to spaces as well as the difficulties they have to face in their everyday 'practicing' of the spaces of the campus. Postcards with images of

station for sky studies/ - christina kousgaard hansen

performative projects - architectural intervention and cultural consequences - liai 7

the doors and border (threshold) technologies and devices were sent and distributed through the spaces of the campus with questions about the possibilities for collaboration and communication within the campus and across the three institutions that make it: the Art Academy, the School of Architecture and the Institute of Design.

christina kousgaard hansen - **/station for sky studies**

performative projects - architectural intervention and cultural consequences - liai 7

Answers should be shared through the circulation of the postcards that were pre-filled with names and addresses of different people in the campus, and the results were collected and exhibited. This was part of a one-week intensive workshop on collaboration and antagonism.

station for sky studies/ - christina kousgaard hansen

take an object for a walk: mask - architectural intervention and cultural consequences - liai 7

In the case of Christina Kousgaard's work, an interest in the sky as a site emerged during the first explorations of the city that she carried out with the help of a 'mask' that allowed her to bring the sky down into the visual experience of walking in the city. The mask she made included several mirrors that were capable of 'brightening' up

christina kousgaard hansen - **/station for sky studies**

take an object for a walk: mask - architectural intervention and cultural consequences - liai 7

the otherwise not-so-full-of-light streets of Umeå, introducing the sky and its colors in the marketized and grey urban environments. The mask brought the sky down, or in. This interest in the sky was developed further into a series of Stations for Sky Studies, or S.S.S., that she conceived, speculated upon and in some cases built. These

blanket/ - audingas sumskas

take an object for a walk - architectural intervention and cultural consequences - liai 7

stations were perhaps more interesting as ideas and in their provocative and sensitive understanding of the sky as a place and as a construction of relations with light, than they were as built prototypes when they happened, although the prototypes also served the purpose of testing different conditions and the relationships a person

audingas sumskas - **/blanket**

take an object for a walk - architectural intervention and cultural consequences - liai 7

has with different framings of the sky and its varying light. Her work has been more centered around her own subjectivity and around the ways in which she perceives the world than related to ideas of collaboration or intra-vention. She has developed her own artistic projects in relationship with notions of space, locating them in spaces

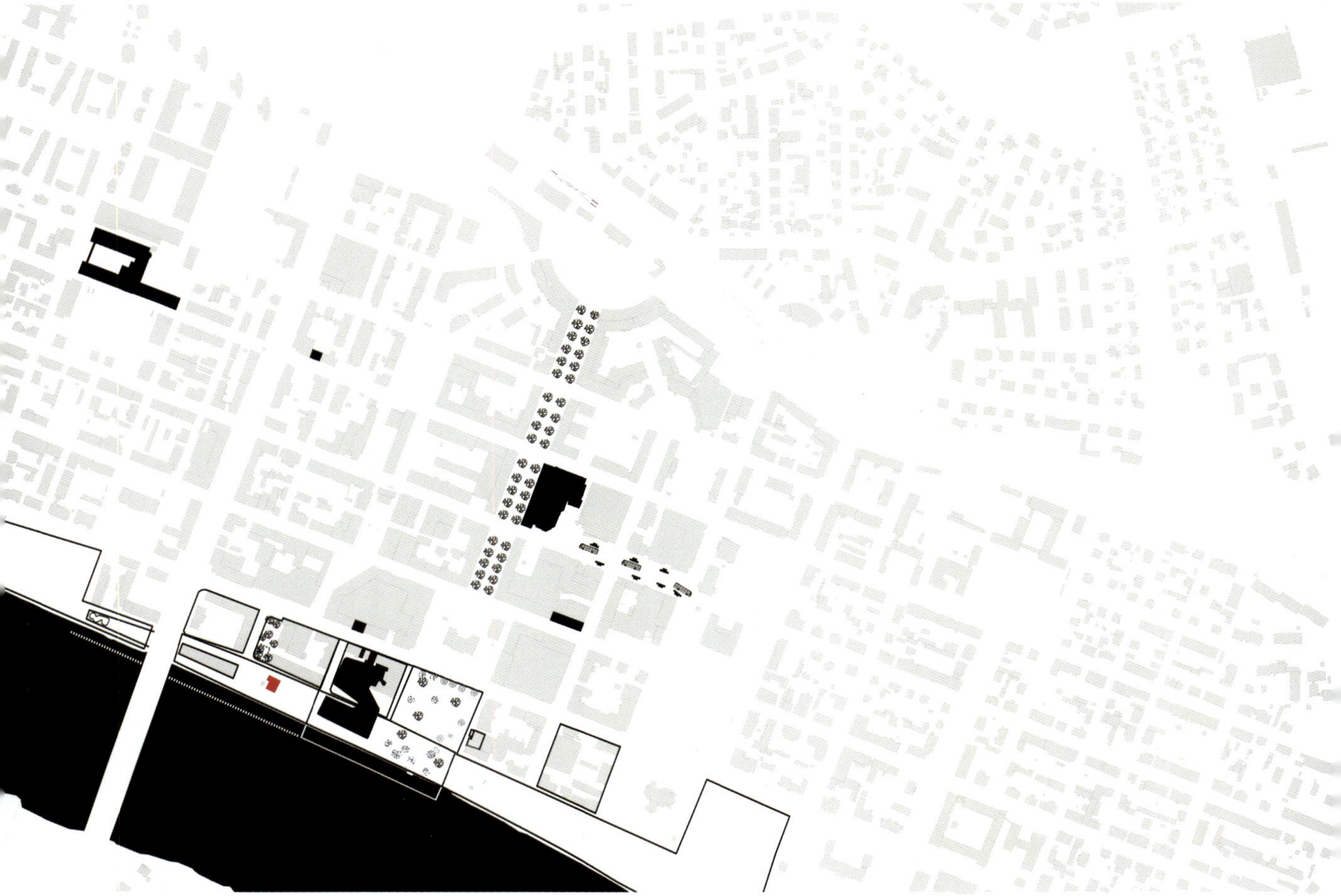

a parked house/in our own backyard/ - erika henriksson

architectural intervention and cultural consequences - liai 7

but seldom through a dialogue with others. Still, we have seen and discussed certain visual qualities and sensibilities that have been mobilized and developed through her work, which has been perhaps more related to issues of representation/diffraction and body/apparatus than to any of our other matters of concern.

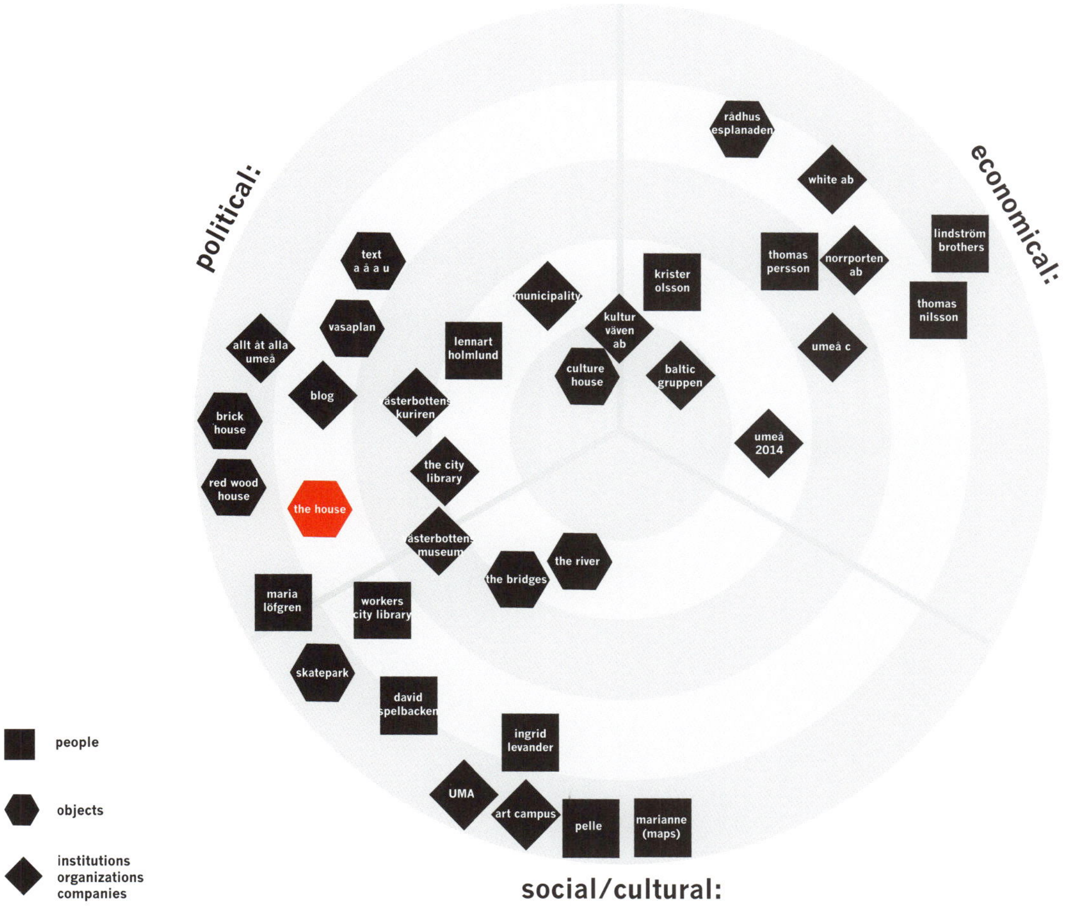

erika henriksson - /**a parked house/in our own backyard**

architectural intervention and cultural consequences - liai 7

Another example of exploration of the city through a domestic object is the one carried out by Audingas Sumskas with a brightly coloured blanket that guided him through the spaces that could host the actions 'it' wanted to (or could) perform: cleaning, blowing in the wind, lying on the ground, protecting, holding leaves, indicat-

a parked house/in our own backyard/ - erika henriksson

architectural intervention and cultural consequences - liai 7

ing directions and positions, hanging, rolling, or many others... The blanket, as the other domestic objects for the other students, helped him put his body back at the center of action: exploring the city happens first and foremost by moving through it. But the body exists always in relationship with other things, devices and apparatuses, like

erika henriksson - **/a parked house/in our own backyard**

architectural intervention and cultural consequences - liai 7

his shoes, his clothes, the pavement under his feet, or the blanket, which co-determine the effects of his presence in the city and in the world.

In other occasions, explorations of the city have happened and evolved through 'things' found in Umeå and their relationships to different people, institutions and actors of all

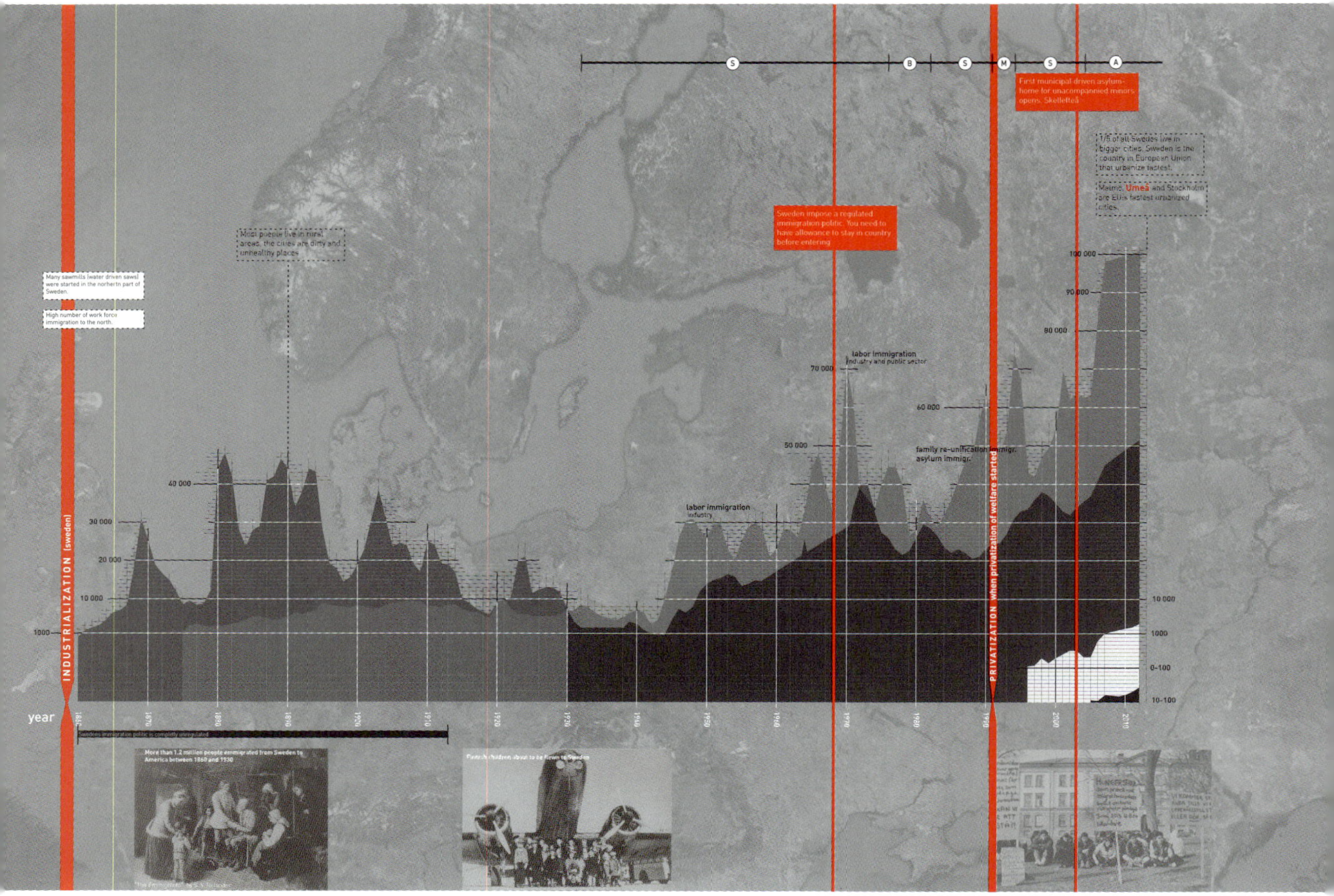

activists in movement/ - erika henriksson

unaccompanied minor refugees and the formal and informal approaches to life - liai master's thesis

kinds. It was the case for instance of Erika's work around a 'house', a building that was literally 'parked' close to the river, after having been displaced from its original location, lifted on top of a steel structure/foundation and forced to wait until a new 'place' was found for 'her'. The displacement of the building was related to current develop-

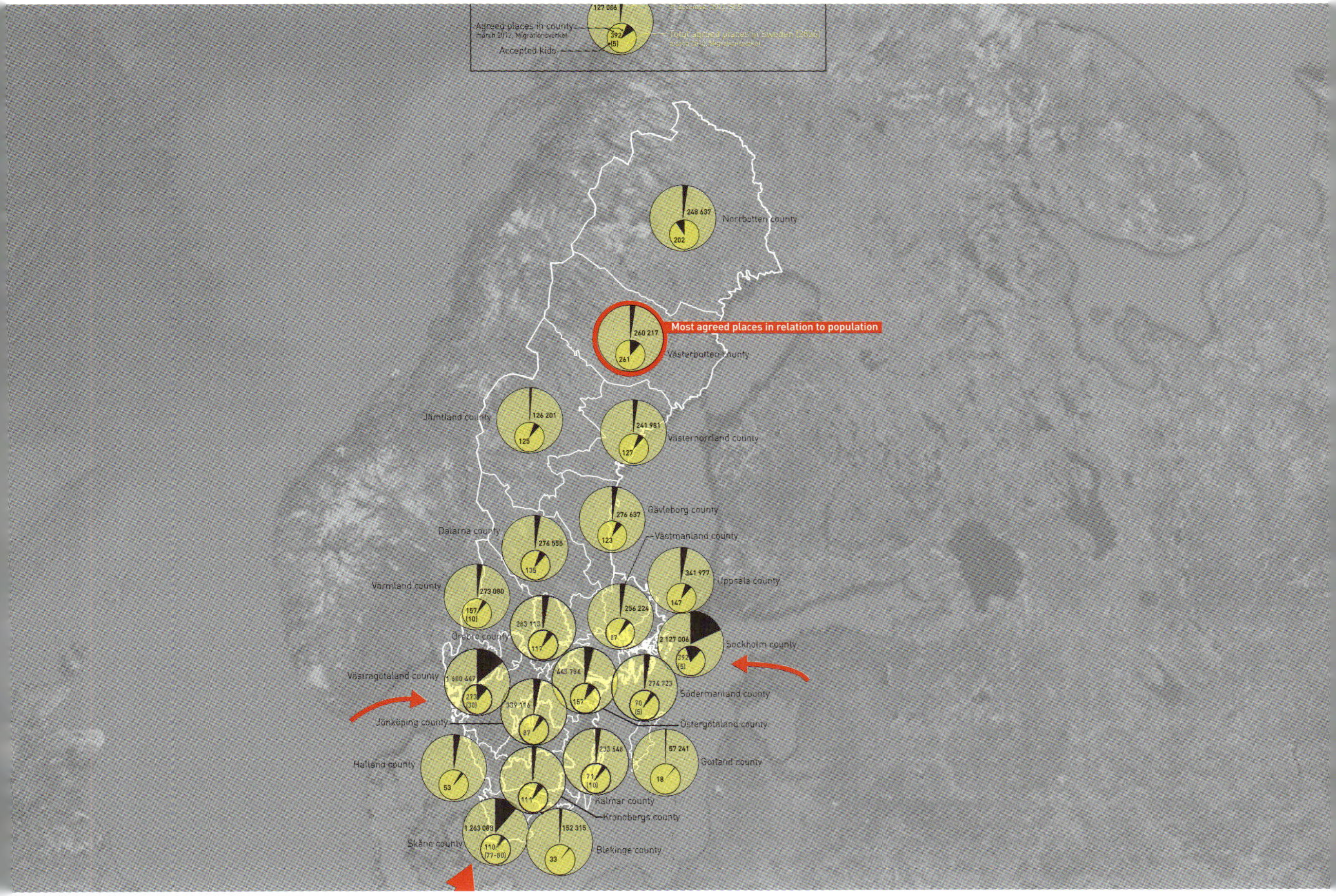

erika henriksson - /**activists in movement**

unaccompanied minor refugees and the formal and informal approaches to life - liai master's thesis

ments of the city and to the construction of the new 'House of Culture', but at the same time its history, its past, was entangled with the stories of other inhabitants of the area, neighbors, shop-owners, archeologists and historians, that could in turn help her/ us connect those stories with the on-going processes of transformation of the city. The

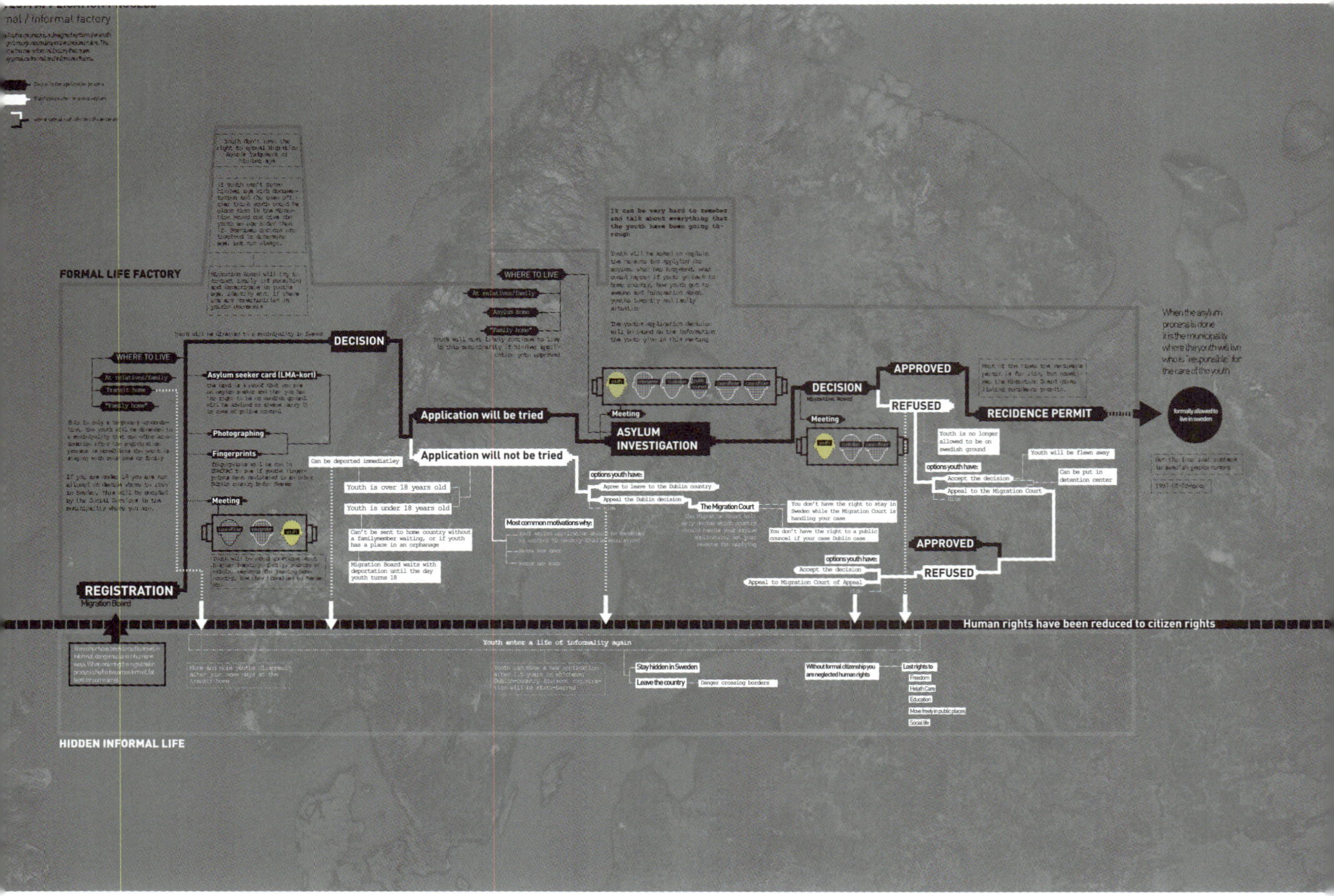

activists in movement/ - erika henriksson

unaccompanied minor refugees and the formal and informal approaches to life - liai master's thesis

house was another actor in a meshwork of relations instead of 'just-a-building', and the lines along which those relations were built, happened and evolved could be followed, explored and inhabited. Those lines allowed Erika to understand many things about the city beyond the house itself, and in relationship with the flows of power and

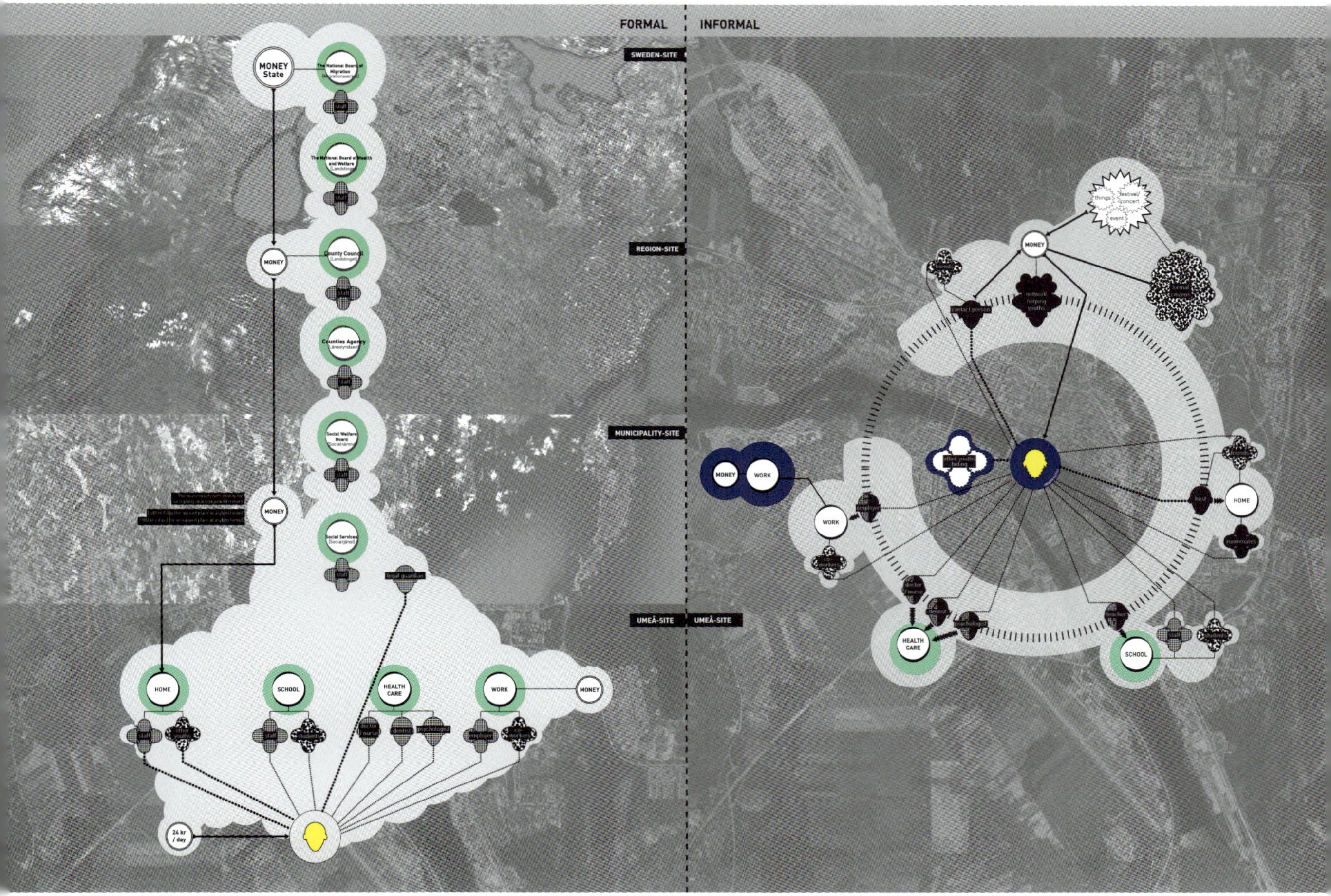

erika henriksson - /**activists in movement**

unaccompanied minor refugees and the formal and informal approaches to life - liai master's thesis

money, the moving of the city library and a history of protests against it, the struggles of a shoe maker to keep his shop alive in spite of the increases in the rent he had to pay, the historical and archeological interest of some of the buildings in the area, and many other political, economic and socio-cultural conditions and situations that were

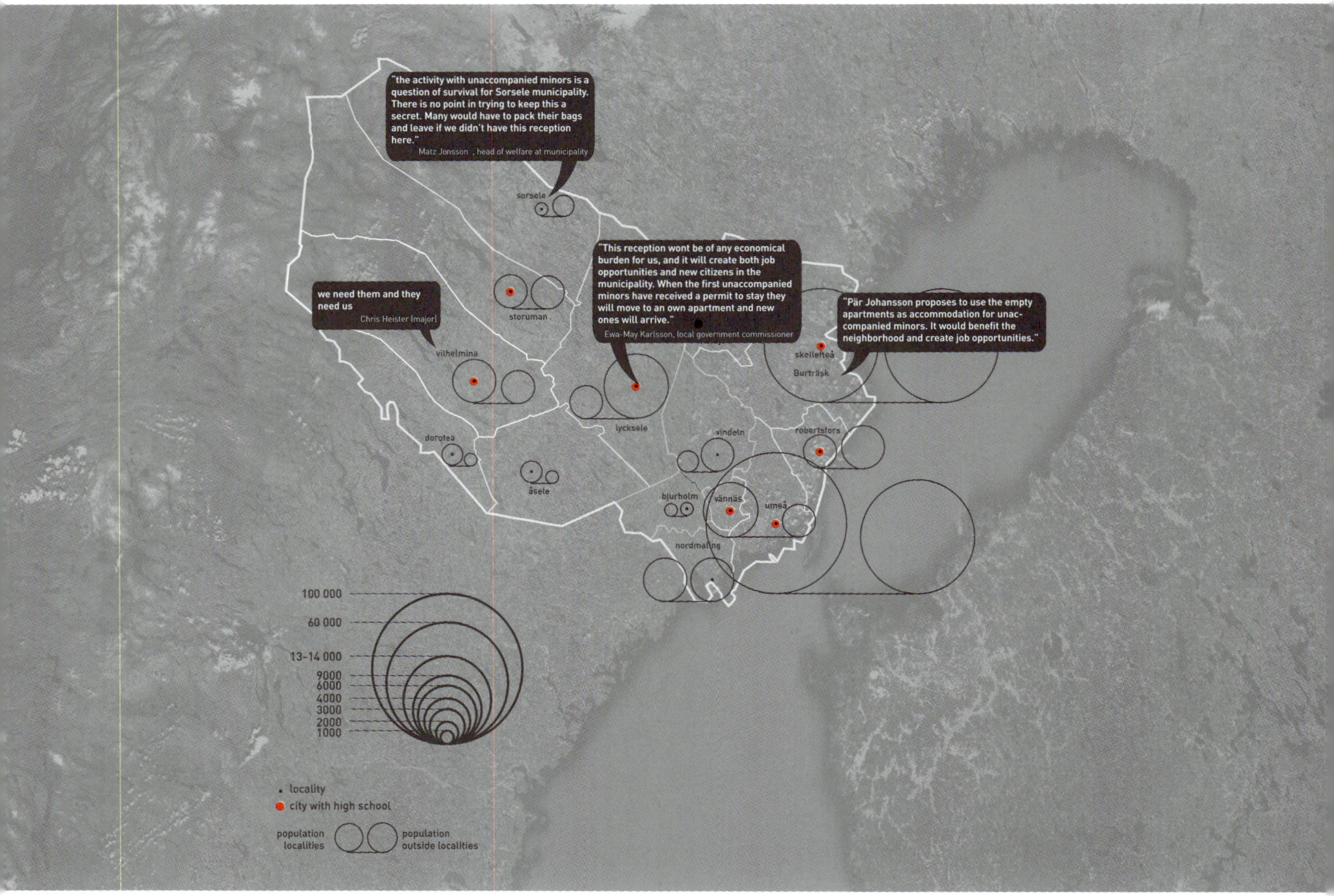

activists in movement/ - erika henriksson

unaccompanied minor refugees and the formal and informal approaches to life - liai master's thesis

at work in the city at the time.

Erika's work shifted towards the presence of unaccompanied minor refugees in Umeå and to an exploration and analysis of the asylum homes in which they were placed and the conditions of their everyday life in Sweden.

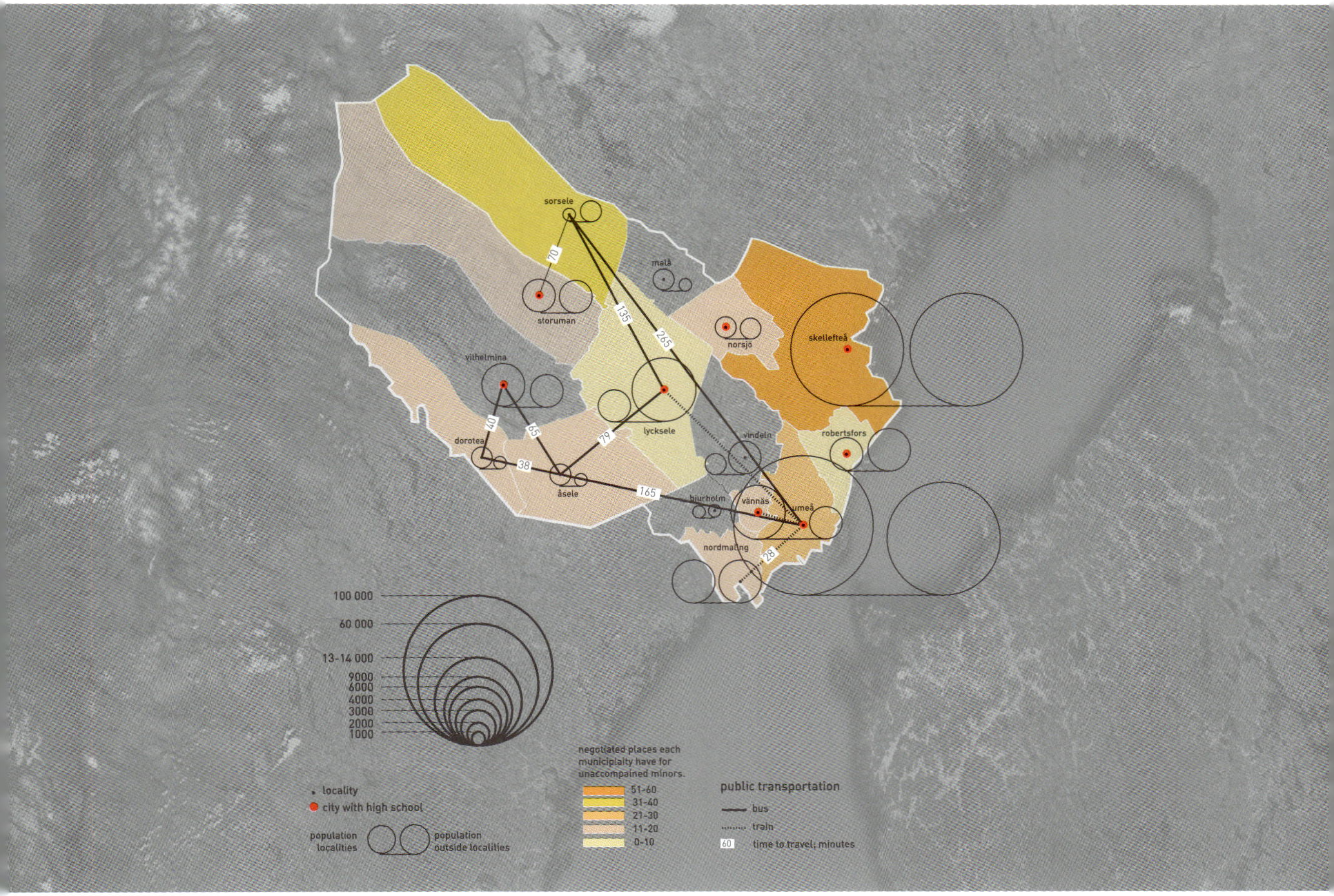

erika henriksson - /**activists in movement**

unaccompanied minor refugees and the formal and informal approaches to life - liai master's thesis

The intensity of her work, which included the development of three individual projects together with three of the girls living in one of the asylum homes, turned into a Master's Thesis that addressed the different approaches to the organization of life in exile, exploring on the one hand the formal management of minor refugees through

activists in movement/ - erika henriksson

unaccompanied minor refugees and the formal and informal approaches to life - liai master's thesis

the bureaucratic state-led administration, and the informal networks into which some of these kids end up with the support and help of diverse individuals, on the other. By encountering the refugees as 'activists in movement', she not only acknowledges their creativity and agency and willingness to move forward, but takes the chance to

erika henriksson - /**activists in movement**

unaccompanied minor refugees and the formal and informal approaches to life - liai master's thesis

learn about other ways of being and living together, testing the possibilities of a distributed home environment that encourages the construction and maintenance of meshworks of relations that support coexistence and require the establishment of solid bonds with others. As opposed to an individualized, consumerist model, life

activists in movement/ - erika henriksson

unaccompanied minor refugees and the formal and informal approaches to life - liai master's thesis

in her proposal is only possible 'together'. And this very 'togethernes', along with the fragmentation of spaces, allows the refugees to 'hide': in such a complex meshwork of spaces and relations it is hard to know if or where they are at any given moment.

Her work looks at immigration in Sweden

erika henriksson - /**activists in movement**

unaccompanied minor refugees and the formal and informal approaches to life - liai master's thesis

historically and focuses particularly in the case of minor refugees, tracing also the shifts in a society that seemed to be ready to host them 'in the name of human rights' and solidarity, but that has now in fact created *an economy of the refugee* in which these kids are seen as an asset that is mobilized according to political agendas

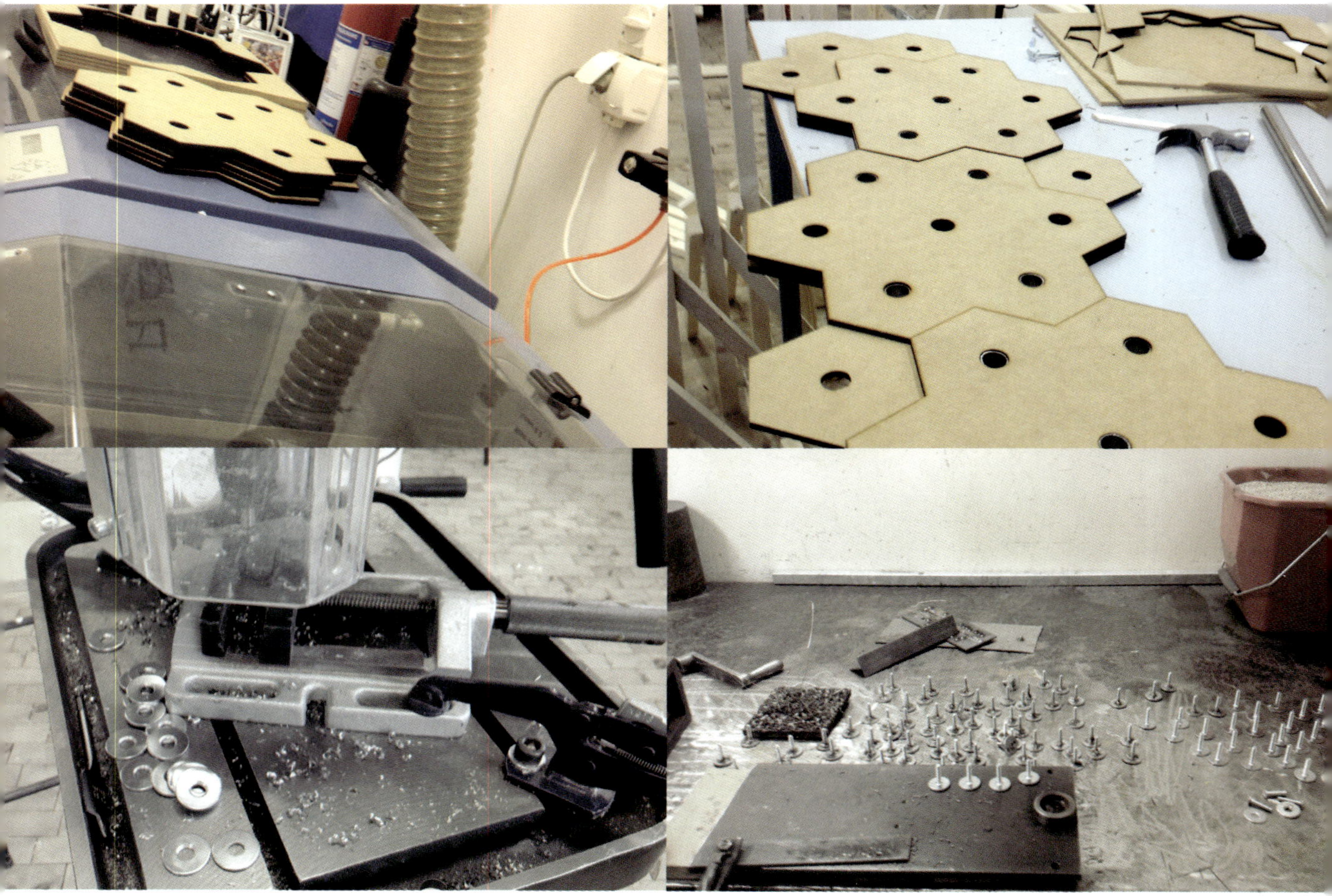

activists in movement/ - erika henriksson

unaccompanied minor refugees and the formal and informal approaches to life - liai master's thesis

in order to repopulate the shrinking cities of the almost empty North, and thrust the economies of small municipalities. These geopolitical, territorial and socio-economic dimensions of her work are inseparable with her conversations with the kids and their guardians at the asylum homes, her presence in those homes as well as in the

erika henriksson - /**activists in movement**

unaccompanied minor refugees and the formal and informal approaches to life - liai master's thesis

kids' rooms, and her careful design and fabrication of the various interventions/gifts that she made with/for the kids. Her work transformed the world not only through the projection of unseen (new) drawings of a distributed domestic environment as a plan that could be implemented in the residential development of Ålidhem, but rather,

activists in movement/ - erika henriksson

unaccompanied minor refugees and the formal and informal approaches to life - liai master's thesis

and fundamentally, through her presence in spaces in which 'she was not supposed to be', and through her asking uncomfortable questions, and through her subtle but persistent 'disturbance' of the on-going bureaucratic 'life' at the asylum homes, with

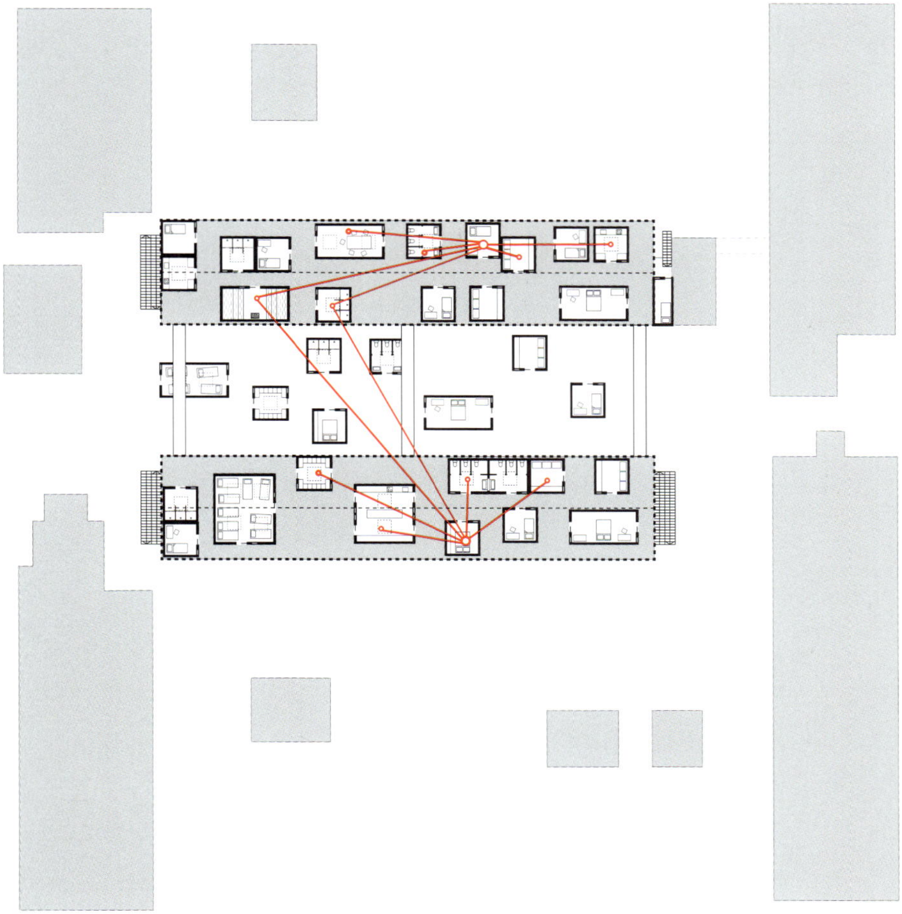

erika henriksson - /**activists in movement**

unaccompanied minor refugees and the formal and informal approaches to life - liai master's thesis

words, bodies and devices that challenge the distribution of what can be said, heard and done (the sensible) with the unexpected, the inadmissible, dissensus and action.

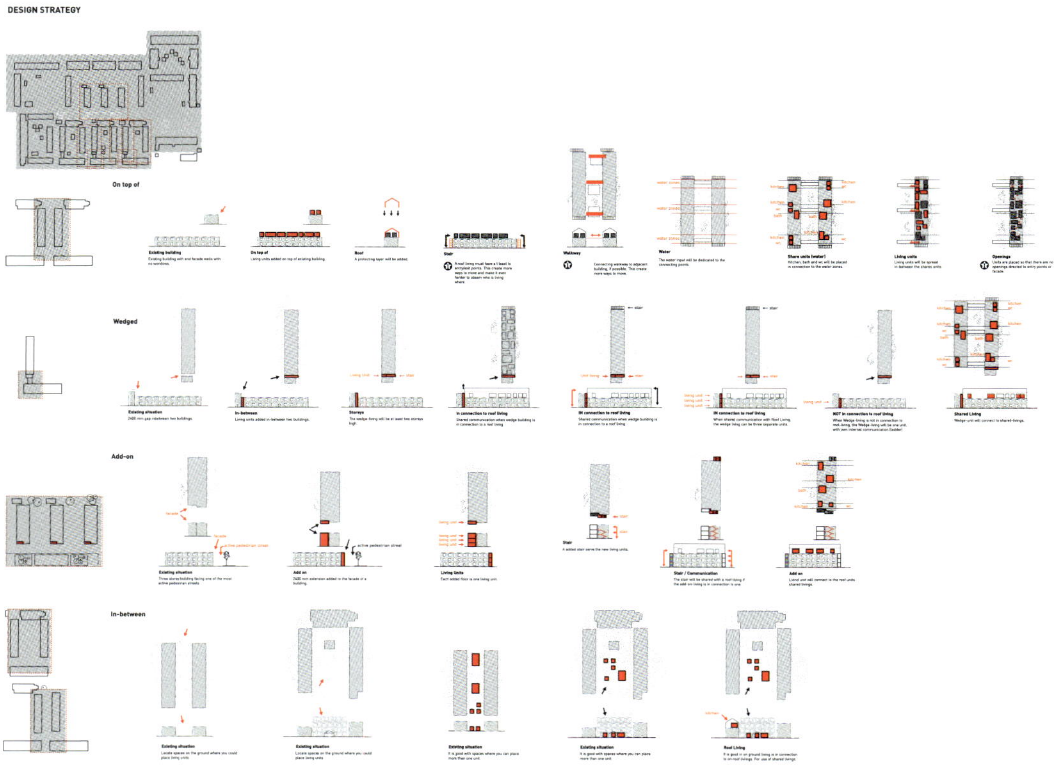

activists in movement/ - erika henriksson

unaccompanied minor refugees and the formal and informal approaches to life - liai master's thesis

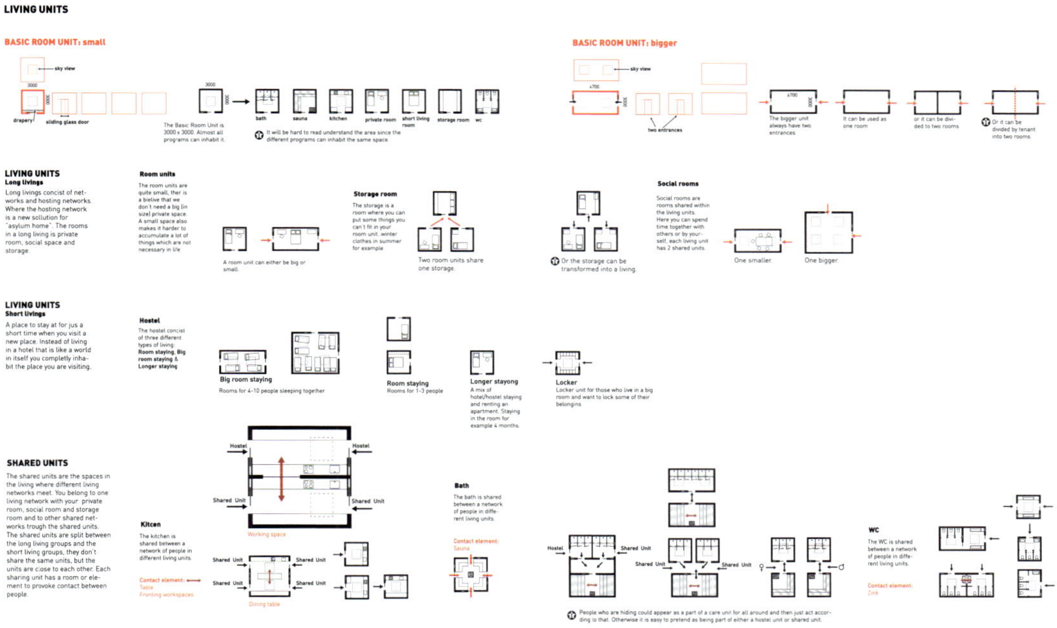
LIVING UNITS
BASIC ROOM UNIT: small
sky view
3000
3000
drapery
sliding glass door
3000
3000
The Basic Room Unit is 3000 x 3000. Almost all programs can inhabit it.
bath
sauna
kitchen
private room
short living room
storage room
wc
It will be hard to read understand the area since the different programs can inhabit the same space.
BASIC ROOM UNIT: bigger
sky view
6700
3000
two entrances
6700
3000
The bigger unit always have two entrances
It can be used as one room
or it can be divi-ded to two rooms
Or it can be divided by tenant into two rooms
LIVING UNITS
Long livings
Long livings concist of net-works and hosting networks. Where the hosting network is a new sollution for "asylum home". The rooms in a long living is private room, social space and storage.
Room units
The room units are quite small, ther is a bielive that we don't need a big (in size) private space. A small space also makes it harder to accumulate a lot of things which are not necessary in life
A room unit can either be big or small.
Storage room
The storage is a room where you can put some things you can't fit in your room unit..winter clothes in summer for example
Two room units share one storage.
Or the storage can be transformed into a living.
Social rooms
Social rooms are rooms shared within the living units. Here you can spend time together with others or by your-self, each living unit has 2 shared units.
One smaller.
One bigger.
LIVING UNITS
Short livings
A place to stay at for jus a short time when you visit a new place. Instead of living in a hotel that is like a world in itself you completly inha-bit the place you are visiting.
Hostel
The hostel concist of three different types of living: Room staying, Big room staying & Longer staying
Big room staying
Rooms for 4-10 people sleeping together
Room staying
Rooms for 1-3 people
Longer stayong
A mix of hotel/hostel staying and renting an apartment. Staying in the room for example 4 months.
Locker
Locker unit for those who live in a big room and want to lock some of their belongins
SHARED UNITS
The shared units are the spaces in the living where different living networks meet. You belong to one living network with your private room, social room and storage room and to other shared net-works trough the shared units. The shared units are split between the long living groups and the short living groups, they don't share the same units, but the units are close to each other. Each sharing unit has a room or ele-ment to provoke contact between people.
Hostel
Hostel
Shared Unit
Shared Unit
Working space
Kitcen
The kitchen is shared between a network of people in different living units.
Contact element:
Table
Fronting workspaces
Shared Unit
Shared Unit
Shared Unit
Shared Unit
Dining table
Bath
The bath is shared between a network of people in diffe-rent living units.
Contact element:
Sauna
Hostel
Shared Unit
Shared Unit
Shared Unit
People who are hiding could appear as a part of a care unit for all around and then just act accor-ding to that. Otherwise it is easy to pretend as being part of either a hostel unit or shared unit.
WC
The WC is shared between a network of people in diffe-rent living units.
Contact element:
Zink

activists in movement/ - erika henriksson

unaccompanied minor refugees and the formal and informal approaches to life - liai master's thesis

erika henriksson - /**activists in movement**

unaccompanied minor refugees and the formal and informal approaches to life - liai master's thesis

public spaces in umeå/in our own backyard/ - veronica gerini

re-appropriating the neighborhood - architectural intervention and cultural consequences - liai 7

In Veronica's case, her work started through an approach to Swedish public and open space, after a first encounter with the Swedish spread-urbanism of distances and open spaces that contrasts with the urbanism of densities, congestion and narrow streets of her Italian and mediterranean background. The spaces that she had ini-

veronica gerini - **/public spaces in umeå/in our own backyard/**

re-appropriating the neighborhood - architectural intervention and cultural consequences - liai 7

tially understood as empty or wasted, could also be seen, after a second, more careful exploration, as spaces full of diverse potential, spaces of encounter, spaces of opportunity; and her work from that moment on evolved towards different attempts at activating those potentials, enabling those encounters and taking those opportunities,

public spaces in umeå/in our own backyard/ - veronica gerini

re-appropriating the neighborhood - architectural intervention and cultural consequences - liai 7

working with the elements that already existed in the situations she was inhabiting/ creating. A careful and detailed analysis of the different elements and hierarchies of a complex layering of responsibilities, rights and obligation in relationship with the areas and spaces of an urban quarter, did not prevent her from talking to the inhabitants of

veronica gerini - **/public spaces in umeå/in our own backyard/**

re-appropriating the neighborhood - architectural intervention and cultural consequences - liai 7

its homes and engaging in the organization of meetings and activities that led to the transformation of their yards and the construction of a series of paths and spaces in the snow, as well as to enabling a series of dialogues. The immediacy and economy of means of this work was remarkable: with next to no materials it was actually pos-

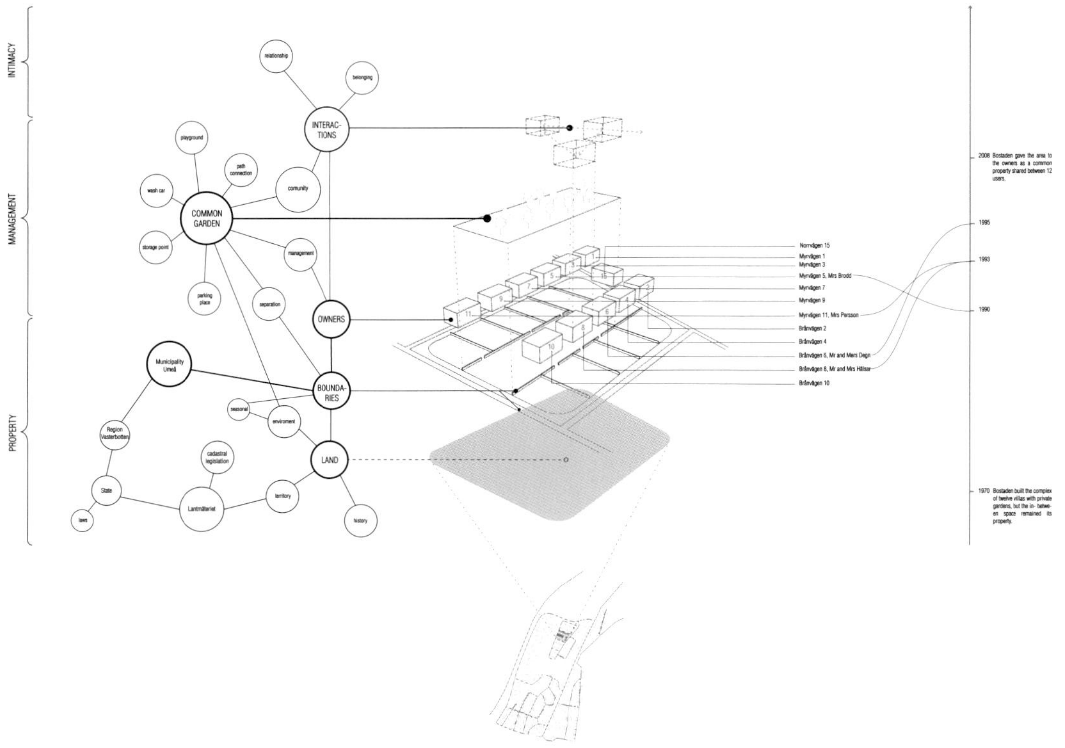

public spaces in umeå/in our own backyard/ - veronica gerini

re-appropriating the neighborhood - architectural intervention and cultural consequences - liai 7

sible to re-articulate spaces for encounter and transform an urban quarter, while at the same time foregrounding the role of our bodies in the making of the world.

One of the central dimensions of our laboratory is the one defined by the interplays of these two notions: the other/coexistence. They are very useful to rethink, explore and

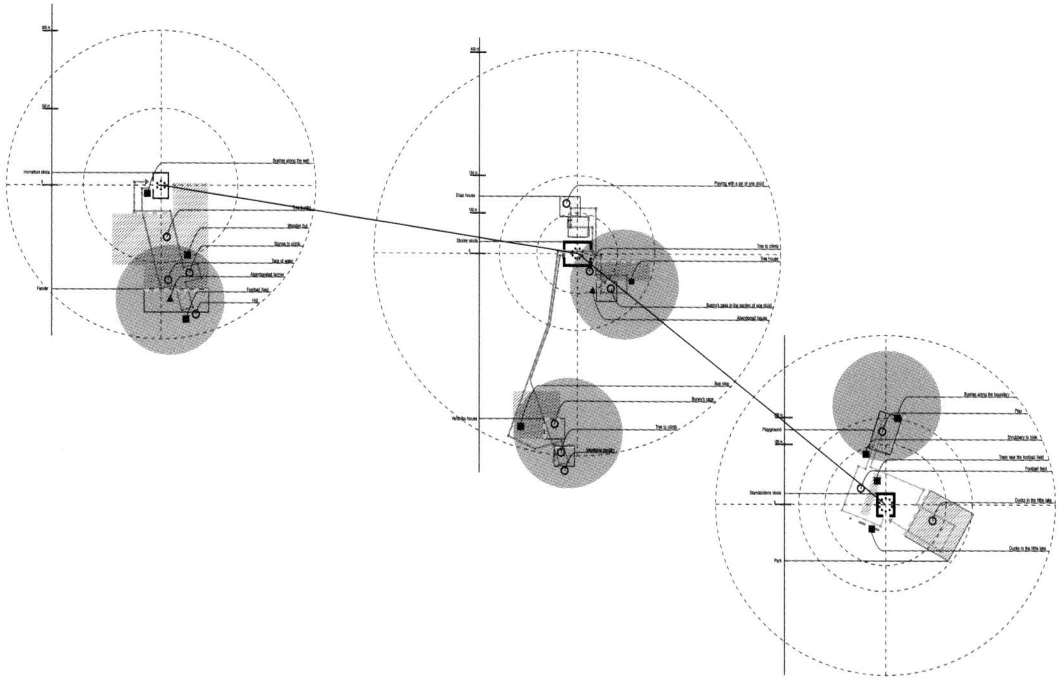

veronica gerini - **/public spaces in umeå/in our own backyard/**

re-appropriating the neighborhood - architectural intervention and cultural consequences - liai 7

test the role of architecture in the production of spaces for being and living together and to reflect upon ways of approaching/ encountering difference. Paula Idun's work around old people in Umeå evolved from an initially distant analysis of the elderly homes, their distribution in the city, the rules and regulations that determined their func-

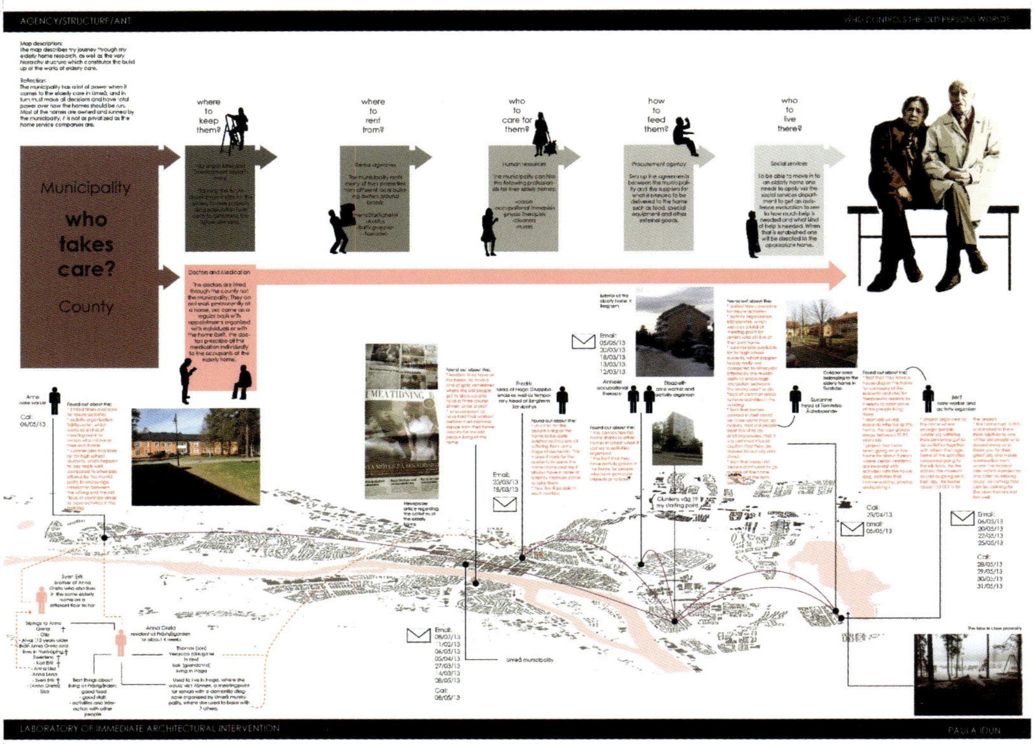

meeting the elderly: awakening curiosities/the other/coexistence - paula idun

elderly homes in umeå - architecture as acupunctural strategy - liai 8

tioning and other urban conditions that affected them as 'buildings' and 'homes', to a more careful exploration of the possibilities of establishing relations among the different homes, connecting them physically through a network of paths and routes. The direct involvement in the homes required to understand and measure the everyday lives at

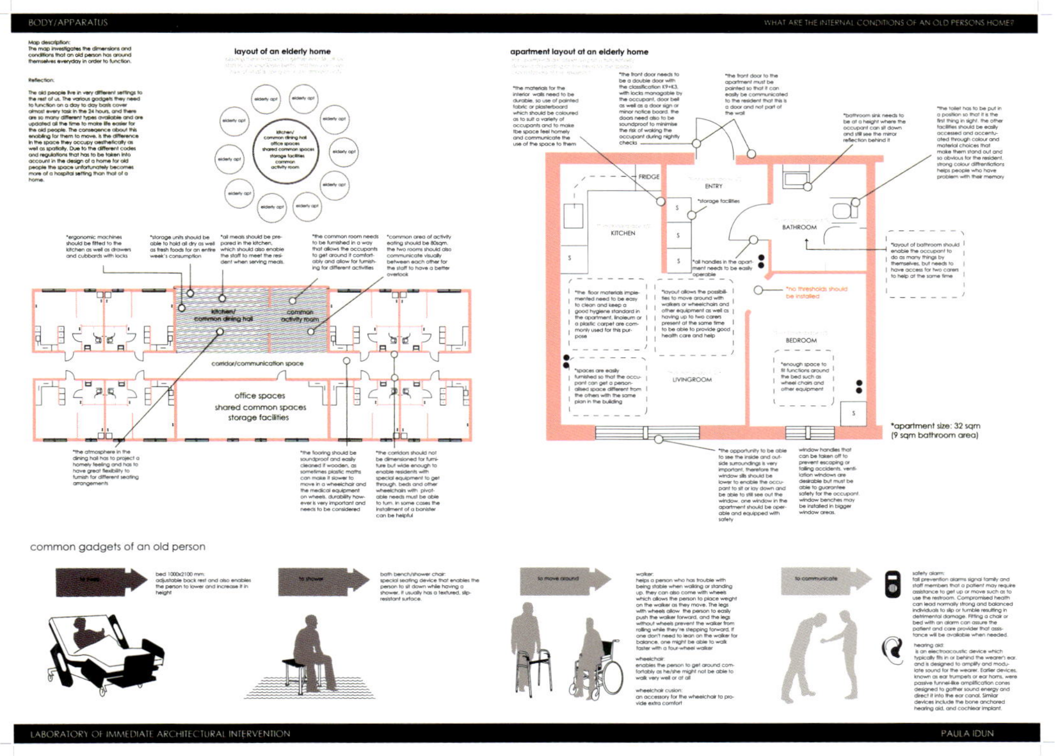

paula idun - **/meeting the elderly: awakening curiosities/the other/coexistence**

elderly homes in umeå - architecture as acupunctural strategy - liai 8

some of them, allowed her to identify a series of opportunities for intervention among which one was received with great enthusiasm by the directors of the home when she communicated it as a proposal. A gardening apparatus was built outside one of the homes in such a way that it would grant the old people living there another degree

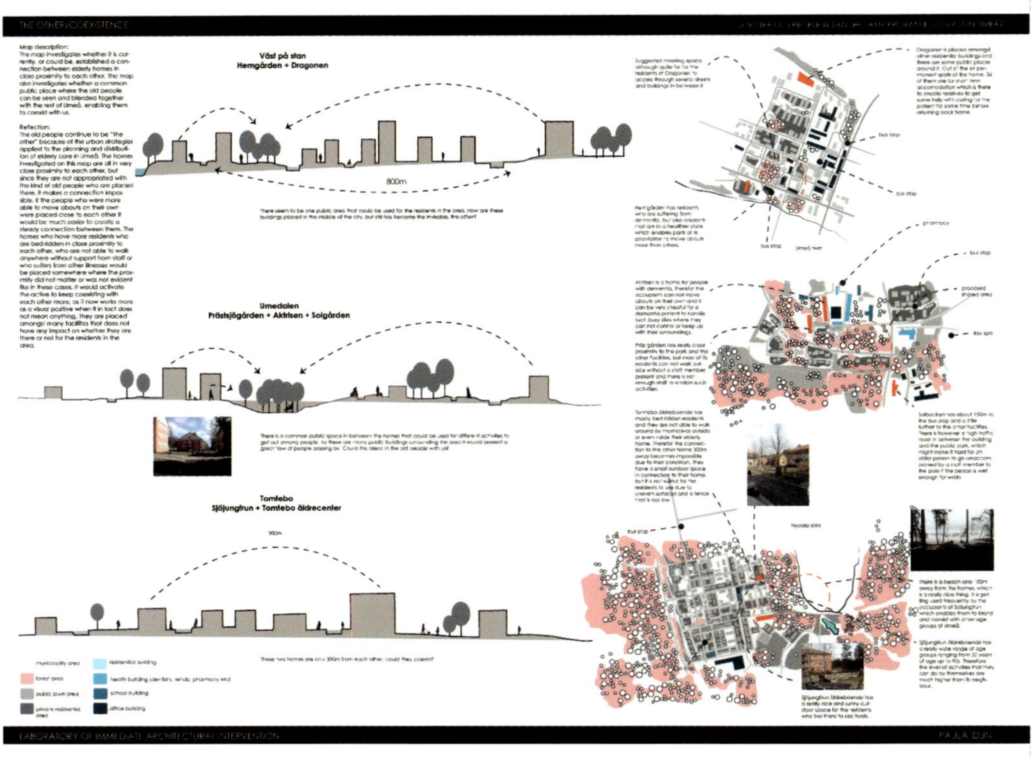

meeting the elderly: awakening curiosities/the other/coexistence - paula idun

elderly homes in umeå - architecture as acupunctural strategy - liai 8

of autonomy, by making it possible for them to plant, take care and grow vegetables or flowers without the constant help and supervision of the staff, thanks to a relatively 'safe' platform, a especially designed gardening desk and some benches. Although the intervention awakened certain curiosities and generated expectation among the

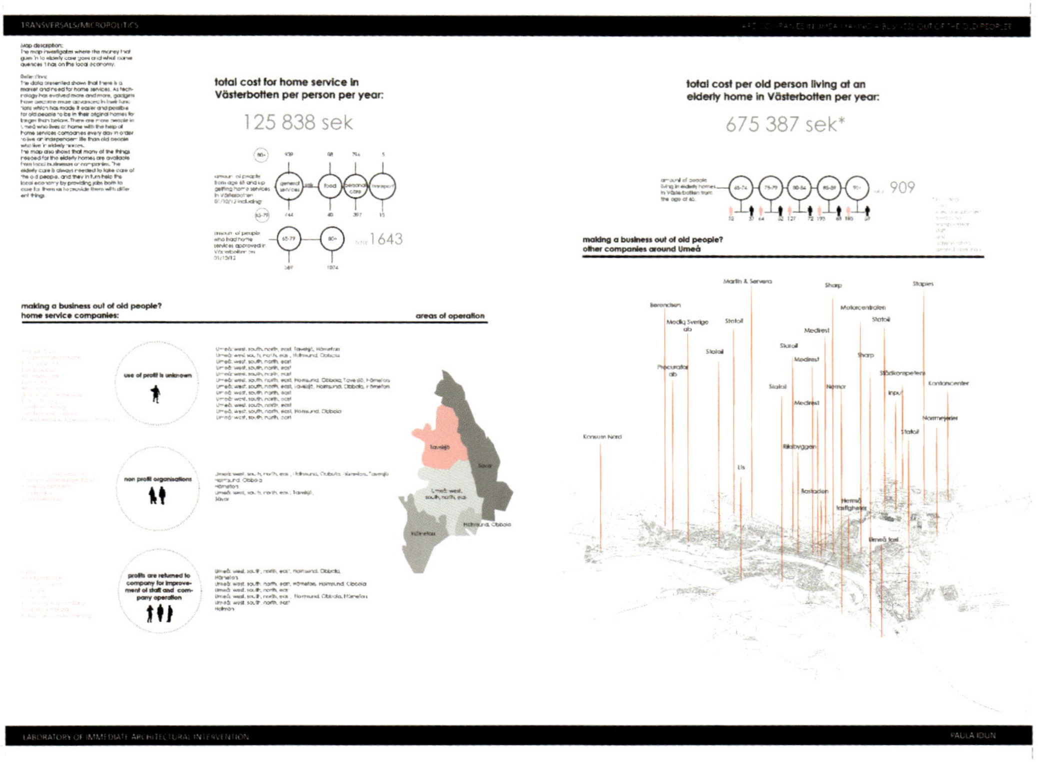

paula idun - **/meeting the elderly: awakening curiosities/the other/coexistence**

elderly homes in umeå - architecture as acupunctural strategy - liai 8

old people, it may have had greater activating effects through closer and more direct involvement of these old men and women in the process of conceiving, designing, producing, and most importantly, building 'the thing' on site, something that could have happened in collaboration with them at all times. Still, as with most of the work car-

meeting the elderly: awakening curiosities/the other/coexistence - paula idun

elderly homes in umeå - architecture as acupunctural strategy - liai 8

ried out at the LiAi, in this case things were not only imagined, thought of, designed or projected - opening doors and spaces for dreams and horizons - but also tested, constructed, installed, and put to work in-the-world, transforming it here-and-now.

paula idun - **/meeting the elderly: awakening curiosities/the other/coexistence**

elderly homes in umeå - architecture as acupunctural strategy - liai 8

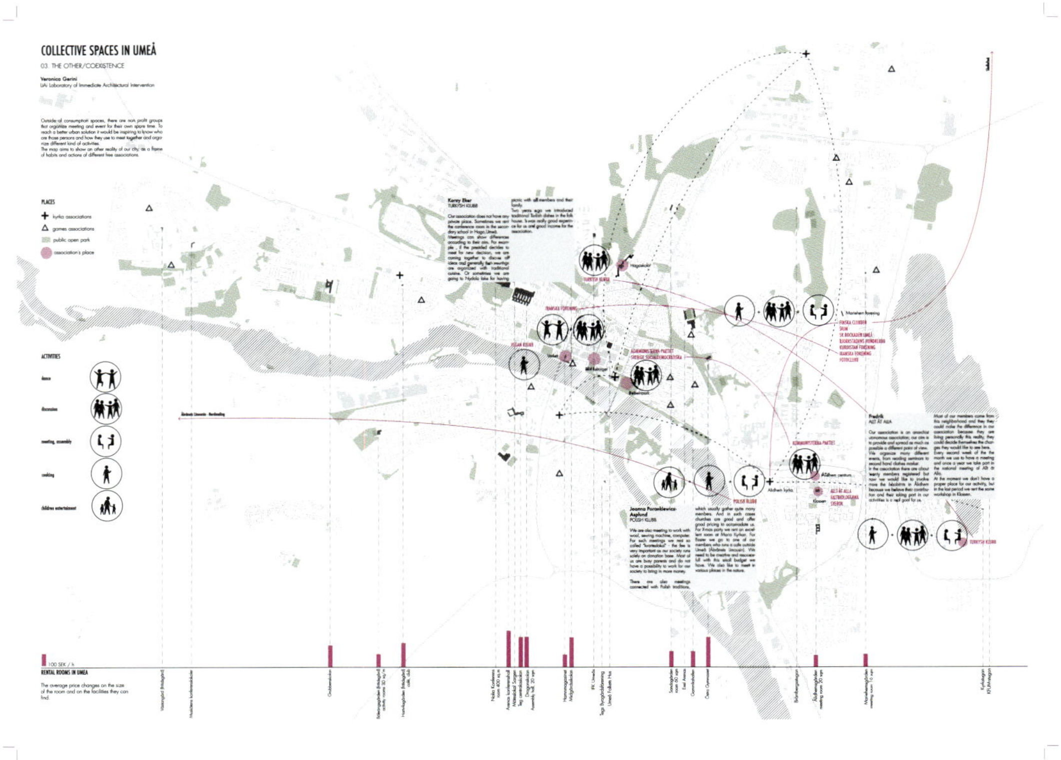

leisure and publicness in the city/the other/coexistence - veronica gerini

collective spaces in umeå - architecture as acupunctural strategy - liai 8

Veronica continued her exploration of public space in Umeå by shifting her focus to leisure. She studied the ways in which associations and individuals spend their free time and how their activities and actions configure and/or produce collective spaces and different forms of publicness.

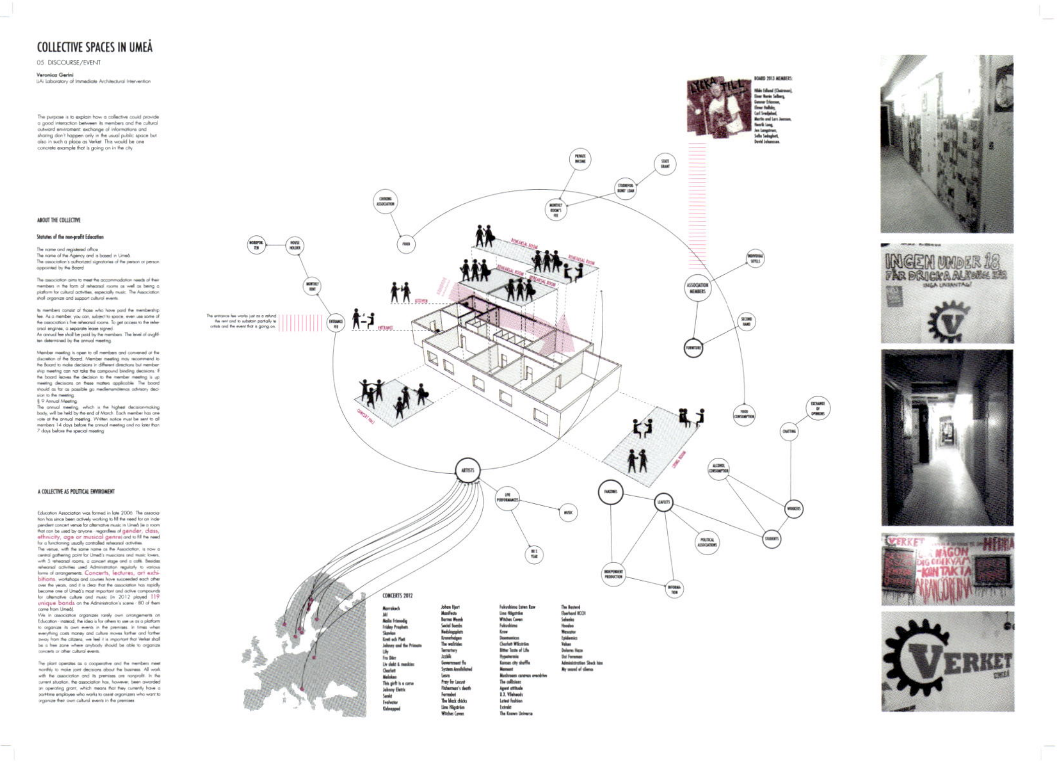

veronica gerini - **/leisure and publicness in the city/the other/coexistence**

collective spaces in umeå - architecture as acupunctural strategy - liai 8

Her investigation took her from the spaces made available by the municipality for the associations to rent, and the norms that regulate their management, to the cultural and activist associations that carry their activities outside this formal system, including sport-clubs, art-groups, ethnic associations and many others, finally 'landing' on the

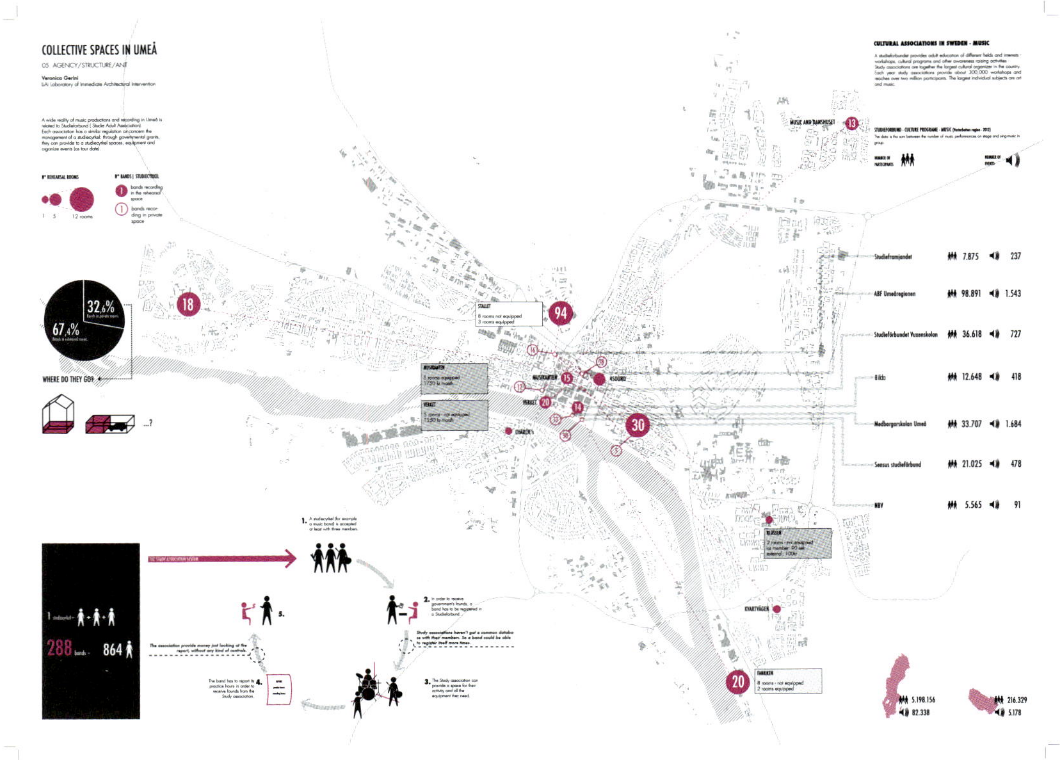

leisure and publicness in the city/the other/coexistence - veronica gerini

collective spaces in umeå - architecture as acupunctural strategy - liai 8

musical scene of the city, which turned out to be incredibly rich and active. While studying the way in which musical associations, groups and musicians are supported in Sweden and how the municipality of Umeå seems to have put in place an extremely attractive policy in this respect - through both fieldwork and research - she got in touch

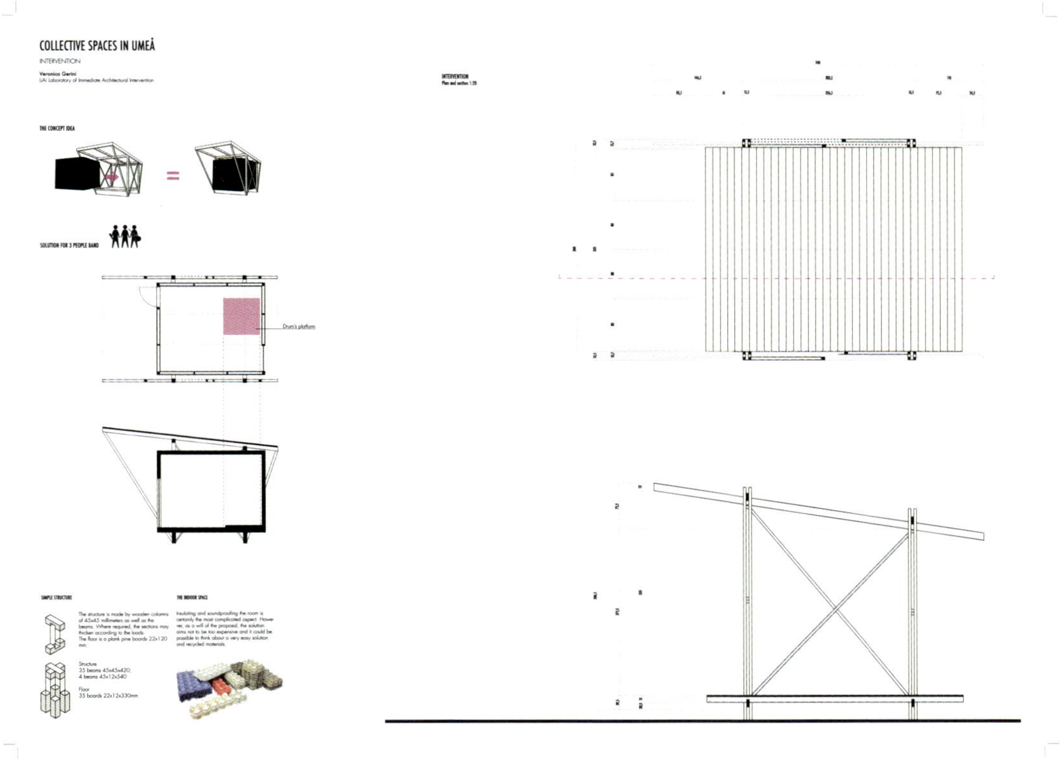

veronica gerini - **/leisure and publicness in the city/the other/coexistence**

collective spaces in umeå - architecture as acupunctural strategy - liai 8

with numerous groups and actors involved in the musical scene and understood there was a lack of both rehearsal and performance spaces. The conversations and discussions with these people helped her come up with a proposal for a simple structure that could be both a rehearsal room when closed, and a small stage when open.

leisure and publicness in the city/the other/coexistence - veronica gerini

collective spaces in umeå - architecture as acupunctural strategy - liai 8

The initial idea was to gather materials from around the city with the help of the musicians and members of the associations but this part of the intervention did not turn out so well and the timber had to be obtained otherwise. Her proposal was to build several of these structures also with the help of the musicians and place them in strategic

veronica gerini - **/leisure and publicness in the city/the other/coexistence**
collective spaces in umeå - architecture as acupunctural strategy - liai 8

locations she had agreed upon with them. Time was too short for her to carry out the whole plan but she managed to build a prototype of the structure and place it outside the school where it was quickly 'tested' by different people.

architecture through other ways of eating/the other/coexistence - tobias westerlund

food and spatial organization - architecture as acupunctural strategy - liai 8

Tobias' exploration of architecture through other ways of eating started with his observation that some old people went regularly to the supermarket with the aim of talking to the cashier rather than willing to buy anything they were really needing. Could supermarkets be spaces for encounter and dialogue? In fact, they were huge machines

tobias westerlund - **/architecture through other ways of eating/the other/coexistence**

food and spatial organization - architecture as acupunctural strategy - liai 8

for the handling and selling of food, and they had even huger parking spaces outside! He started thinking about the amount of food that is thrown away in these kinds of shops and decided to look closer into the origins of food in Umeå: where is it produced, how does it arrive to the city, how is it distributed to all shops, where are those

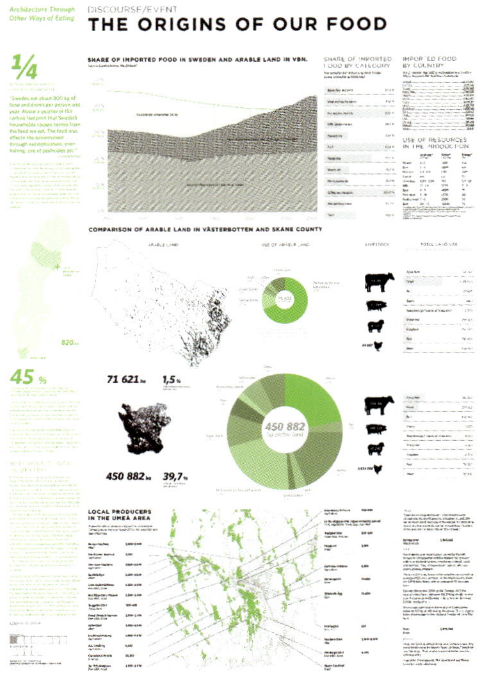

architecture through other ways of eating/the other/coexistence - tobias westerlund

food and spatial organization - architecture as acupunctural strategy - liai 8

shops located and what are their characteristics? Particularly, he placed a lot of attention to the ways in which waste food was generated and handled throughout the chain of food production, distribution and consumption, locating a series of sites for intervention in which 'improvements' and 'actions' could be invented and carried

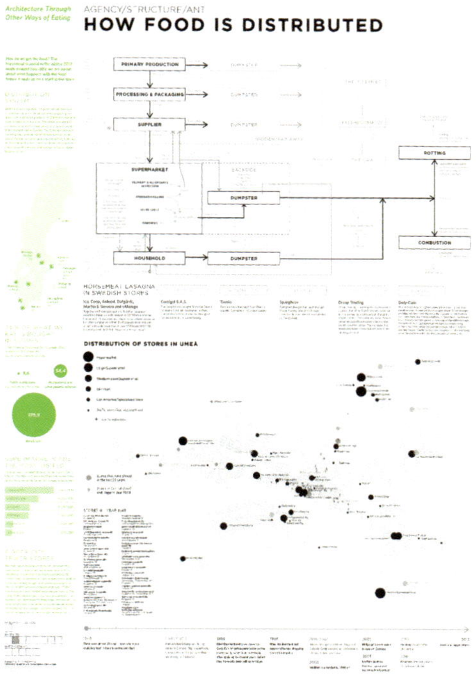

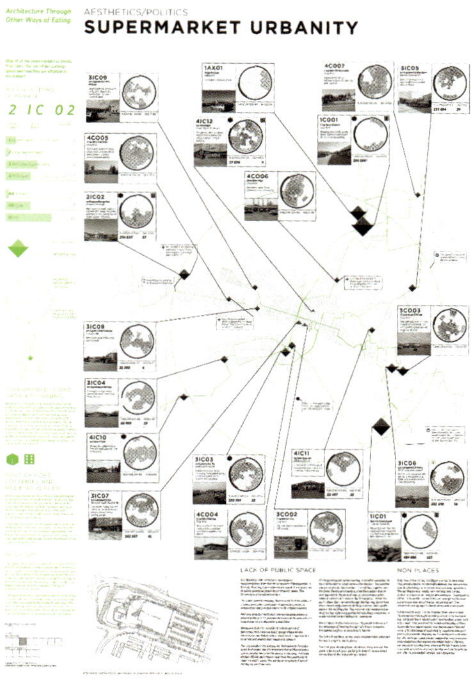

tobias westerlund - **/architecture through other ways of eating/the other/coexistence**

food and spatial organization - architecture as acupunctural strategy - liai 8

out. He was not only able to explore a kind of supermarket urbanity emerging in and around these monster-shops but also to find out, locate and examine the 'backside boutiques' associated to them: the accessible dumpsters related to some of these shops into which lots of food and other goods are regularly thrown. His engage-

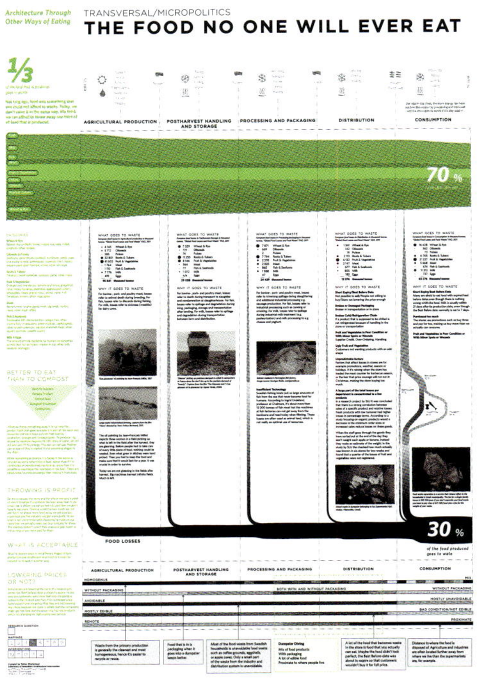

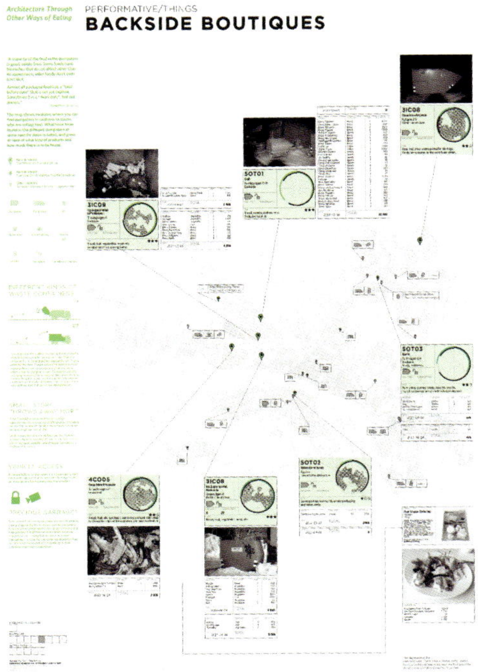

architecture through other ways of eating/the other/coexistence - tobias westerlund

food and spatial organization - architecture as acupunctural strategy - liai 8

ment went on to a regular and patient visiting of these dumpster sites where he collected, with help from other students, many different amounts and kinds of food in perfect condition that they checked, counted, measured, and.. well, ate together.

His work continued with the design of sev-

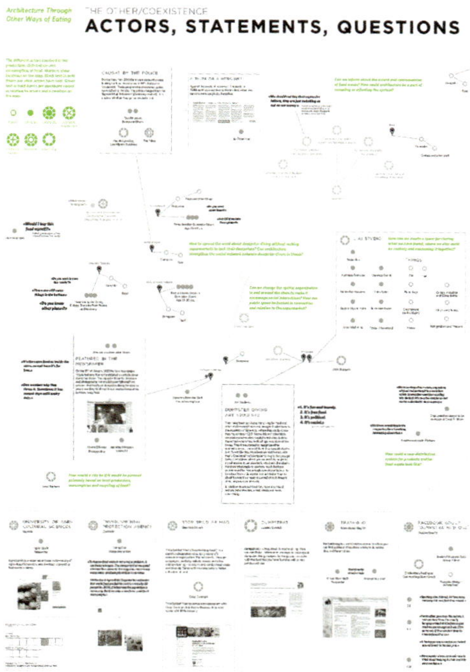

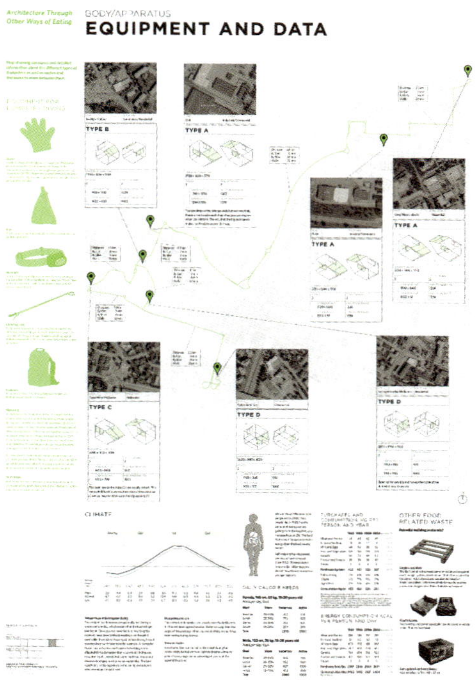

tobias westerlund - **/architecture through other ways of eating/the other/coexistence**

food and spatial organization - architecture as acupunctural strategy - liai 8

eral tools and devices that would make it easier for them to examine the dumpsters and to get a hold of their content, making sure that they had at the same time an innocent appearance. Since the amounts of food they found were way larger than they expected -and than they could eat themselves- he also organized an intervention

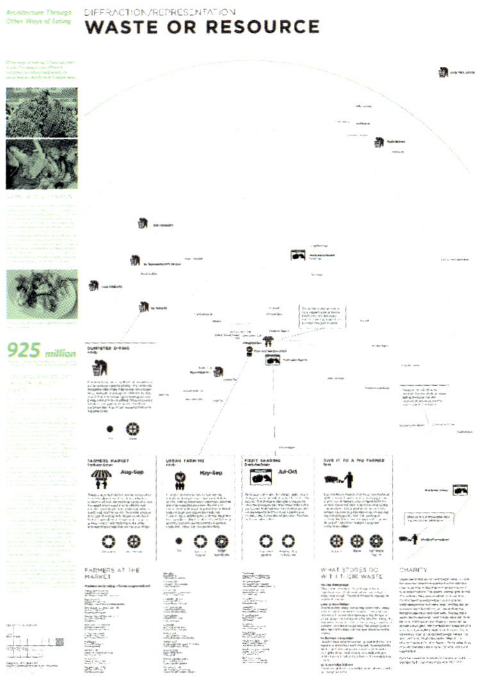

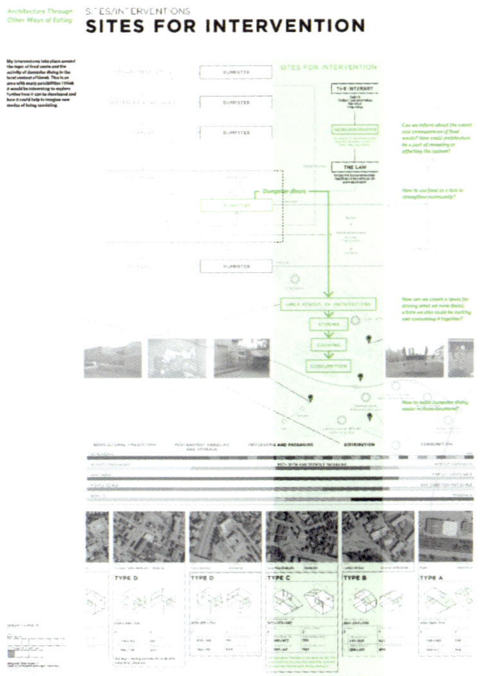

architecture through other ways of eating/the other/coexistence - tobias westerlund

food and spatial organization - architecture as acupunctural strategy - liai 8

through which the food was given away to people that they encountered in the city and to whom they explained the whole project. Some of this food was also given to a local association that distributes it to other people that need it, but that is unable to sign agreements with the shops and supermarkets as they are worried that they

tobias westerlund - **/architecture through other ways of eating/the other/coexistence**

food and spatial organization - architecture as acupunctural strategy - liai 8

might be sued if the food is not in good condition and someone gets sick. Tobias work, exploration and careful identification of the best 'sites' for intervention, allowed him to act as a by-pass in this transaction that turns waste into food. Beyond these very 'real' and physical interventions, he also designed an architectural projection, a

architecture through other ways of eating/the other/coexistence - tobias westerlund

food and spatial organization - architecture as acupunctural strategy - liai 8

small building that would help them in the process of collecting, keeping and consuming food from the city dumpsters. A huge fridge, that takes room-proportions and therefore generates a lot of excess heat, is used to maintain the large amounts of food they find in good condition, while heating a very well insulated kitchen and dining room.

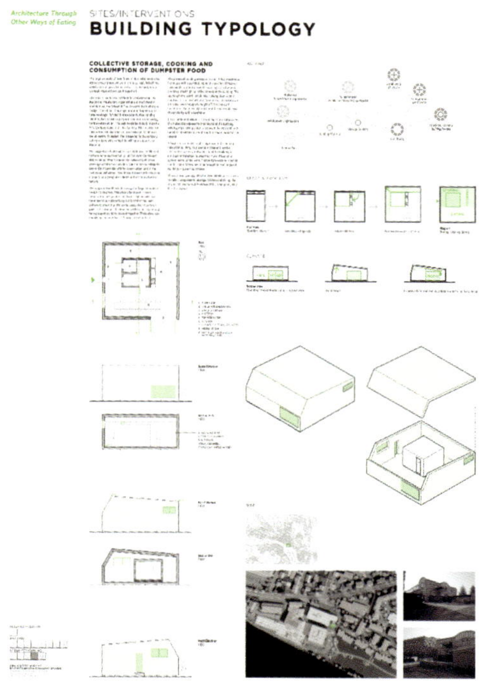

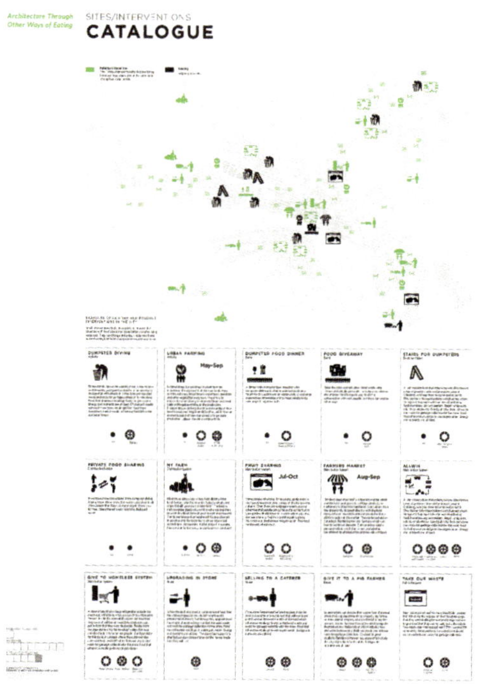

tobias westerlund - **/architecture through other ways of eating/the other/coexistence**

food and spatial organization - architecture as acupunctural strategy - liai 8

This is located very close to the school of architecture and could be a student union meeting place as much as a cooking workshop, and it is of course built with local wood, materials and technologies. It not only looks good but it smells good too!

norrland's productive hinterland/ - audingas sumskas

immigrate, inhabit, develop! - liai master's thesis

Audingas' Master's Thesis emerged from his personal involvement in an enormous company that produces all kinds of salads, spices, flowers and other vegetables in huge extensions of greenhouses, which are located in a small village of the hinterland, in the north of Umeå. His work points out and explores the paradox of a landscape of

audingas sumskas - /**norrland's productive hinterland**

immigrate, inhabit, develop! - liai master's thesis

shrinking local economies and dying villages in the hinterland of Norrland - the northernmost of the three 'lands' into which Sweden is divided - and the explosive growth of transnational companies that benefit from streamlined market regulations, global capital flows, immigration and the availability of cheap land and energy, precisely

norrland's productive hinterland/ - audingas sumskas

immigrate, inhabit, develop! - liai master's thesis

in and around those shrinking communities. His analysis and engagement in the company as one more temporary worker allowed him to come into close contact with the CEO and to understand the techniques, processes and rhythms of the company: greenhouses are almost constantly built to increase the production in order to

audingas sumskas - /**norrland's productive hinterland**

immigrate, inhabit, develop! - liai master's thesis

satisfy the (ever?) increasing demand. His first speculative interventions included a proposal to interfere in this expansion by redesigning the greenhouse and managing to insert a housing module between the original greenhouse and its extension, so that it would benefit from the excess-heat generated by the greenhouses. Elevated

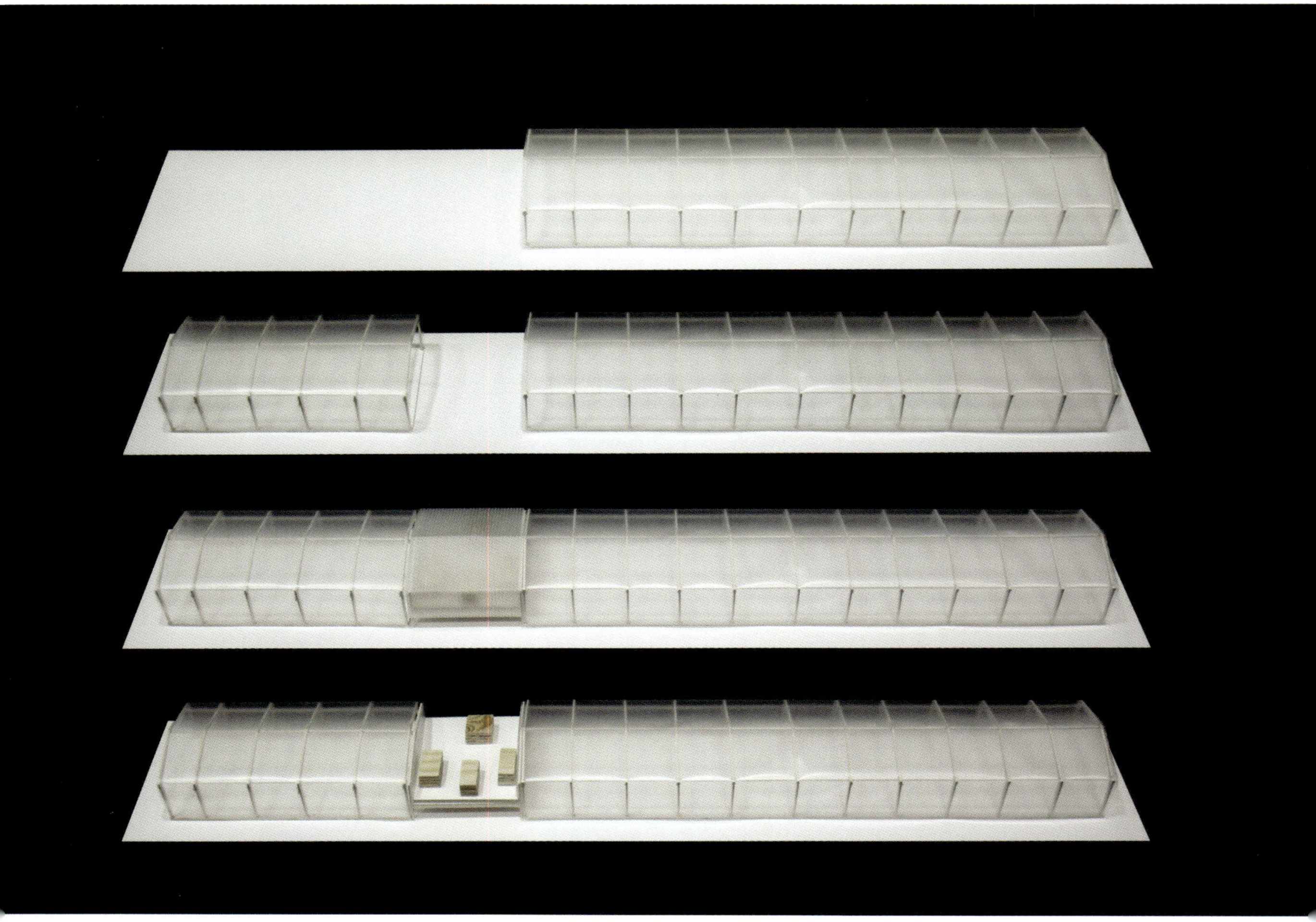

norrland's productive hinterland/ - audingas sumskas

immigrate, inhabit, develop! - liai master's thesis

one-floor height from the ground, the housing module would not interfere with the company's work in the greenhouse, but it could provide cheap and adequate accommodation to immigrant workers that were otherwise placed in very poorly equipped and not properly maintained old villas, now turned into communal barracks. Further re-

audingas sumskas - /**norrland's productive hinterland**

immigrate, inhabit, develop! - liai master's thesis

search and in-depth analysis allowed him to develop a clear understanding of the territorial condition, and to propose a regional strategy that could change the way we look at the hinterland and plan its uses. His project also included a detailed analysis of the village and a speculative proposal suggesting that the community could engage in

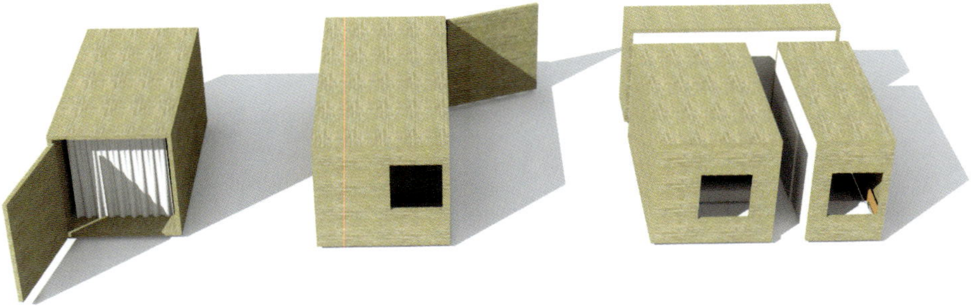

norrland's productive hinterland/ - audingas sumskas

immigrate, inhabit, develop! - liai master's thesis

close collaboration with the salad company in order to establish synergies that would enable a better use and reuse of the excess energy generated in the greenhouses as well as the construction of affordable housing and other public facilities, while at the same time allowing the expansion of the company's activities, and transforming

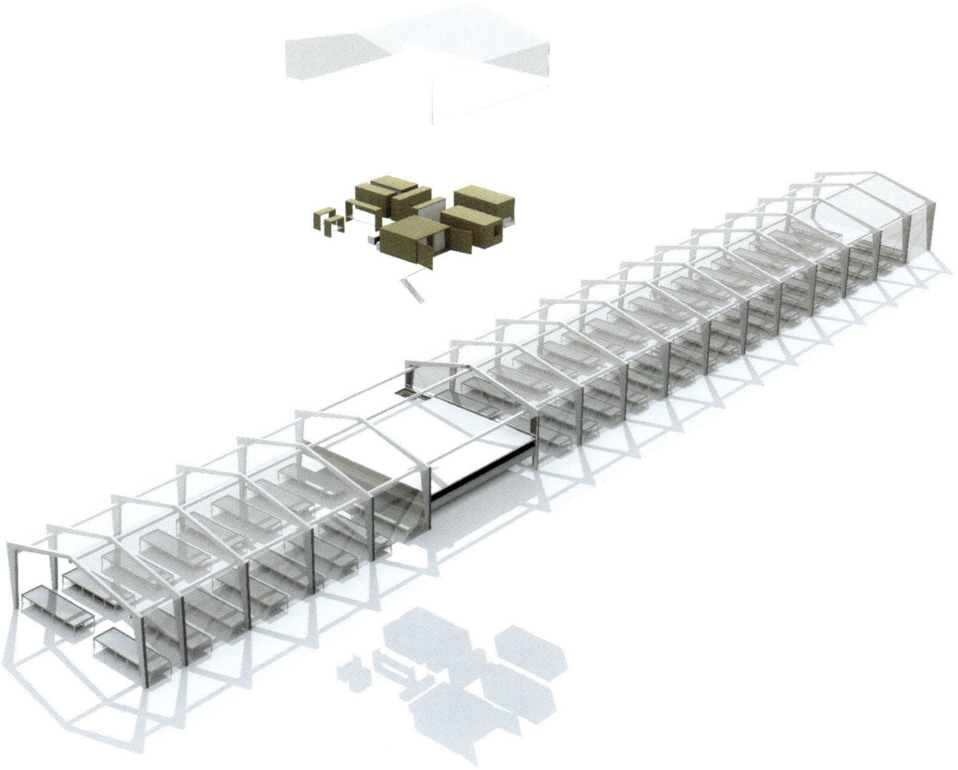

audingas sumskas - /**norrland's productive hinterland**

immigrate, inhabit, develop! - liai master's thesis

the local identity and economy. Integrated in his work were also several smaller interventions through which the local conditions and specificities were tested, active local actors were contacted and interviewed, and greenhouse technologies and construction techniques were rehearsed.

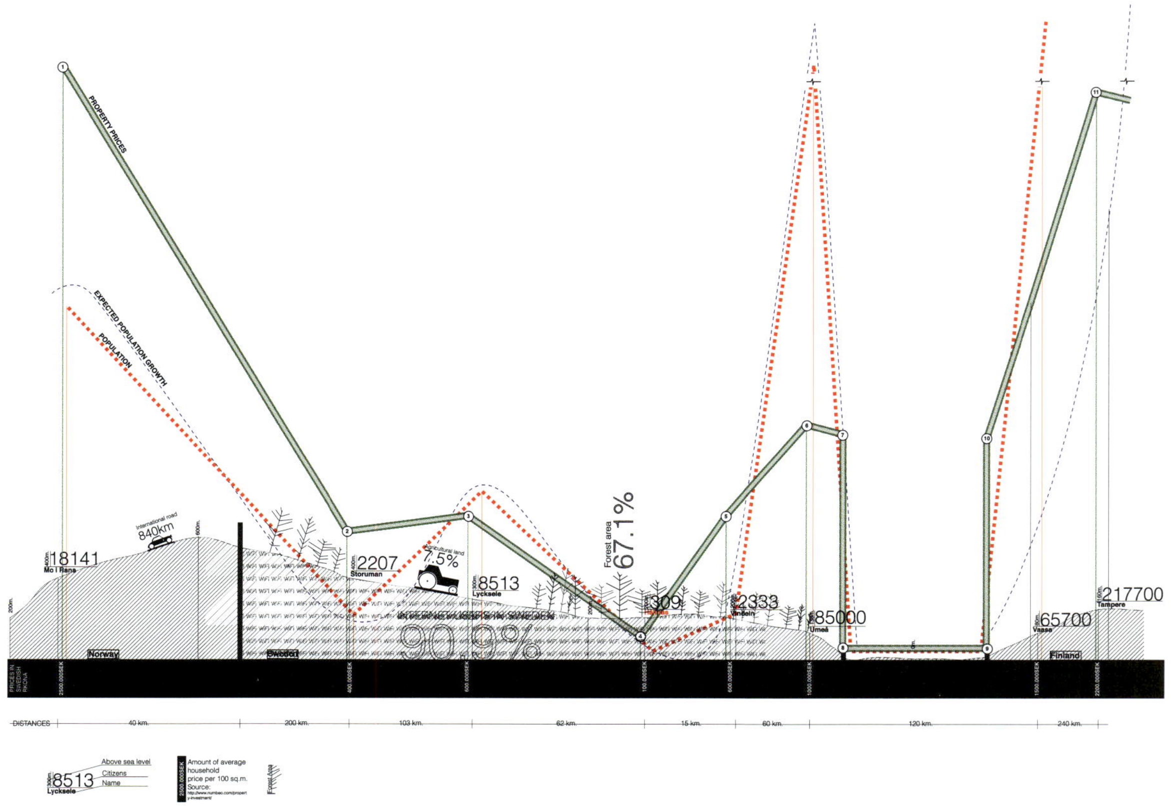

norrland's productive hinterland/ - audingas sumskas

immigrate, inhabit, develop! - liai master's thesis

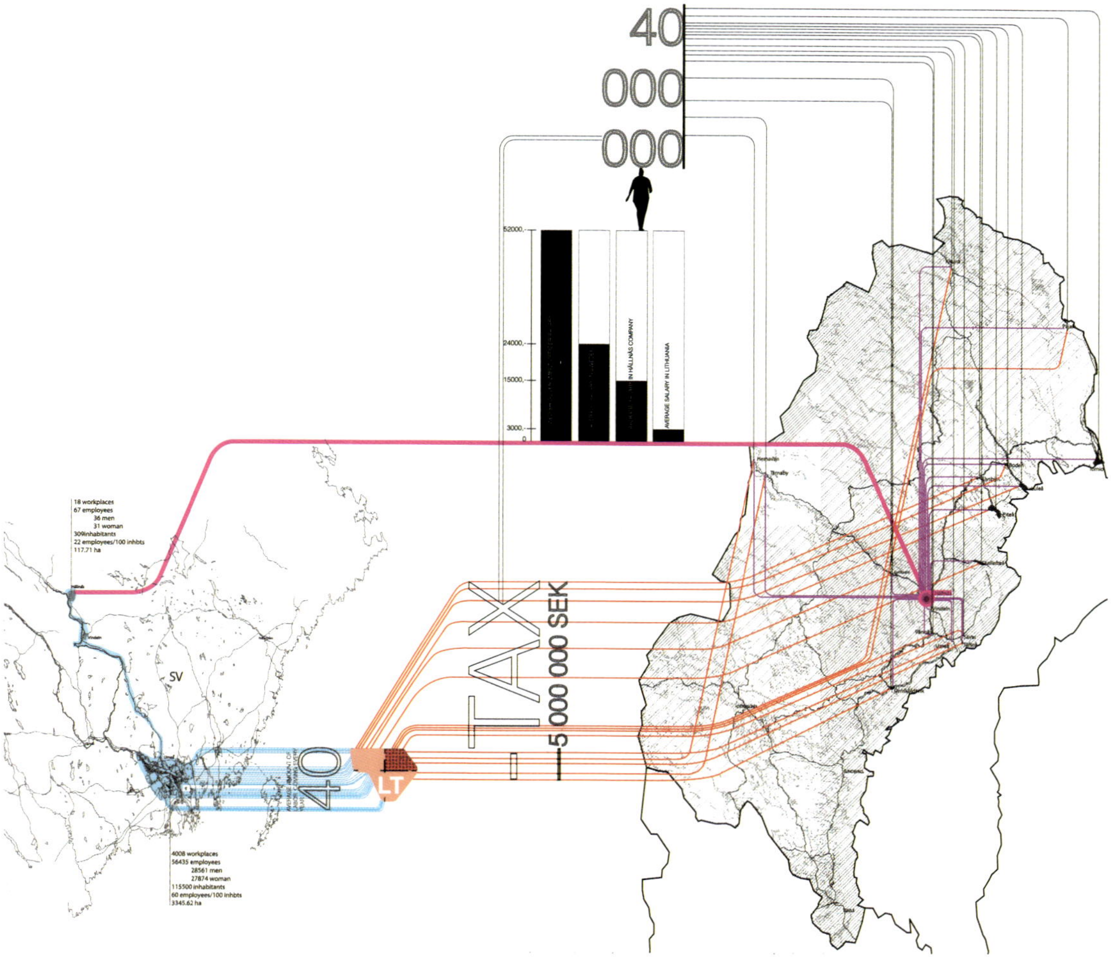

audingas sumskas - **/norrland's productive hinterland**

immigrate, inhabit, develop! - liai master's thesis

taking place/ - anna misharina

urban intervention - architectural intervention and cultural consequences - liai 7

Anna started her work on urban commons by exploring the dance scene in Umeå. She got in contact with dancers and dance associations and understood the precarity they live in. Only a few are lucky enough to have stable jobs or to grab some of the few available funds in order to maintain their already scarce income and incredibly inse-

anna misharina - **/taking place**

urban intervention - architectural intervention and cultural consequences - liai 7

cure agendas. One of the structural conditions affecting them is the lack of dancing stages in which their performances can be scheduled. Organizing dance events is therefore difficult. This led to speculations about the possibilities of designing an affordable but portable dance-floor that could be easily moved from one place to

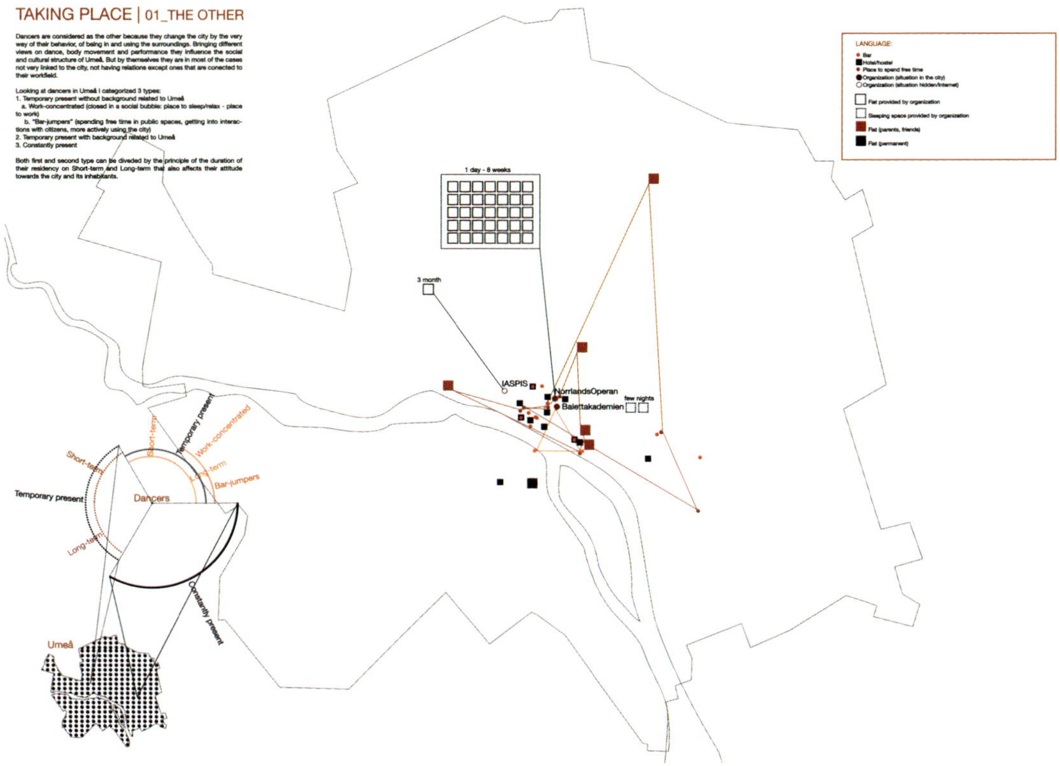

taking place/ - anna misharina

speculative mapping - the other/coexistence - architecture as acupunctural strategy - liai 8

another, turning conference rooms, auditoriums, schools or other public spaces into dance stages. While continuing to develop her exploration of Umeå through many and diverse interventions, Anna engaged in a parallel process of collaboration with a local dance group that led to the production of first a prototype and several variations,

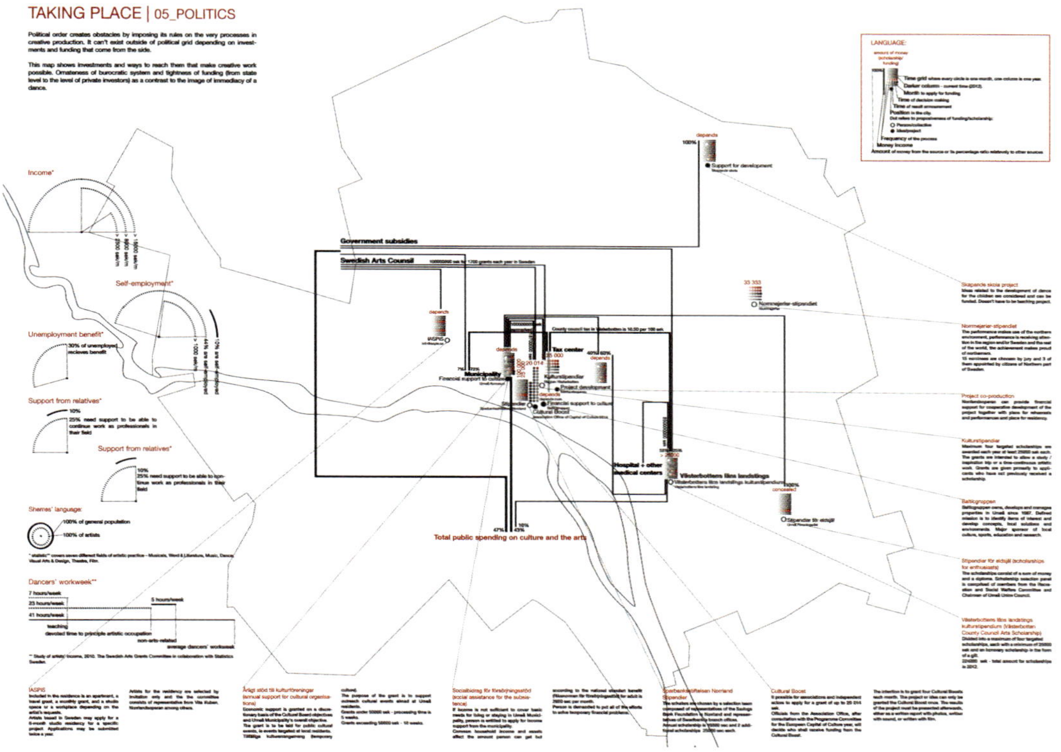

anna misharina - **/taking place**

speculative mapping - the other/coexistence - architecture as acupunctural strategy - liai 8

then a full scale dance floor thanks to some funds they applied for together and managed to obtain. The floor is now another 'real' urban commons, as it remains in the custody of a local association but can be used by anyone on the condition that it is well taken care of and returned after use.

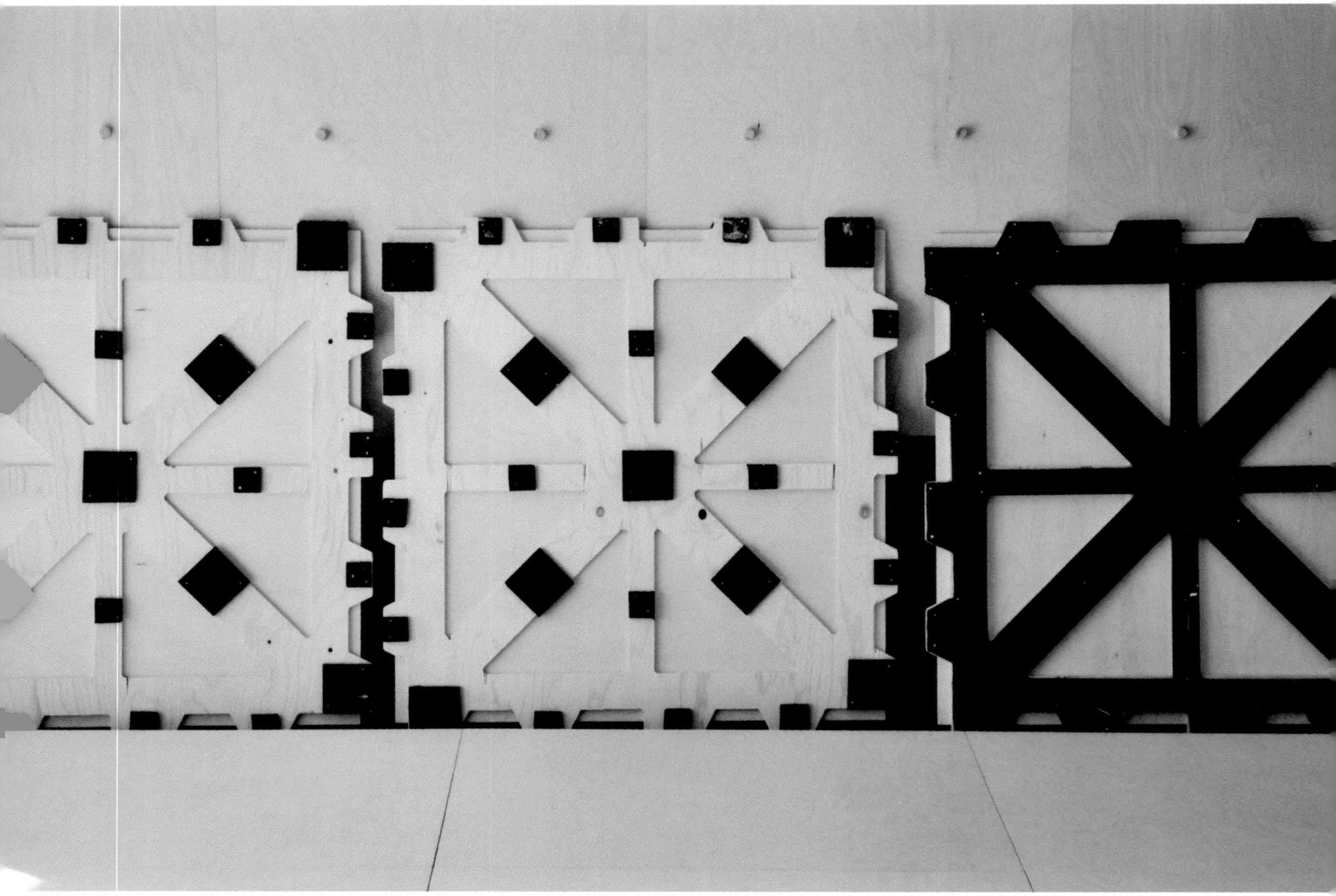

taking place/movable dancing floor/ - anna misharina

developed prototype - architectural intervention, realization and consequences - liai 9

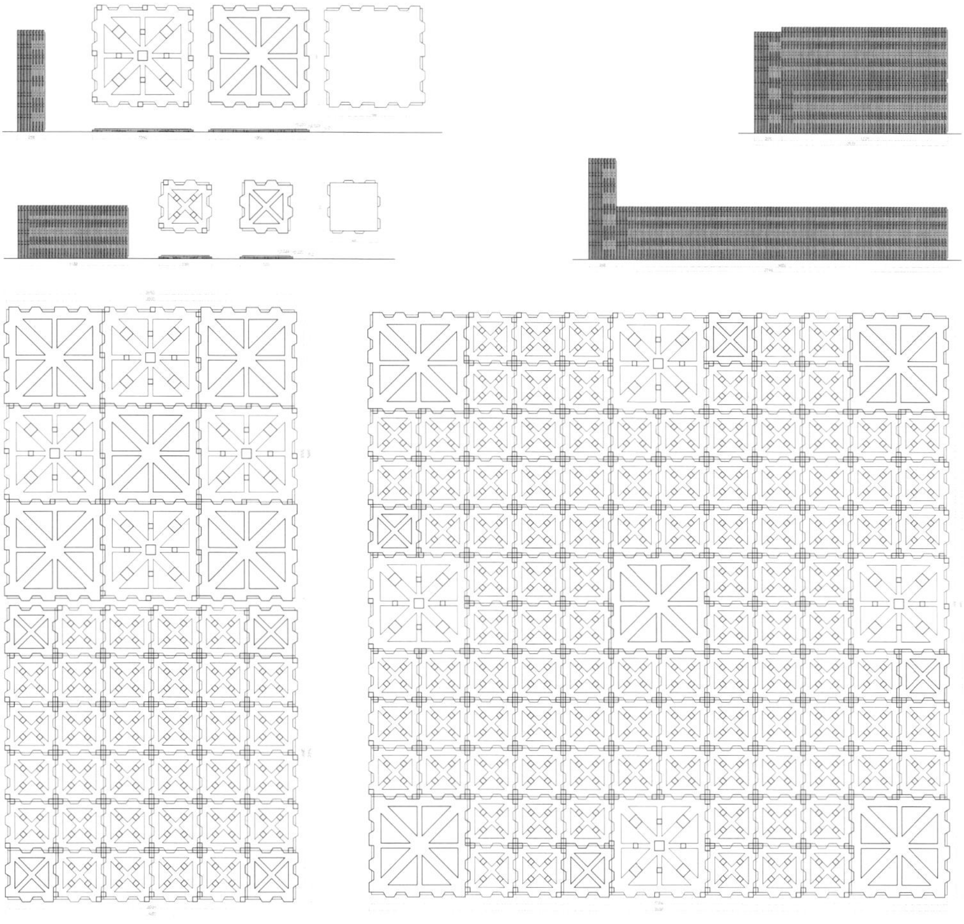

anna misharina - **/taking place/movable dancing floor**

overview basic drawings - architectural intervention, realization and consequences - liai 9

taking place/movable dancing floor/ - anna misharina

developed prototype - architectural intervention, realization and consequences - liai 9

anna misharina - **/taking place/movable dancing floor**

developed prototype - architectural intervention, realization and consequences - liai 9

non figurative urban commons/ - anna misharina

interventions within / anticipations of alternative public spaces - liai master's thesis

The process described above is one among many of the interventions that make up the landscape of actions-in-the-city that constitutes her work and that ended up becoming her Master's Thesis. There isn't a linear process and a final outcome or result in the form of a projective design, but multiple interventions: some of them are

anna misharina - /**non figurative urban commons**

interventions within / anticipations of alternative public spaces - liai master's thesis

speculative, some are projective, most of them are collaborative and performative. All of them transform the world and produce effects that challenge the conditions of the situations in which she participates. They have very real effects, sometimes through the constitution of stable urban commons, sometimes in the form of very located and

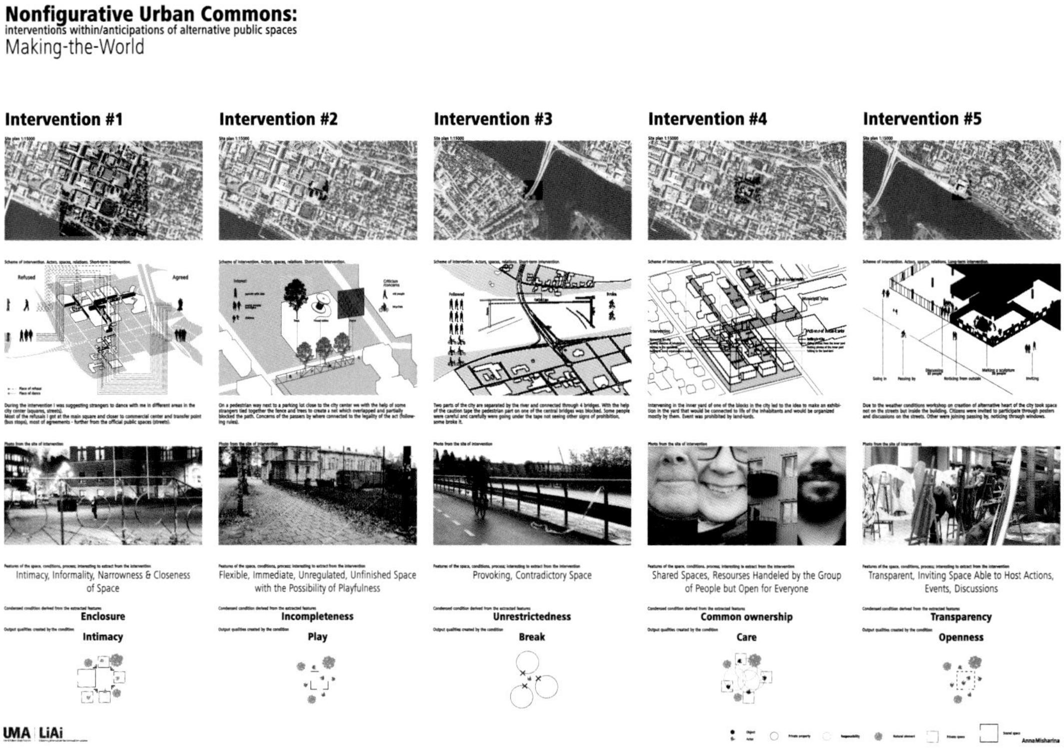

non figurative urban commons/ - anna misharina

interventions within / anticipations of alternative public spaces - liai master's thesis

short term events that can be enjoyed only as they last. They are also performative in their discursive power, as they construct and propose other ways of conceptualizing and imagining what the commons are or can be, effectively shifting the limits of what is or can be shared and suggesting alternative ways of being together and of sharing.

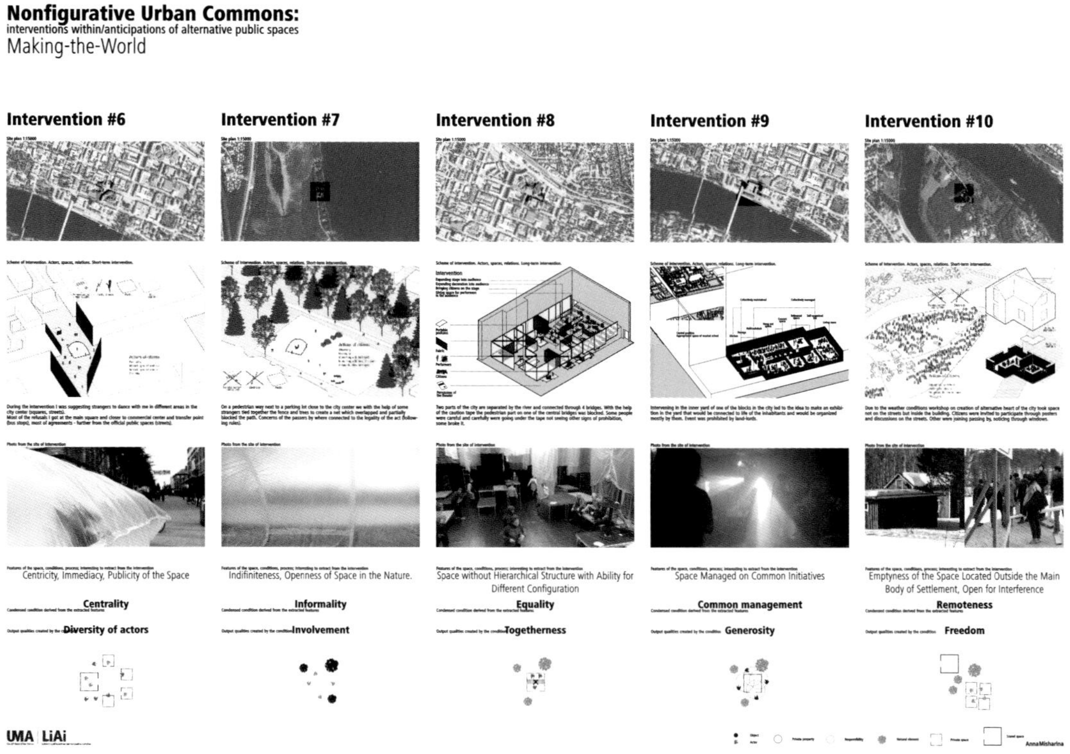

anna misharina - **/non figurative urban commons**

interventions within / anticipations of alternative public spaces - liai master's thesis

The speculative and projective 'tracks' of her research led her to proposing a design for a complex urban community in an island located in the river - very close to the city center - where the municipality has plans for a high-rise residential development which has been highly criticized and debated. Her proposal draws instead from

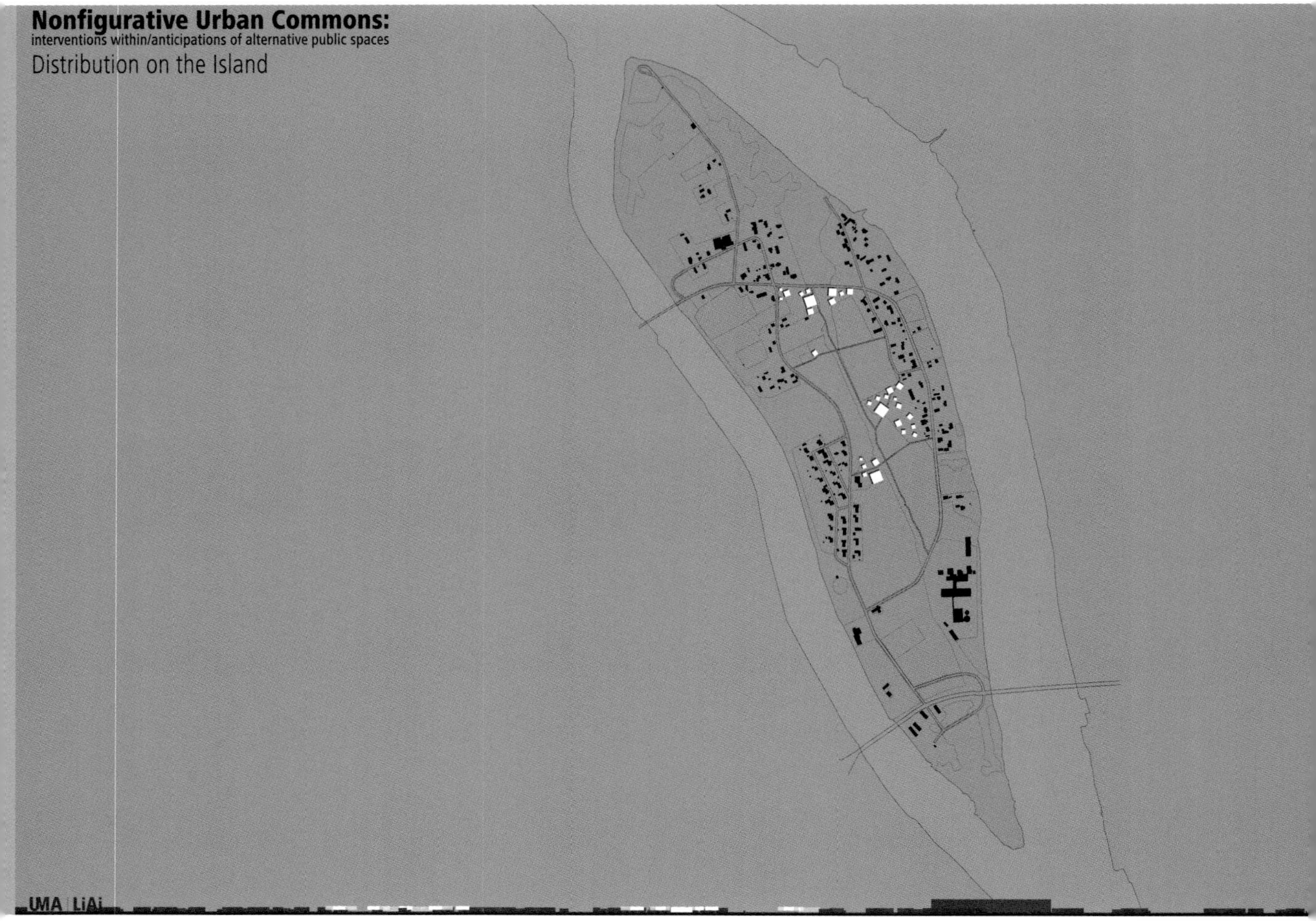

non figurative urban commons/ - anna misharina

interventions within / anticipations of alternative public spaces - liai master's thesis

the experiences of her interventions and is conceived on the basis of the principles she has found at work in the different situations as generators of 'commonness' and openness, anticipating alternative forms of conceiving public space and announcing another way of living together.

anna misharina - /**non figurative urban commons**

interventions within / anticipations of alternative public spaces - liai master's thesis

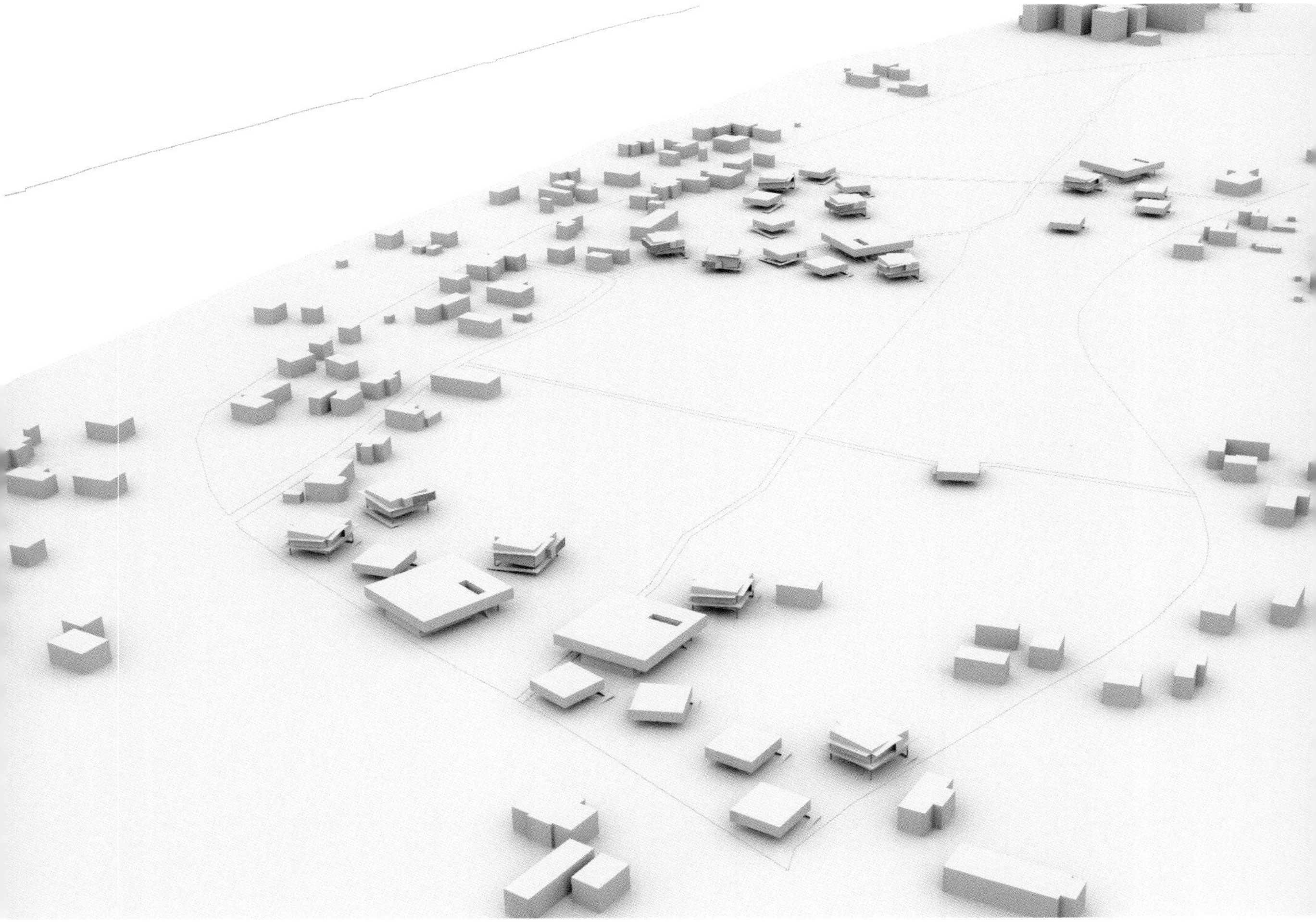

non figurative urban commons/ - anna misharina

interventions within / anticipations of alternative public spaces - liai master's thesis

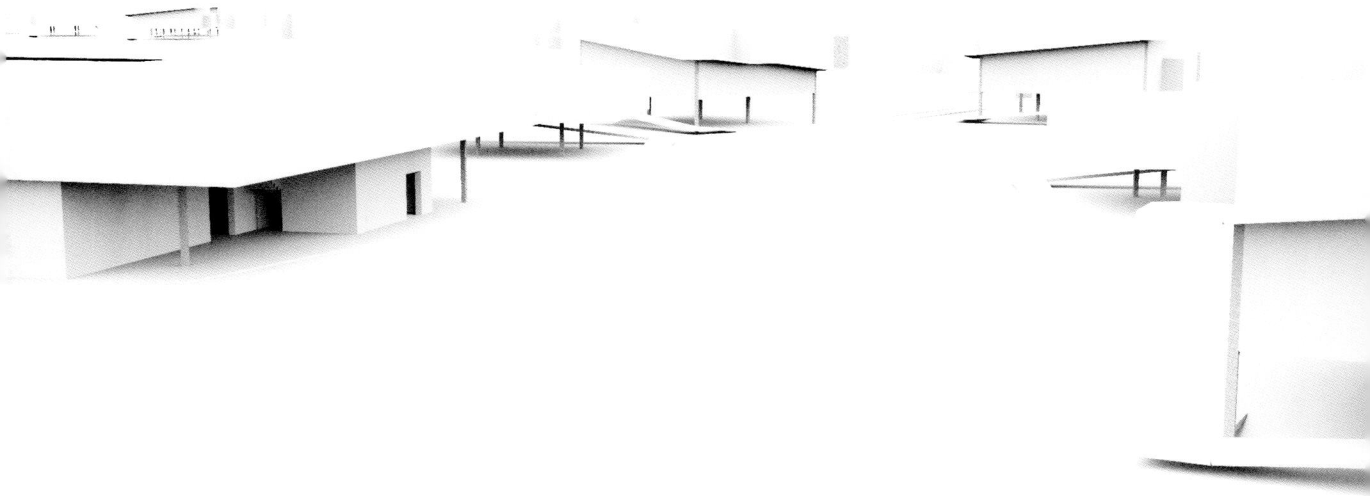

anna misharina - /**non figurative urban commons**

interventions within / anticipations of alternative public spaces - liai master's thesis

year exhibition/ - liai

liai faculty and students working together in the construction of the year exhibition at umeå bildmuseet

The work produced at the LiAi was shown along other work produced at UMA in a joint exhibition at Umeå Bildmuseet (the museum of contemporary art of the city) that was curated by Peter Kjaer and Ellen Skånberg. Peter's and Ellen's idea of 'work in progress' was a perfect starting point for us: we engaged in the design and produc-

liai - **/year exhibition**

liai faculty and students working together in the construction of the year exhibition at umeå bildmuseet

tion of a central space that could host diverse events during the exhibition but that was to be clearly connected with the idea of a roundtable. We adapted and improved the design for the moving structures we had built during one of the workshops (the 'flyttblock') and built three more of them. We completed them with six smaller 'cous-

year exhibition/ - liai

the roundtable setting for the year exhibition at umeå bildmuseet "in-the-making"

ins' that were easier to move and therefore more flexible in terms of the multiplicity of configurations that they allowed. One of the big 'flyttblock' was built as part of a performance in the museum, during which all the parts that had been previously arranged in a particular order on the ground, were put together in an orchestrated and collaborative

liai - **/year exhibition**

a view of the year exhibition at umeå bildmuseet

effort by all LiAi participants. In our space we also exhibited images of the laboratory's experiences, field trips, interventions, research and work, through film projections, prints, posters and models as well as a big table-on-wheels that was fabricated during a workshop with the spanish art collective 'sitesize' with the aim of collecting infor-

year exhibition roundtable/ - liai

professor walter unterrainer in one of the roundtable discussions organized at umeå bildmuseet

mation about the history and development of 'Kulturväven' - a local project to build a new 'house of culture' which has been designed by Snöhetta and is currently under construction. Several thematic roundtable discussions were organized in the central space, involving students, professors, local activists, politicians, and other people that

liai - **/year exhibition roundtable**

a setting for a series of roundtable discussions as part of the year exhibition at umeå bildmuseet

were invited to participate. These discussions were a success not only as discussions but also as a way of activating the otherwise static and representational space of the exhibition and as a way of creating an actual space and time for encounter, where the laboratory and the school could meet the city and its inhabitants.

year exhibition roundtable/ - liai

participants in one of the roundtable discussions organized at umeå bildmuseet

liai - **/year exhibition year exhibition**

participants in one of the roundtable discussions organized at umeå bildmuseet

fair city project/trälager paviljong - liai

a project to build an experimental timber pavilion in collaboration with kids and kulturverket (umeå)

The Fair City project came as an opportunity to collaborate with Umeå municipality through 'Kulturverket', a section within the local administration that encourages children and young people to be creative involving school pupils in arts and culture projects. In the framework of Umeå being the European Capital of Culture in 2014, the

liai - **/fair city project/trälager paviljong**

a project to build an experimental timber pavilion in collaboration with kids and kulturverket (umeå)

municipality runs a parallel project in which 1000 children will participate in a grand exhibition displaying their visions of Umeå in the future. Working with nine topics inspired from the Convention on Children's Rights, the kids were to inspire designs for nine pavilions that the School of Architecture, through the LiAi, was to design. One

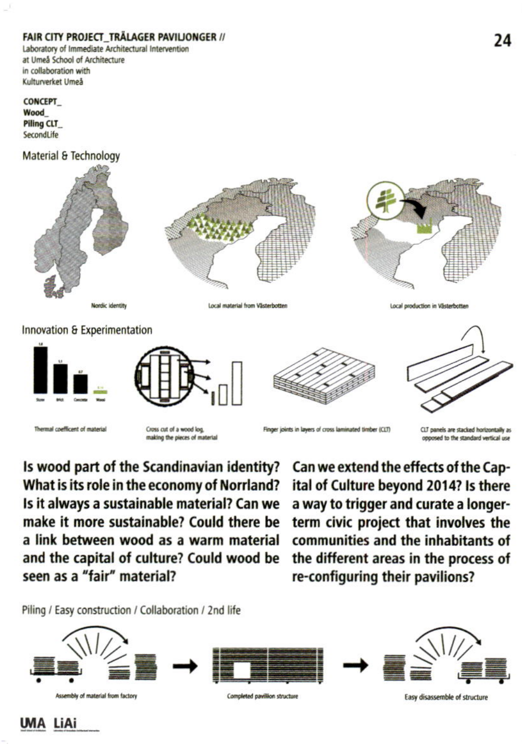

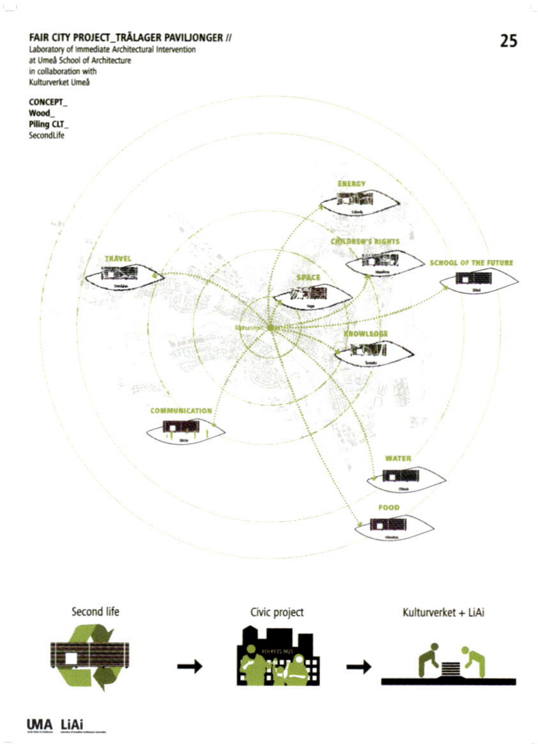

fair city project/trälager paviljong - liai

a project to build an experimental timber pavilion in collaboration with kids and kulturverket (umeå)

of these pavilions was to be built as part of the activities of the LiAi during 2013. We integrated the work with the kids at their schools in the explorations carried out by our students at the LiAi. They engaged the kids to guide them through "their city and their world" in order to locate interesting and exciting sites for the pavilions. During

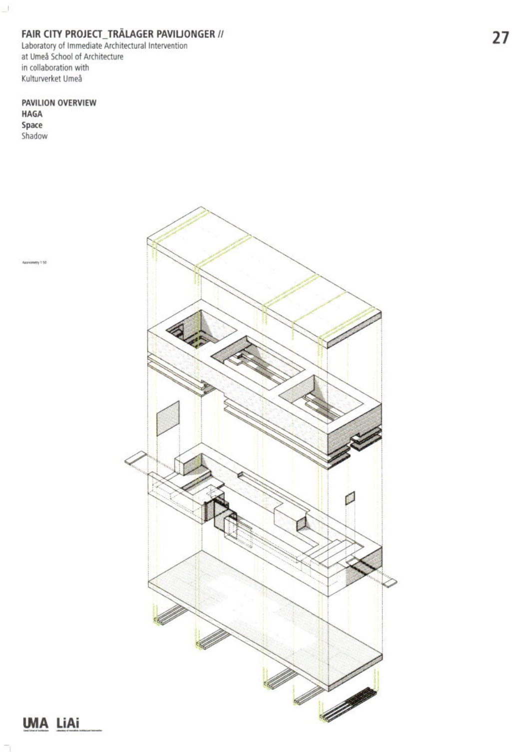

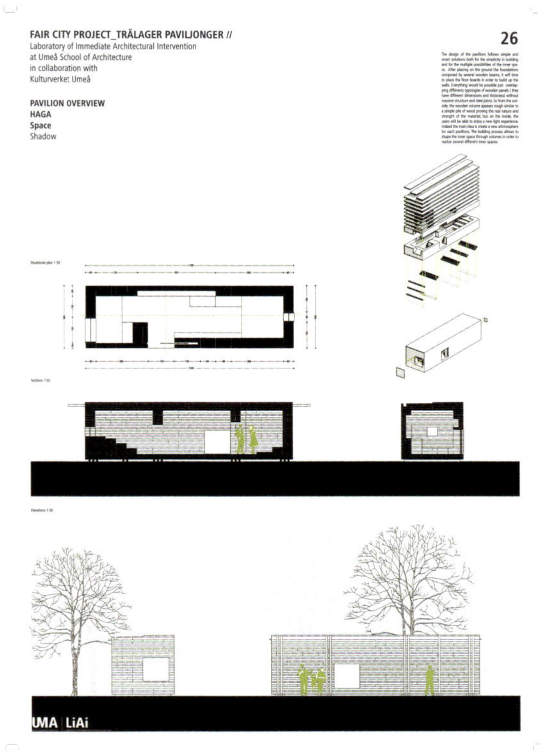

liai - **/fair city project/trälager paviljong**

a project to build an experimental timber pavilion in collaboration with kids and kulturverket (umeå)

a very intense workshop run in collaboration with Claudi Aguiló and Roger Tudó, from the architectural offices 'dataAE' and 'HARQUITECTES', from Barcelona, the students developed a design proposal for an architectural system that could generate nine different pavilions for the nine different sites. A basic design was then pro-

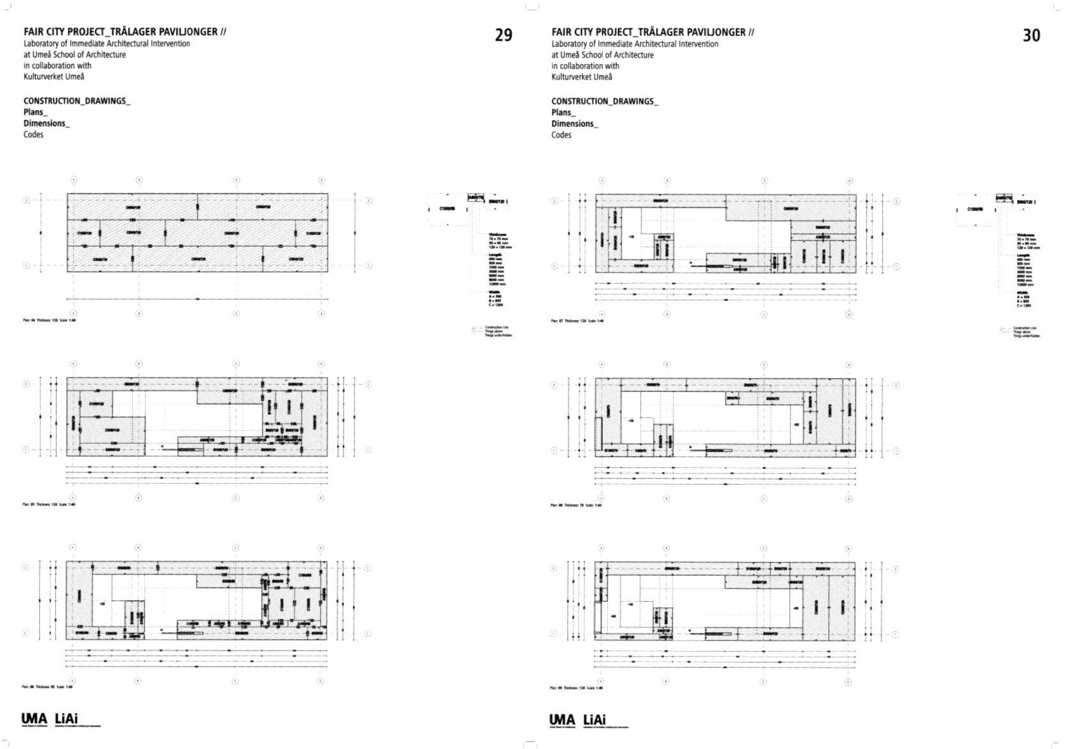

fair city project/trälager paviljong - liai

a project to build an experimental timber pavilion in collaboration with kids and kulturverket (umeå)

posed for each site in relationship to their specific characteristics, conditions and themes, and finally, one of the pavilions was developed in detail, down to the construction scale, in order to be built outside the school before transportation to its final location. The proposal subverts the usual and logical use of cross laminated timber (CLT) and elaborates a strategy based on 'piling' the CLT panels that allows the

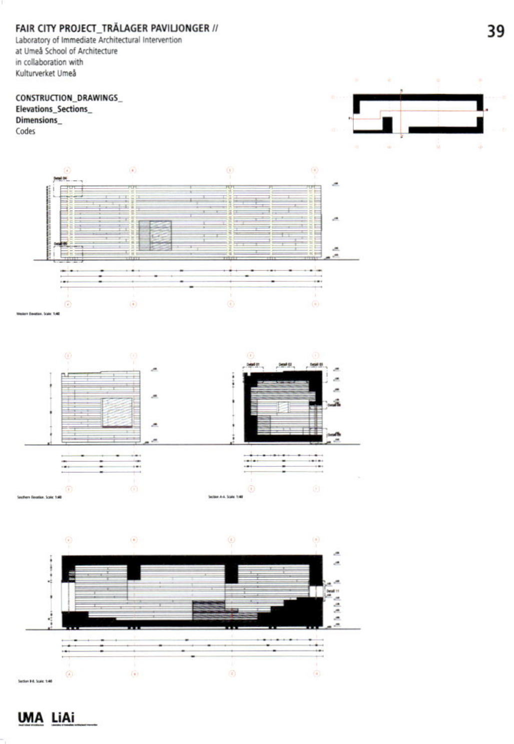

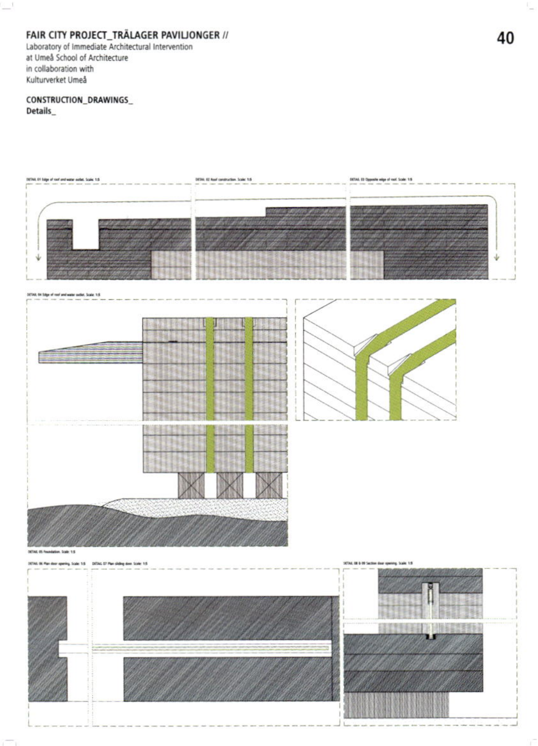

liai - **/fair city project/trälager paviljong**

a project to build an experimental timber pavilion in collaboration with kids and kulturverket (umeå)

whole to be stable without the use of any screws, glues or other fixing techniques. Such a strategy simplifies the construction process and makes the dismantling of the pavilion not only possible but also easy and affordable. The ease of construction opens doors to the involvement of students, faculty, kids and other citizens in the actual building process, while the piling strategy introduces the possibility of a 'second life'

fair city project/trälager paviljong - liai

a project to build an experimental timber pavilion in collaboration with kids and kulturverket (umeå)

for the material and a longer-term civic project that could extend the idea of co-creation beyond the events related to the year 2014. The pavilions, once in their final locations, could become interesting activators in the communities that were to host them, by 'asking' their people to engage in deciding upon their 'second lives', their possible uses, their collective management and the collaborative processes of dismantling and

liai - **/fair city project/trälager paviljong**

a project to build an experimental timber pavilion in collaboration with kids and kulturverket (umeå)

re-configuration required for the pavilions to continue existing. Unfortunately, the construction of the pavilion was cancelled late in the process, for reasons beyond the LiAi's control. Nevertheless, the students were very proud of their work and happy about the intense and challenging experience of working with the kids and with institutional partners, and an exhibition was organized in the school to show the results.

erika henriksson, anna misharina and tobias westerlund/ - uma public lecture series
small intervention on the snow in order to prepare the lecture by tim ingold on "making"

uma public lecture series - **/erika henriksson, anna misharina and tobias westerlund**

small intervention on the snow in order to prepare the lecture by tim ingold on “making”

//

ONCE
BAR
BIBLIOTECA
AUDITORI
20

"[...] we are faced with a paradox where at the very moment in which political discourses proliferate, we assist in a progressive depoliticisation of the social sphere and of language."[1]

against critical content: transversality and the intervention

susan kelly

It is August 2011, and I am attending a talk at Auto Italia, an artist run gallery space on the Old Kent Road in South London, UK. The talk is part of a series on notions of self-organisation and includes an impressive speakers list: Bifo, Mark Fisher, Nina Power, and more. This gallery space is in a glass fronted former

---

1 Colectivo Situaciones, (2009). 'Disquiet in the Impasse', paper given at seminar *Micropolitics Studies in Transversality I: Militant Research*, Goldsmiths College, London, translated by Mara Ferreri, Esther Gabara and Valeria Graziano. From the book *Conversations on the Impasse: Political Dilemmas of the Present*, Buenos Aires: Tinta Limón, 2009, which is a dialogue in Spanish between Colectivo Situaciones, Suely Rolnik, León Rozitchner, Sandro Mezzadra, Raquel Gutiérrez Aguilar, Peter Pál Pelbart, Santiago López Petit, Michael Hardt and Arturo Escobar.

car show room near Peckham. It is a poor area, and around 80% of the local population is made up of either recent African and Latino immigrants or people of second and third generation Afro-Carribean descent. The road is famous as the cheapest property on the London Monopoly game board, and as the only street on the board from South London. It is two weeks after the riots that gripped the city for days after the police murder of Mark Duggan in Tottenham in the north of the city. Most of the large chain stores on the street are still boarded up and the stink of smoke has just lifted. There are still police everywhere and the noise of helicopters is heavy in the sky. I live nearby and I've never seen this many white people like me in one place on this road, or as many bicycles. None of the speakers mentions the riots, or comments on this display of our gathering in a glass box. And yet, we are supposedly doing some critical thinking about self-organisation.

The dynamics and contradictions of gentrification are more than familiar in this scene, but the absolute division between the ostensible content of the discussion and the palpable and still reeling context in which it took place, reached new, almost unbearable heights on that day. For in the cultural field, with its attendant rounds of intellectual and political debate, we can see an ever intensifying split between the 'themes' cultural organisations and many artists and intellectuals 'work on' - and how those issues take shape in the social field. In these spaces, speech and discourse too often become self-referential, inter-textual loops, symptomatic of the academic and mediatised cultures from which they emerge.

This detachment is also symptomatic however, of a series of larger issues: our frightening inability to find ways to address the enormous divides in our cities which are increasingly entrenched along class and racial lines; and our lack of capacity to challenge the ways in which the micropolitics of neoliberalism have caught us in complex layers of complicity and contradiction. For many artists and intellectuals, one of the ways in which to tackle this problem of disconnection and to experiment with its micropolitics, is through the concept and the form of the intervention. The intervention would seem to promise a more concrete form of action, a more direct engagement with issues in the social and cultural field. But how has the form of the intervention worked in the practices of critical artists, architects and intellectuals who operate in the cultural field, and what are the openings and limits of these modes of action? Can they really circumvent the problem of the production of increasingly abstract and detached social critique?

To intervene in the most general sense, means to come between two things or two points in time. The term as it has been used in politically and socially engaged cultural practices however, has drawn on the more active sense of the notion of intervention as an imperative to construct and insert something into a situation with a view to changing it's functioning. Linked to the military definition of the term – to the interference of one state in the affairs of another usually through force or threat of force – this notion of the intervention explicitly aims to reconfigure a given situation. The intervention in cultural practices is understood to be primarily concerned with 'real life' and 'real politics', with effecting some kind of change 'on the ground'.

The notion of intervention in the art field is of particular interest therefore, as it not only conjures up notions of directness and transformation, it also links to earlier artistic movements that sought to question and at times dissolve the division between art and life. Writing in the catalogue of a 2004 exhibition at the Massachusetts Museum of Contemporary Art entitled *The Interventionists*, Gregory Sholette linked the work of contemporary interventionist artists and collectives specifically to the Soviet Constructivists and their calls for 'Art into Life!', 'Art into Production!', and to 'Liquidate Art!'. Sholette: "*The Soviet avant-garde artists of the 1920s and early 1930s sought to intervene directly into life by developing an art that would be useful for the advancement of an unprecedented revolutionary society.*"[2]

Sholette cites artists such as Mayakovsky, Rodchenko, Tatlin and others, who often left their studios and entered factories, or developed designs for buildings, workers clubs, portable propaganda, and art laboratories *"where experimentation with new Constructivist principles ideally preceded real world implantation"*.[3] While taking care to differentiate the profoundly different contexts of Soviet Russia and early 21st Century North America and Europe, Sholette nevertheless draws comparisons between the constructivists and the contemporary interventionist's desire for art to be useful. For

---

2 Sholette, Gregory. (2004) 'Interventionism and the Historical Uncanny' catalogue essay in The Interventionists, Massachusetts Museum of Contemporary Art, MASS MoCA Press.

3 *ibid*

soviet constructivist artists, *"art would never again be treated as mere décor or serve as a luxury item for the wealthy"*.[4]

Setting aside the social and revolutionary context of soviet Russia, for Sholette, the contemporary equivalent of this desire for directness and utility can be found the notion of the artist as tool-maker and tool provider. The curator of the exhibition *The Interventionists* goes further: citing the work of artists such as Mike Rakowitz, who produces low-cost shelters for homeless people that are inflated by heat exhaust from city buildings and subways, or that of 'Critical Art Ensemble' who set up a temporary lab to test the veracity of organic and non-genetically modified foods labels, Nato Thompson declares that these artists *"[...] do not preach. They do not advocate. As opposed to providing a literal political message, these artists provide tools for the viewer/participant to develop their own politics."*[5]

Sholette and Thompson applaud this directness and utility of the intervention but caution simultaneously against over-stating the efficacy of such tools that emerge from the small and in the end, rather limited field of art. This gesture toward the limit of the art field however, seems inadequate for understanding the limit of the intervention in the cases they cite. For it is surely the act of producing and subsequently displaying such works in and for these cultural contexts that mark their limit, not some inherent scale problem with art or the art work. In drawing parallels between these contemporary projects and the earlier avant-garde trope of 'art into life', they insert this work in an art historical lineage and largely ignore the relationships between the practices on display and the social and political contexts from which some of them emerge. In other words, it is the mode of relation between these projects and the cultural sphere that is the problem, not some given, ontological condition of the field.

While Rackowitz's shelters and 'Critical Art Ensemble's labs temporarily enact and prototype some really interesting and important experiments, it is surely the case that context is everything in determining the social and political value of their interventions. Framing this work as a kind of pragmatic tool art however, disavows the frame of the institution and the mediation of these

---

4 *ibid*

5 Thompson, Nato. (2004) 'Trespassing Toward Relevance', *The Interventionists*, Massachusetts Museum of Contemporary Art, MASS MoCA Press, p.48.

projects. The seductive rhetoric of directness circumvents the conditions of possibility that produce these projects and places them in the public eye.

While there may be a case to argue for the use of the museum as a kind of public 'info space' that points viewers to something going on elsewhere, it would be disingenuous to claim that any of the interventionists mentioned above for example, are somehow autonomous from the currency of the cultural field, be it aesthetic or economic. Furthermore, we know that it is a very particular public who visits the contemporary art museum, especially those with a $10-$15 entry fee. In short, it is possible to see that in these interventionist projects, there is already a relation to the cultural field and to the institution that the rhetoric of directness cannot simply make go away.

Moreover, the libertarian and supposedly non-ideological gesture toward a notion of 'tool provision' claimed by the curator, masks a whole range of positions, contexts and strategies central to the work of many of the artists, groups and activists in the exhibitions.[6] Drawing attention to this frame however, is not a call to insist on the 'art-ness' of these projects, or to draw them back into an aesthetic discourse they may wish to ignore. Pointing to the limit of the notion of the intervention as it appears in this example, rather aims to highlight *where* the actual blockages to social and political transformation in such practices may lie. For in assuming a direct and transparent relationship between the display of the project and the 'real world', such curatorial projects do nothing to experiment with the form or the mode of relation between the cultural field and broader social and political forces. Despite their overt references to the 'real world', within this institutional setting, these projects very much adhere to the behaviours and grammars of other art works to be found within the same walls.

It would be untrue to extrapolate from the above that the concept of the intervention is somehow worthless and compromised. Like any other concept, it is claimed and reclaimed and put to multiple, often-contradictory use. What the example of the Interventionists exhibition shows us however, is what happens when in a given period, a concept is designated as something

6 Look for example, at Yo Mango's work in the Spanish social movements at that time. See, Robert Andrews, 'Shoplifting as Social Commentary', *Wired*, August, 2005 http://www.wired.com/culture/lifestyle/news/2005/08/68609 [accessed August, 2012]

closer to an artistic genre. In this move, a grammar of operation is established which marks and contains within it already given systems of operation and value.

In other words, the intervention through being designated a quasi-art genre, becomes destined to sit as critical content within the institution, leaving the museum and the cultural field unquestioned and intact. In containing the intervention as content, it becomes unnecessary to do the work of tracing its experimentation and effects through the territories and fields it inhabits, paying attention to its truth claims, its positioning and blind spots. It also becomes unnecessary to look at the cultural institution and field within which is displayed and to implicate that place in the issues, the critique and the reconfigurations at work.

In another related and more recent example of this problem of the production of detached critical content, we can look to London's Institute of Contemporary Art (ICA) *Season of Dissent* in 2010.[7] Here, we see an even more cynical claim to the concretely political, enacted alongside non-engagement with the urgent political and social issues that were occurring in the city and within the institution at that time. In 2010, when the ICA mounted its *Season of Dissent*, London was in the midst of the explosion of student demonstrations which were taking place physically right outside the institution's doorstep at that time. Through its exhibition title and press releases, the institute claimed a direct link to urgent political issues in the 'real world', while simultaneously doing everything it could to close down those relations.

The 'season' proceeded with little reference to and no solidarity with those events outside its front door. Indeed, artists and groups who wanted to turn over their residencies in the galleries to space for supporting the developing student movement were dis-invited from the institution, and in their place, panels of intellectuals and social commentators were invited to talk at length on yet more panels about the crisis in education for a £10 ticket price.

What do these examples tell us about the way in which our once public institutions are being branded and neo-liberalised, and what do they tell us about the possibilities today for practices of cultural and political intervention as

7 See: http://www.ica.org.uk/microsite/dissent/ At the time, the ICA was also in major turmoil. Its funding was cut by over 20%, staff were being made redundant or jumping ship and a series of private sponsorship deals had gone belly up.

foreseen by the constructivists? It is a difficult problem, because by containing social and political issues as content within the curatorial frameworks of an institution, it can appear as if important issues are being addressed.

However, as 'Collectivo Situaciones' observed in the opening epigram to this essay, what seems to be taking place within that discourse might actually have the opposite effect – a depoliticisation, a limiting of knowledge, a blockage of the operations of interventionist work.

In processes akin to financial outsourcing and privatisation, critical content is subcontracted by the institution exclusively to some artist or collective's work – or a panel of talking heads – while the institution's role in passing down government cutbacks to unpaid interns and artists and to outsourced cleaning and security companies paying poverty wages, remains unchallenged - along with their continued renewal of toxic sponsorship deals. In the cases of MASS MoCA and the ICA, it is clear that the demand to promote institutional branding, to market, to tightly control press releases, and to control and design the curatorial and institutional message, leaves no space to deal with complex constituencies and contexts or to respond meaningfully to contingent 'real world' political developments. It also leaves no time or inclination to consider what is happening to the institutions' own cultural sector or to fight back. For the legitimacy of the thoroughly marketised, brand obsessed public-private institution that is the mainstay of the neo-liberal cultural sector in the UK and North America, is grounded in its responsibility to that brand-market and its wealthy sponsors, and not to the public, not to the arts communities, not to the social movements artists are part of, or the issues they seek to address. In this scenario, art has not moved so far away from being *"treated as mere décor or serve as a luxury item for the wealthy"*, as the soviet constructivist artists might have wished.[8]

So can the work of the critical intervention inhabit this cultural field at all, and if it can, can it mobilise that frame transversally in the context of its critical work?

The term transversality has recently become closely linked to forms of experimentation with modes of politi-

8 *ibid*

cal organisation, and to practices that explicitly aim to produce new connections between subjects, territories and disciplines.[9] In Deleuze and Guattari's thought, the movement of transversality signals a non-representational, additive form of alliance that explicitly sets out to de-territorialise the disciplines, subjectivities, fields and institutions it works across.[10] Within the context of art theory, the term has also been used by Gerald Raunig to describe new terrains of open co-operation between different activist, artistic, social and political practices in the first years of the new century.[11]

Significantly, when analysing the relationships between art practices and social activism, Raunig turns to the notion of the intervention via Walter Benjamin and the figure of the soviet constructivist Sergej Tretjakov. Through a critical re-reading of Walter

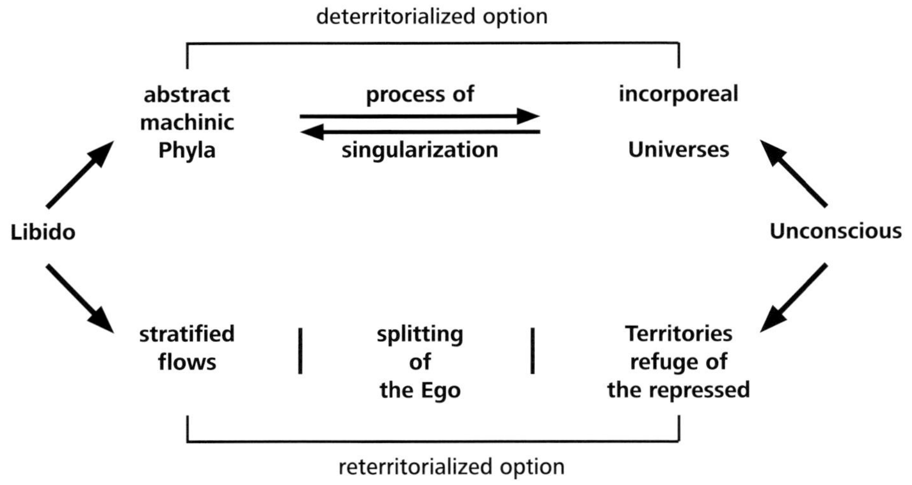

Figure 3.2 Libido-unconscious options. Source: Felix Guattari, *Cartographies schizoanalytiques*, Editions Galilee, 1989.

9 Genosko, Gary. (2004) Félix Guattari: An Aberrant Introduction, (London: Continuum), p.47.

10 Deleuze, Gilles. (1999) Foucault, (London: Athlone Press), p.70.

11 Raunig,Gerald. (2002) 'Transversal Multitudes', Transversal, <http://eipcp.net/transversal/0303/raunig/en>[01/10/2002]

Benjamin's seminal essay '*The Author as Producer*', Raunig looks at the concrete ways in which politicised cultural practices traverse and connect with different fields and institutions.[12] Walter Benjamin famously stated that it is not enough for the 'political artist' to display the correct tendency or commitment to 'the proletarian cause'.

Such a position would amount to what Benjamin calls a 'mere well-wishing' or ideological sponsorship, where separations between the aesthetic 'quality' of the work and its political tendency are maintained.

Benjamin argues that in focusing exclusively on an artist or writer's stated position vis-à-vis the relations of production, and ignoring how their work operates within the relations of production, a writer's work (the content of which often consists of turning depictions of misery into objects of aesthetic consumption) merely supplies an aesthetic for the apparatus of production, rather than working on changing the apparatus of production.[13]

For Benjamin, the task of the political writer is to "*intervene actively*" in the relations of production through the organisation of society.[14] Citing the example of the Soviet writer Sergej Tretjakov, Walter Benjamin describes how Tretjakov worked as a convenor of mass meetings, created travelling newspapers, wrote reports for Moscow newspapers, was involved in introducing radio and cinema to the area where he lived, as well as writing literature. In doing so, Tretjakov developed a practice that intervened in and altered the given organisation of society. In Raunig's re-reading of Benjamin's essay, he identifies contemporary equivalents to Benjamin's 'well-wisher' in certain socially-engaged art practices that commit precisely this error of supplying representations of political content within an institutionally defined structure of artistic production.[15]

---

12 Benjamin, Walter. (1973) 'The Author as Producer' in *Understanding Brecht*, (trans. Anna Bostock), London: New Left Books, pp.85-103 and Gerald Raunig, 'Grandparents of Interventionist Art, or Intervention in the Form. Re-writing Walter Benjamin's "Author as Producer", www.eipcp.net/diskurs/d05/text/geraldraunig02.html, December 2000 [accessed 2/7/03]

13 *ibid*

14 *ibid*

15 Raunig, Gerald. (2000) 'Grandparents of Interventionist Art, or Intervention in the Form. Re-writing Walter Benjamin's "Author as Producer", www.eipcp.net/diskurs/d05/text/geraldraunig02.html, [accessed 2/7/03]

Raunig suggests that such practices present a superficial politicisation that is mediated through a rhetoric of empowerment and moral authority sanctioned by their institutional legitimation as art. As a consequence, such practices might proclaim a social engagement but do little to address the social and political structures, including the institution of the museum and cultural field itself, that produce social inequality.

Following Walter Benjamin's discussion of Tretjakov, Raunig calls on writers and artists to develop political ways of working that directly engage with and intervene in the institutional structures of artistic recognition, production and dissemination.[16] He suggests that artist's work should acquire an organising function (not confined to propagandist use) that would address the means of artistic production as well as the 'products'.

What is striking about this rethinking of the relationship between art and the political is that the notion of form has been shifted from an aesthetic term located within the field or perhaps even a genre of art, to a term that describes the forms of organisation that cultural practices may develop.[17]

In paying attention to where the notion of form might lie in such practices, and by insisting on this focus on political ways of working, Raunig, after Benjamin and Tretjakov, aims to prevent the concept of the intervention becoming either a 'pragmatic' tool that disavows its context, or another bit of critical content for the culture machine. Far from languishing as a minor quasi-genre, or being contained as a piece of political content on display, this notion of the intervention would analyse and take on the complex fields and values that its practice works through and reconfigures.

Practices developed in collectives such as Park Fiction (Hamburg) or the Los Angeles-based group Ultra-Red provide good examples of longer term and deeper level interventionist and organisational work that takes great care in its interface with cultural institutions and the artistic field.

Ultra-Red consists of a fluid, and increasingly international group of artists, musicians, residents, community

---

16 *ibid*

17 Rodchenko asserted in Russia of the 1920s that organisation was to be the principle of all creative activity. See, Rodchenko 'Slogans' (1921), in Art into Life, Seattle: Henry Art Gallery, 1998, pp.69-71

organisers and activists. Based initially in the 1990s in the Pico Aliso district of Los Angeles, their activities began, and to a certain extent continue, to centre on housing, immigration and labour rights. By employing different strategies of sound recording, witnessing, campaigning and organising events in collaboration with other residents and workers in the neighbourhood, Ultra-Red work on making a new collective space. On the ground, Ultra Red have gotten involved in work that has prevented the demolition of several housing projects in Pico Aliso and in securing additional funding from the city of Los Angeles for local education programmes. They work also as sound artists, producing tracks from recordings made on site, which they distribute as albums online, and through independent label Milles Plateaux. Sales from their soundwork also partly fund their activities. They also stage recording and sound events, sometimes in the form of listening tribunals in art museums, often invited through the museum's education and community programmes.

In an interview with Janna Graham in *Fuse* magazine, some members of the group spoke explicitly of their activity as (artistic) organising.[18] For these members of Ultra Red, working in a more straightforward activist context usually involves moving from campaign to campaign, whereas the form of community based organising that they are involved in entails a broader range of activities over a longer period of time. Ultra-Red underline the importance of the long-term and semi-located nature of their practice.

Such a temporality shifts the group's main constituency of what they call 'accountability' from the art world to their own community in Pico Aliso, while also allowing for a series of experimental sound works, guerrilla actions, and legal and political campaigns to take place. In other words, by working and intervening in this way, their issues, constituencies and their invention of forms is activated not only from within the frame of the art world. These forms that are developed through practice and organising, produce a transversality that would never be possible within the strict confines of the art field, and allows Ultra Red to develop a range of practices, spaces and critical communities in which to produce and reflect on what they do.

In Ultra Red's practice, as well as in the practices of many of collectives, artists and cultural workers, this attention to the grounds on which the legitimacy and responsibility of their work rests, seems key. Rather than submit to the logic of the neo-liberal cultural institution whose legitimacy and responsibility has almost completely shifted to the domains of their donors and the market, such practices work across these interests, bringing other constituencies, criteria and values into play.

Rather than operate within the restrictive grammar of the art genre that plays by the rules of the curatorial frame, interventionist practices can reconfigure those frames, articulating and instantiating another set of desires and ambitions.

And surely, smaller artist run spaces can question this emulation of the formats and rituals of more established institutions, and experiment with other forms, other ways of engaging with different social terrains.

---

18 Janna Graham, 'Interview with UltraRed', Fuse Special Issue: 'Democracy Improvised', Vol. 26, No. 2, April 2003, p.26. 'Democracy When?' was curated by Tone O. Neilson. The Hamburg-based 'multi-disciplinary venture' that goes under the name of 'Park Fiction' is another really good example of a long-term, located series of practices that work in this organisational way to produce different events, creative campaigns and mutable organisational forms of community.

For transversal and interventionist practices would not be interested in the undoing of fields, or the taking apart of the institutions for their own sake, or in the name of a potential that is always and forever deferred. Instead, they would involve a series of slow, organised, deliberate processes that work to produce another consistency across and between fields.

In the absence of clear answers or paths out of the impasses of neoliberal institutional life and the intense micropolitical struggles in the fields of culture today, such consistencies might begin to weave a terrain on which we can build new relationships and possibilities of working otherwise. Dismantling the production of abstract and detached social critique, intervening in this proliferation of political discourses that work to de-politicise the social sphere and language, demands not endless analysis, but rather the support and development of practices that build capacity to resist processes of neoliberalisation and their corollary in alienated content production. //

"So the test for political interest is now slightly easier to pass: one must practice sociology in such a way that the ingredients making up the collective are regularly refreshed "[1]

rethinking public practices through collective pedagogies and spatial politics

javier rodrigo montero and antonio collados alcaide

This text emerges as a reflection built from the invitation to develop a workshop in the context of the Master's Program "*Laboratory of Immediate Architectural Intervention*" at Umeå University School of Architecture. Our intention here is to establish a dialogue, starting from the frameworks of Transducers, with concepts such as space politics, political intervention or collective practices. Concepts that

1 Latour, Bruno (2005). *Reassembling the social: an introduction to actor-network-theory.* Oxford/New York: Oxford University Press.

are enunciated and circulated in different ways and within many professional fields (culture, sociology, education, urbanism, or cyberactivism, among many others). In order to do so, firstly we will briefly explain the concepts we use in the text, and secondly, we will articulate four points of tension and complexity, that are issues from which we can understand the political dimension of 'practice' in public space. In this small journey we will accompany Bruno Latour readings with the interpretations and discussions of some friends and colleagues in this field such as Isaac Marrero and Aida Sanchez de Serdio. Our intention in this regard is to compose a short text that can open new debates and questions/paradoxes regarding the political practices that are developed in the field of interventions in public space.

Collective pedagogies/spatial politics/Transducers. What is it all about?

"TRANSDUCERS Collective Pedagogies and Spatial Politics"[2] is a cultural project aiming to research and activate initiatives in which artistic practices, political intervention and education are flexibly coordinated on the basis of actions by collectives and interdisciplinary groups.[3] Collective pedagogies are transdisciplinary initiatives, which approach specific social problems (such as, for example, health, recycling, treatment of residues, clean energy, the concept of citizenship or urban regeneration, among others) through sustainable development, citizens' participation, learning communities and visual culture).[4] This is achieved through the activities of work groups, including both educators and students, as well as artists, architects, landscape artists, residents and town planners, thus giving rise to discourses through which a dialogic and collaborative learning process is established.

This approach through pedagogy also considers the work of *politics operating on space* and the various organizational models of actions in the chosen initiatives. This aspect implies the constant configuration of specific spatial politics, which involve the development of alternative practices that propose a more integrated, participative and interdisciplinary use of space through

2 www.transductores.net

3 Collados, Antonio; Rodrigo, Javier (2009). TRANSDUCTORES. Pedagogías colectivas y políticas espaciales. Granada: Centro José Guerrero.

4 *ibid*, p. 16-17

the collaboration of town-planning and architecture with other fields of knowledge, such as, for example, art, pedagogy, sociology, ethnography, ecology or community work.

Such collaboration is only feasible in frameworks favoring the exchange of skills and 'knowledges'. Such exchanges facilitate the meeting of various professional people with local experts and other groups involved, setting up learning communities in which each contributes their particular knowledge and attitudes. At the same time, they interconnect very different disciplines, institutions and organizational habits, opening up a broad spectrum of collaborations with NGOs, schools, kindergartens, local communities, universities, youth and community centers, trade unions, etc. New forms of praxis thus emerge and, consequently, new politics, at the same time as intervention occurs in the collaborating institutions and their organizational models. Among these experimental practices we can find the creation and management of participative urban gardens, the emergence of self built spaces for learning among university students, research and participative diagnoses with local communities, or the development by artistic cooperatives of communication campaigns for trade unions and pressure groups.

Where are we going now? What is, then, the Transducers framework when we are thinking in terms of political interventions in public spaces? How can we rethink public practices and spatial politics?

Within the perspective described above, it is important that we don't lose sight of the fact that with *Transducers*, even though we are talking about projects, we are actually referring to the creation of networks of different agents and of real work conditions that generate political intervention. This activity implies certain political consequences when analysing projects and rethinking work conditions:

Firstly distancing ourselves from the dominant narratives that describe objects as results in the public sphere, a discourse that is prevalent in art catalogues and in books on participation or informal urbanism. In practical terms this implies no longer seeing an urban garden or an open plaza as a symbol of successful architecture or of participatory urbanism, or simply as a result of new ways of constructing cities. On the contrary, the task here would be to chart and recognise the people involved, the relationships they have, and the invisible tools that actually generate those dynamics, which end up creating and transforming spaces.

The goal is to stop seeing space as a result and start conceptualising the invisible networks that make up work processes in public spaces. In other words, the task is to identify the social magma, the architectonic plates that, as they move and collide, produce the movements necessary for creating transformation on the surface of what we consider public space.

In the words of Bruno Latour, who addresses these issues in his book *"Reassembling the social"*, one must try to understand the incommensurability of social magma, which allows us to trace political relationships. In this sense, the urban garden or the plaza are not interesting in terms of the results of political actions. Instead, they gain meaning when we look at them as the sum of numerous actions and interactions (networks) that give rise to any given space.

The focus shifts from seeing an object to inquiring about the network quality and the specific relationships involved in its creation: which players collaborated with each other? In which scenarios? How did they manage their relationships with one another? How did they design and create a network, which could later become a garden? What materials did they have, and where did they come from?

Secondly, coming down in support of an increased visibility and recognition of the potential of these networks. This involves rethinking the capacity networks have for critical intervention, and considering alternative ways to talk about them. To put it another way: what can we learn from these projects if we see them as the relationships and results of networked actors, working in specific spaces? Following Latour, this is a task of reassembling the social world, in that it involves developing a political view of partnerships and actors on the same plane, at the same level. The work of reassembling entails following the actors and narrating their political partnerships, in all their contradictions and complexities.

In *Transducers*, in some ways we are trying to understand the social topography of the initiatives that we investigate. We aren't so interested in the type of practice, or its categorization within a more conventional, or discipline-based, paradigm. (In fact, the unique nature of each case, where each one is truly its own microcosmos, means they inherently escape restrictive categories or parameters, like *"community participation", "informed urbanism", "critical pedagogies",* or *"public artwork"*, to name some of the most common 'types'). We are interested in looking at practices by placing them on the same plane and learning by representing them as networks.

Thirdly, in relationship to the previous point, we conceptualise these networks as living organisms that grow, develop, multiply, and (why not), even die. This perspective requires presenting these networks of actors, or sets of actors, as both complex and sustainable entities. This step involves understanding that within their organizational and relational models there is an entirely complex politics related to working in public spaces. Therefore, we must observe and understand them slowly, like the universe itself, and really 'take in' the projects. We should observe their development and evolution in terms of organizations that connect various agents. In short, this activity works to localise the network, by understanding the projects' politics as the sum of the assemblages and relationships of the different actors.

A project's politics is, therefore, the power relations it establishes, and the contradictions and complexities that come into play. In this sense, a project's politics is not a 'carte blanche' just because it espouses good intentions, or works toward fostering empowerment, participation or awareness within certain target groups that receive and are activated as consequence of the project. Rather, one's politics refers to the interactions, on the same plane, of all the actors and groups, without distinguishing between target groups and coordinators.

One's politics is defined by the everyday interactions among actors, and the space and tools we use to build relationships, or as it were, which we use to politicize them.

In practical terms, this means that in any project, the morning coffee meeting among a group of women who discuss the urban garden project, the proposal drawn by a group of architects, or a meeting to get permission from the council, are all equally important moments. Each one is a situation where actors and tools interact on the same level, each with their specific moment and space within a project.

There, in these interconnected scenarios, is where the real game of politics is activated, the politics that reveal the multiple relationships among the different actors. That is to say a shift from 'social' politics to 'thing' politics,[5] but moreover a specific translation into a thick description of concrete relations with its complexities, actors, times and limits: 'políticas de lo concreto' or 'concrete politics' as suggested by Aida Sanchez de Serdio.[6]

Fourthly and last but not least, this assemblage leads to yet another consequence in our general outlook. Comprehending the relationships within constructed networks means perceiving the sum of different actors, times, spaces and forms of collaboration, in combination with the sum of diverse and heterogeneous 'knowledges'. The total is, in effect, the political task of articulating and generating practices of political intervention. Political intervention in this context implies understanding, somehow, the intangible working conditions within a network. These working conditions behave like the dark matter of interventions in public space. Meaning, we should understand that the politics of a project is the total sum and construction of such invisible networks, and its effort to reconstruct them in relation to, or within, a common space.

---

5 Latour, Bruno (2005). From Realpolitik to Dingpolitik or How to Make Things Public. In B. Latour and P. Weibel (Eds.), *Making Things Public* . Cambridge, MA: MIT Press / ZKM Karlsruhe. pp. 14-41

6 See Sánchez de Serdio, Aida (2010) "Políticas de lo concreto: producción cultural colaborativa y modos de organización". In Collados, Antonio and Rodrigo, Javier (2010) *Transductores: pedagogías colectivas y políticas espaciales*. Centro José Guerrero. Granada. pp. 44-64

Postscript: Asking ourselves politically

Politics, always, are part of the inevitable tension between breaking down relationships and rebuilding the everyday space we share from the difference among actors.[7] Therefore, the real political struggle occurs when we try to articulate the tension between the various actors, tools, times and spaces within the same framework, while progressively rebuilding a concept of the collective.

However, it is important to note that this reorganization does not imply closed or homogeneous activity, but a continuous reassembly of actors and networks that results in new gaps, disagreements and distances. This approach would lead us to reconsider a minor social science in order to view and activate political interventions in public spheres. A new type of 'becoming-neo-pragmatism' as proposed by Isaac Marrero.[8] This neopragmatism, instead of seeking a totalitarian consensual, parliamentary 'cosmovision' or world-vision about the political and the public sphere, stares at and participates in a composition/putting-together of a repertoire of heterogeneous tools and multiples ways of co-existence and being-together through our differences. In other words: minor sciences for concrete and ground politics.

Spatial politics are always open topographies of actors and networks, at once complex and contradictory, which should always be held in tension. If we can work these tensions and this 'in-process' framework of politics, then we might be able to rethink and build together other tools, methodologies and ways of thinking about political intervention in public spheres, Maybe we can create some 'situated knowledges'[9] about how to be together through our differences and create significant, unpredictable and proactive experiences of the commons. Thus, the question of politics is a question about pedagogies, and vice-versa. Fortunately there's no turning back here. //

---

7 Latour, Bruno (2005). *Reassembling the social: an introduction to actor-network-theory.* Oxford/New York: Oxford University Press.

8 Marrero, Isaac (2012). "Por una teoría del actor-red menor: perspectivismo y monadología". In Tirado Serrano, F. & López Gómez, D. (eds.) *Teoría del Actor-Red. Más Allá de los Estudios de Ciencia y Tecnología* Barcelona: Amentia. (on press)

9 Haraway, Donna (1988). "Situated Knowledges: The Science Question in Feminism and the Privilege of Partial Perspective". Haraway, Donna. Feminist Studies Vol. 14, No. 3. pp. 575-599.

at the edge of antagonism: exploring dissensus at the liai - aida sánchez de serdio

at the edge of antagonism: exploring the limits of dissensus at the laboratory of immediate architectural intervention

aida sánchez de serdio

In the last two decades, collaboration has emerged as a key concept in several fields of cultural practice (arts, education, social activism, urban planning etc.).[1] Although it is defined in substantially different ways, and it is deployed in varying degrees, collaboration seems to be the new shibboleth for progressive

---

1 See Kravagna, Christian. *Working on the Community. Models of Participatory Practice.* European Institute for Progressive Cultural Policies, 1998 [Online] <http://eipcp.net/transversal/1204/kravagna/en>; Billig, Johanna; Lind, Maria; and Nilsson, Lars (eds.) (2007) *Taking the Matter into Common Hands. On Contemporary Art and Collaborative Practices.* London: Black Dog Publishing; Butler, David and Reiss, Vivienne (eds.) (2007) Art of Negotiation. Manchester: Corner House; and Collados, Antonio and Rodrigo, Javier. *TRANSDUCTORES. Pedagogías colectivas y políticas espaciales / TRANSDUCERS. Collective Pedagogies and Spatial Politics.* Granada: Diputación de Granada y Centro José Guerrero, 2010.

cultural and social action. One may argue that by definition any social process involves collaboration between agents, be they individual or collective, and therefore it would be redundant to postulate collaboration as something that has to be brought or introduced into cultural practices. It becomes obvious that here collaboration is understood quite differently as a particular way of bringing together disparate social or individual positions (materialised in organisations, lay and expert people, citizens, etc.) in a common project of transformative nature through debate, negotiation and eventually consensus —or at least a sufficient degree of agreement.

The debates on collaborative cultural projects seem to be dominated by two main perspectives. One privileges conviviality, conflict resolution and personal development —as in many versions of community arts—, jumping perhaps too quickly to shared projects and celebration of community.[2] The other —reading Laclau and Mouffe in a rather partial way— focuses on conflict and dissensus as the main feature of the social, leading ultimately to the impossibility of conciliation.[3]

Both are problematic for different reasons. In the first case, we can be led to the denial of difference and therefore to the cancellation of politics in social relations. In the second perspective what is denied is the possibility of any agreement, and it seems as if the aim of the cultural practice were to deliberately produce alienation and antagonism.

Public space offers an exceptional battlefield for relationality, collaboration and antagonism. Any intervention in such a field involves tensions in many levels, ranging from the phenomenological transformation of daily life experience —as in the controversial sculptures by Richard Serra— to the huge investment of political and economic capital in strategic urban developments (of course, both dimensions can coexist and usually do).

We must also consider the struggles surrounding the definition of 'public' in a context of increasing privatisation and branding of urban space. The pro-

---

2 Bourriaud, Nicholas. (1998) *Esthétique relationelle*. Paris: Les presses du reél; Harding, A. (2005) *Magic Moments. Collaborations Between Artists and Young People.* London: Black Dog Publishing.

3 Bishop, Claire. (2004) *Antagonism and Relational Aesthetics* in October, N.110, Fall (51-80); and Bishop, Claire. (2006) *The Social Turn: Collaboration and Its Discontents.* Art Forum. XLVI, N.6, February.

liferation of regulations issued by public agencies and local governments are often justified in the name of 'civility' or 'coexistence'. These public policies define (or rather target) deviant identities and behaviours that must be eradicated from public space, conceived as a clean stage for the narratives of cultural success (meaning the defeat of a troubled past) and the pleasures of undisturbed consumption. But conflict resurfaces when individuals and organisations contest this neutralised and mercantilist definition of 'public' with notions of collective production of sociality, and with practices of common owning of the public. The most recent and conspicuous example is the *Occupy* movements all over the world that have gathered massively in squares and streets bringing politics literally back to public space. This politics is neither harmonious nor formally regulated but based on conflict and disagreement, and on a fracture of the traditional formalizations of dialogue (rational, self-regulated, bourgeois).

Therefore, when the MA *Laboratory of Immediate Architectural Intervention* at Umeå School of Architecture invited me to participate with a one-week seminar and workshop, I thought that it would be interesting to share a debate about dissensus and antagonism in public space with the students. My proposal involved the reading of Ernesto Laclau and Chantal Mouffe's *Hegemony and Socialist Strategy*[4] in order to grasp its complexity regarding the notion of antagonism beyond a simplistic reduction to opposition or conflict. As the authors argue, antagonism refers to the fundamental non-closure of identities and discourses that defines contemporary social struggles after post-structuralist critique. Given this impossibility of an essentialist definition of collective identities, hegemony (unlike power or domination) emerges as a tension and precarious balance between antagonist forces: entities whose relation is determined by the fact that they can never be fully defined because they reciprocally subvert their content. As a complementary reading, Oliver Marchart[5] allowed us to explore how this non-closure and unstable balance of forces can be brought from the field of political theory to the field of urban theory. In order to contribute to this ontological and epistemological displacement, we connected the readings to films by Hito Steyerl (*The Empty Centre*, 1998), J. P. Sniadecki (*Demolition*, 2008), and Thom Andersen (*Get Out of the Car*, 2010) in which the city is explored as a space of dissensus, fracture and friction subject to constant transformation but never to be solved.

The discussion with the students and with Alberto Altés, the co-director of the MA, produced complex interpretations of the films that located tensions not only in the processes represented in the films but also, importantly, in the filmic strategies used by the documentaries to activate a different kind of spectatorship in the audience (non-linear narrative, out of field, long static shots, etc.)

The second half of the seminar/workshop was oriented towards the search in the city of Umeå of traces, signals, narratives, etc. that evidenced the irreconcilable antagonist dynamics of contemporary and past society. This would be done by explorations of the city, or other processes that the group might decide. Then, instead of rushing to a proposal of collaboration that tried to 'solve' or 'reconcile' in any way

---

4 Laclau, Ernesto and Mouffe, Chantal. (1985) Beyond the Positivity of the Social: Antagonisms and Hegemony. *Hegemony and Socialist Strategy*. London: Verso, (93-149).

5 Marchart, Olivier. (1998) *Art, Space and the Public Sphere(s). Some basic Observations on the Difficult Relation of Public Art, Urbanism and Political Theory.* European Institute for Progressive Cultural Policies, [Online] <http://eipcp.net/transversal/0102/marchart/en>

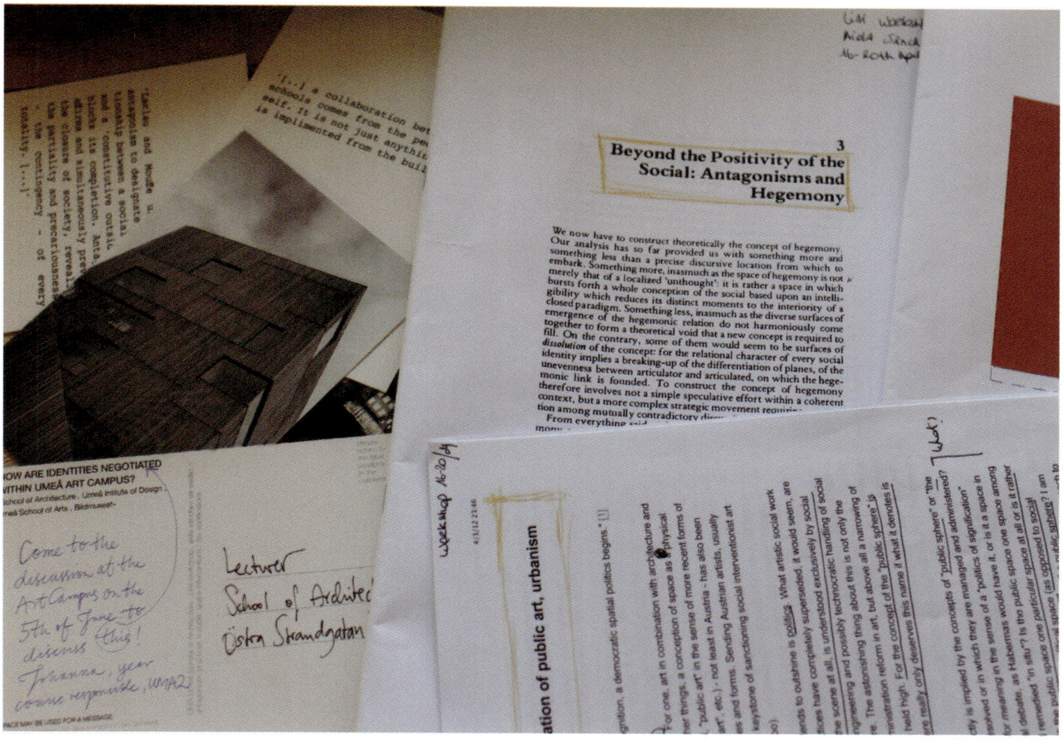

the antagonist relations perceived, the participants were invited to take a step back and explore that very antagonism as fully as possible, either by devising a representational/signalling intervention in public space or producing a short visual/audiovisual essay.

These proposals had to have a research dimension based on the theoretical frameworks we had been discussing in the first days of the seminar, and articulated around a question that oriented the exploration and its final materialisation. Here the students showed an enthusiasm and commitment that brought them to present almost finished visual projects by the end of the workshop. Interestingly enough, instead of locating dissensus in the city in general, two of the three projects explored the much more near context of the art campus where Umeå School of Architecture is located —a very interesting project of urban development through culture and knowledge economy in itself. The third one focused on the Ume River that runs just next the campus, a line along which a number of future urban transformation plans are articulated.

The projects about the campus took as a main concept the notion of limit/border (one of the notions present in Laclau and Mouffe's book) in very different manifestations.

The first one identified the spots —both discursive and physical— where the interconnection of the different schools present in the campus (Architecture, Arts and Design) was at the same time postulated and prevented. They also interviewed students about the possibilities they saw of a real interrelation between the students of the three schools. While the campus is organised in a way that promotes active exchange among the different schools (and so it is expressed in the institutional website), the visual communication allowed by the glass walls is interrupted by locked doors, security cards, differences in institutional cultures, etc. Using a typical strategy of corporative publicity, the group printed postcards with photographs of the identified 'check-points', combined with statements from the students interviews or from the University website.

The second project focused in discursive/symbolic borders within the School of Architecture. The group was aware of the contesting notions of architecture present in the school (and also among themselves), and carried out several video interviews with teaching staff of the school about those definitions and how limits were experienced and located, both symbolically and physically, in the school.

The third project about the river was also a short film in which different voices (visible and invisible) tell different stories about the experience of the river while the camera films different spots along the riverbank from the water so that we never get to see the river itself. Both the narratives and the urban elements by the river tell the viewer about the lack of consensus about that element of the city in which past and future struggle producing a complex present.

The workshop ended with a public discussion of the projects that gave all of us a different perspective over the work done. And we surely needed that after being obsessed by it for three days! The visual essays had explored public space in such a way that allowed frictions and limits to emerge, and did not rush into solving them, as conventional community art does. The idea that intervening does not mean solving anything but rather getting entangled in lines of tension and creating new ones is an interesting learning for anyone working in the cultural field.

I would suggest that taking dissensus and antagonism seriously is at the basis of a critique of architecture as a purely technical or operational intervention. But during the discussion an important issue came out that had been muffled during the workshop and that was inherent to the definition of the seminar.

The three projects, though presenting antagonisms and borders, did not imply any conflict in their presentation or institutional articulation. As I said, the limit was already present in the proposal to the groups, and it was not so much a limitation of the projects. In planning the seminar and workshop my concern was not to create a real conflict in the MA, so in a way we were trying to explore the nature of conflict and avoiding it at the same time. On the other hand the format of the public presentation contributed to that neutralisation, but surely the projects can be reactivated politically in other contexts or through other forms of circulation in the future.

Actually I am not really sure we can open up a space for radical antagonism in a planned way, as the workshop was. Antagonism takes over the situation, it simply happens, and it cannot be articulated because, as Laclau and Mouffe say: *"Antagonism, as a witness of the impossibility of a final suture, is the experience of the limit of the social. Antagonisms are not internal but external to society; they constitute the limits of society, the latter's impossibility of constituting itself"*.[6]

How would it be like to work educationally at the limits of society, at the limits of what is intelligible for us? What kind of travel companions would we need for such a border crossing? How would be institutions pushed to their very limits of existence if these educational practices took place? And, what are the limits of education as a context to do this? (Suggestion for an alternative reading: try these questions with the word architecture instead of education). //

---

6 E. Laclau and C. Mouffe, op. cit., p.125

سقط الطاغيه

art, or developing amphibians

per nilsson

Art does not only strive for bringing its content forward. The style in which content is presented is at least equally important since style and content in art are intertwined. They are not related as content to a predetermined form for expression. Moreover, artistic expression comes from individuals, but when it comes to individuals and their selves it might be felt that viewing oneself in the midst of it, life, art or space, requires a distance that distinguish the viewing eye from the self that is viewed, as applying a pre-determined form in relation to its content; mind to body. According to one interpretation of Socrates, the body itself constitutes a problem for such viewing: the further from the body the closer to truth, the closer to the body the further from truth. This distance of mind from body is commonly referred to as reflection, a practice also labelled philosophy. At the same time the reflexive distance needs to be located somewhere apart from that distance; it needs the body that is an integrated part of the self that reflects, its presupposition rather than obstacle. The material for self-reflection comes from that self's embodied experiences gathered on its journey through, and dwelling in, space and time; life. Reflection in general - and self-reflection in particular - is part of a becoming of self; a becoming that can be a creation by the self that becomes. Selves then are here viewed as embodied minds, something noted in thoughts on performance art.[1] Self-creation is viewed as a practice of such an embodied mind as it is moving through time and space while also creating space for its own dwelling together with other dwellers. Embodied minds, therefore are more akin to artworks, intertwined, than to a separation between mind and body.

Self-creation is part of philosophy as a practical discipline rather than theoretical. Admittedly philosophy today is regarded more as a theoretical discipline providing highly universal and general statements combined with claims to necessity and truth in all possible worlds for these statements.[2] But there is, and have always been, a strand of philosophy more focused on the self of *the philosopher as an individual creating him or her self.* Alexander Nehamas names this discipline *the art of living* and writes:

"With the notable exception of Socrates, with whom their tradition originates, and a few others (the sceptic Pyrrho comes immediately to mind) who did not compose any works of their own, they are both the characters their writings generate and the authors of the writings in which their characters exist. They are creators and creatures in one."[3]

Nehamas connects the art of living intimately to a particular form of philosophical/aesthetic writing. It is through such writing that a character that is the

---

1 Fischer-Lichte, Erica *The Transformative Power of Performance: A New Aesthetics*, eng. transl. S. I. Jain (New York: Routledge, 2008), pp 82-83.

2 Danto, Arthur, C. *The Philosophical Disenfranchisement of Art* (New York: Columbia University Press, 1986), p 154.

3 Nehamas, Alexander *The Art of Living* (Berkeley: University of California Press, 2000) p 3.

creator and creature in one can emerge and be developed. Style becomes a key trait of writing through which character as self is brought forward. Style is here taken as something developed by an individual rather than something belonging to a culture. However, no one creates ex-nihilo. Styles are developed through the crossing of paths with other styles already developed. One could therefore object and say that style is something used by an author or artist, something one *imitates*, a manner. Hence when style is acquired, art disappears and artifacts are construed. Such is Octavio Paz's notion of style, to which I am sympathetic since imitation is rather common as cultural expression.[4] This we can see by the use of the prefix *re-* everywhere today. We no longer think, make or do but re-think, re-make and re-do. However, I use style here as the developmental means through which an individual expresses him- or herself through time and in space and individuals are always situated in space and time, they are dwellers in specific historical cultures. That means that the style I am talking about is intertwined with the self who is expressing him- or herself, style is therefore also a becoming.

Style is part of the becoming of self; at the same time it is a tool through which the self becomes. Therefore the style of, for instance Nietzsche is detectable only after his death and his style included the use of many different styles connected to the different perspectives he used to create his self and exemplify his art of living.[5] Style here, therefore, is connected to individual expressions; it is used to create the taste by which one will be judged, while that judge primarily is oneself. It is not regarded as a manner, but as a becoming. Says Richard Rorty: *"The perfect life will be one which closes in the assurance that the last of his final vocabularies, at least, really was wholly his."*[6]

The art of living is an individualistic endeavour and the aim is to create oneself as a unique being, as a character, but this cannot be done without crossing paths with others, regardless the claims of Rorty. Self-creation is, as all forms of art, relational. This means that one tries to make an example out

4 Paz, Octavio The Bow and the Lyre, Eng. transl. R. L. C. Simms (Austin: university of Texas Press, 1972), p 7-8.

5 Nehamas, Alexander Nietzsche: Life as Literature (Cambridge. Mass: Harvard University Press, 1985).

6 Rorty, Richard Contingency, Irony and Solidarity (Cambridge: Cambridge University Press, 1989), p 97.

of oneself, and this example has to be recognised by others if its uniqueness is to be realised, and what is exemplified is that a possibility in fact was realised as a creation of a particular self. Moreover, the realisation of one possibility entails that other possibilities also can be realised, it entails that *"the realm of possibilities is not exhausted."*[7]

But if imitation, acquiring a manner, means that art is gone, what is to be learned from examples of the art of living? What did Montaigne,[8] for instance, *learn* from Socrates? According to Nehamas, Montaigne learned *"that there is little to learn 'from' him [Socrates], even though one can learn a lot 'through' him."*[9] But at the same time, Montaigne as Socrates had to go through others in order to fashion his own self as a unique human being: *"There is no such thing as a direct confrontation with oneself: that way only emptiness lies. To the extent that Montaigne uses earlier texts for his own purposes [he is] using them to fashion something truly his own by their means."*[10] There are no rules for that relational aspect, *"the path to the self must cross the paths of others, sometimes, cruel as that seems, almost purely as means."*[11]

The writing through which one creates ones self as a character by expressing one's paroles stands in a particular relationship to language; it views language as originating in ambiguity. With parole Ferdinand de Saussure means empirical instances of speech.[12] They are utterances made in, for example, everyday conversation. However, I also include non-linguistic instances of personal expressions in parole as for example bodily expressions as they come out in performance art or contemporary dance. Parole is akin to a poetic dimension since individual, personal, expressions in themselves are ambiguous. Therefore I distinguish parole from discourse, which here is

---

7 Nehamas, *The Art of Living*, p 127.

8 Montagne, Michel de *The Complete Essays of Michel de Montaigne*, eng. transl. C. Cotton (Stilwell: Digireads.com, 2009).

9 Nehamas, *The Art of Living*, p 126.

10 Nehamas, *The Art of Living,* p 117.

11 Nehamas, *The Art of Living*, p 117.

12 Saussure, Ferdinand de *Course in General Linguistics* (Glascow: Fontana/Collins, 1974), on the broader use of the term and its application to works of art, see Nilsson, Per *The Amphibian Stand: An Essay Concerning Research Processes in Fine Art* (Umeå: h:ström — Text & Kultur, 2009), pp 91-99.

regarded as a rational construction of language through which language is capable of exercising violence, for example on human bodies.[13] Octavio Paz tells us that even though we think we do, no one speaks prose. It is even more incomprehensible that we should speak discourse. We do, however express ourselves through parole akin towards poetic expression. Therefore our speech is closer to poetry than it is discourse or even prose.[14] Parole, therefore is intimately linked to the becoming of style, while prose and especially discourse is more akin to learning a manner. In parole style and content are intertwined while discourse aims at providing a rational form for expressing content.

Through the ambiguity of artistic/poetic expression parole opens up the possibilities for uniqueness in creating oneself as a form of art. But from a discursive point of view parole, ambiguity and uniqueness are *ironical*. Thomas Mann in his *The Magic Mountain* writes:

"Isn't it grand, isn't it good, that language has only one word for everything we associate with love—from utter sanctity to the most fleshly lust? The result is perfect clarity in ambiguity, for love cannot be disembodied even in its most sanctified forms, nor is it without sanctity even in its most fleshly . . . Caritas is assuredly found in the most admirable and most depraved passions. Irresolute? But in God's name, leave the meaning of love unresolved! Unresolved—that is life and humanity, and it would betray a dreary lack of subtlety to worry about it."[15]

In this passage of aesthetic writing content and style are intertwined, and since the content is the ambiguity and embodiment of love it cannot be otherwise. Love itself is likening to a constant becoming in an ambiguous in-between. An epistemological objectivistic discourse on love with the intent of reaching certainty about its definition would indeed *"betray a dreary lack of subtlety."* According to Octavio Paz such discourse only brings forward the shortcomings of philosophy as a theoretical discipline with too high ambitions that result in a partial philosophy: *"Reflecting on Eros and its powers is*

13 Nilsson Per, *The Amphibian Stand* (Umeå: h:ström — Text & Kultur, 2009), pp 122-125.

14 Paz *The Bow and the Lyre*, p 11.

15 Mann, Thomas *The Magic Mountain*, here quoted from Nehamas *The Art of Living*, p 19.

not the same as expressing them: expression is the gift of the artist and the poet."[16] More complete visions - clear rather than clear and distinct - demand therefore that we also turn to art and poetry, since they provide the ambiguous in-between character of Eros' powers, the bitter-sweetness of erotic desire and love.[17]

Paz sees modern philosophical reflections on Eros as descending from the writings of Marquise de Sade:

"Sade was a prolix and dull writer, the opposite of an artist; Shakespeare and Stendhal tell us more about erotic passion and its mystery than do Sade and his modern disciples as they struggle bitterly to transform it into a philosophical discourse. The dungeons and beds of razors of sadomasochism have turned into a tedious university chair in which the pleasure/pain pair engages in endless arguments."[18]

Love then has perfect clarity, but is not clear and distinct, in ambiguity of becoming in-between *"utter sanctity"* and *"the most fleshly lust."* The ambiguity of love therefore can be *discursively* experienced as *ironical* since discourse aims at providing a manner for expressing content in an un-ambiguous way.

Irony feeds on the ambiguity of language. Admittedly there are vulgar forms of irony where a speaker expresses the opposite of what he means in an ironical way.[19] Hopefully then there are listeners who can detect the ironical tone in voice and gesture and then through inferring the opposite of the said deduct the speakers correct meaning. However, that is not by far the subtle form of irony I am striving for uncovering here in relation to the quote from Mann. In the case *when the meaning of speech is contrary to the words used in the uttering* there is an implicit presupposition that the speaker knows what he means in a clear and distinct way and deliberately hides it through irony. This strategy may make some listeners look stupid, which also often is one aim of irony.

However, the refined form of irony I am thinking about is connected to the sub-

16 Paz, Octavio *The Double Flame: Love and Eroticism*, eng. transl. H. Lane (New York: Harcourt, INC., 1996), p 25.

17 Carson, Anne *Eros: The Bittersweat* (Champaigne: Dalkey Archive Press, 1998), pp 3-10.

18 Paz *The Double Flame*, p 25-26.

19 Nehamas, A *The Art of Living*, p 51.

ject matter of what is talked about. Lets say that the meaning of speech is not captured by the words used *because there are no words that can capture that meaning in an un-ambiguous and certain, clear and distinct, way,* which often is the case with, for example, new metaphors as part of a persons parole or with concepts like love, which then are examples of clarity in ambiguity.

As I said above, irony feeds on the ambiguity of language but it might also feed on the ambiguity of a subject matter as well as the ambiguity of a self's desire for uniqueness. Such ambiguity makes uncertainty the intrinsic essence of irony, *which means that irony not always can be deciphered and that a speaker can be completely truthful in being ironic.*[20] Again style becomes important if art of living is aimed for. If uncertainty is intrinsic to expression we can understand Rorty's characterisation of the ironist as one who *"wants to be able to sum up his life in his own terms,"*[21] and it would *"betray a dreary lack of subtlety to worry about it."*

This, for me makes the connection between such sophisticated irony and *Art* hopeful since art is intrinsically connected to uniqueness of style as becoming rather than to manner. In art style and content are intertwined. The ambiguous self chooses the ambiguous style of expression that best brings ambiguity of self forward, while ambiguous style of expression chooses the best ambiguous self for its expression. This is the embodied mind as *chiasm.*[22] Ambiguity that makes uncertainty intrinsic to expressions is therefore for me one great promise of art and provides art with what can be learned through it; *'through' is here more important than 'from'.*

Poetry views ambiguity as the essence of language, its character as image, while *prose*, whose most sophisticated version is *discourse*, rather views the essence of language as un-ambiguity, its character as visual.[23] Visuals strive for clear and distinct unambiguity, while images are perfectly clear in (their?) ambiguity. Poetry and image are examples of parole while un-ambiguity and visuals are part and parcel of the dream of discourse, a

20 Nehamas, A *The Art of Living*, p 51.

21 Rorty *Contingency, Irony and Solidarity*, p 97.

22 Merleau-Ponty, Maurice The Visible and the Invisible, eng. transl. A. Lingis (Evanston: Northern University Press, 1969), ch. 4.

23 Paz *The Bow and the Lyre*, p 11, on images vs. visuals, see Daney, Serge *Before and After the Image*, www.earthlink.net

dream that *"betray(s) a dreary lack of subtlety."* With Octavio Paz I regard the ambiguity of language as an asset, a poetic asset that saves language from the un-ambiguous reductive treatment in discourse: *"The poet . . . never assaults the ambiguity of the word. In the poem language recovers its pristine originality, mutilated by the subjugation imposed on it by prose and everyday speech."*[24] Through parole and poetry language can proliferate, and feeding expressions of parole into discursive language - for example by introducing new and vivid metaphors - can develop into a critique of discourse, a critique of manner.

Through parole, poetry and art make sense of the clarity of the world in all its ambiguous abundance. Dance and Performance Art make sense of *bodies in motion through time and space as parole*, through world and life, in all their abundance. Through Contemporary Dance bodies in motion can reach their thresholds, approximating *Amphibian bodies in littoral landscapes* or *bodies without organs swinging between surfaces of stratification and planes of consistency.*[25] Disciplined instrumental bodies can through *de-creation* of movements and limbs proliferate, bring forward an abundance of meanings, and free themselves from instrumentality; and they do so through submitting to the harshest discipline: a paradox? No. It is through discipline we reach freedom, it is when something is internalised that we can direct, interpret and invent what we have internalised in novel fashions and styles, or rather *de-create* the instrumental reduction that broke off discipline before it reached the threshold of freedom. Again we enter the difference between style as becoming and style as manner. This we can learn *through* contemporary dance. It is through de-creation we again can reach language and body as poetry and thereby explode both language and bodies un-ambiguity into ambiguous abundance, from manner to style as becoming. *Dance* is the poetry of the body.[26]

De-creation is characterised by Simone Weil as a process where something is brought from the created to the un-created. She contrasts de-creation with destruction, which means that something is brought from being cre-

---

24 Paz *The Bow and the Lyre*, p 11

25 On Amphibians and Littoral landscapes see: Nilsson *The Amphibian Stand*, pp. 77-110, on bodies without organs see: Deleuze, Gilles & Guattari, Felix *A Thousand Plateaus*, eng. Transl. B. Massumi (Minneapolis: University of Minnesota Press), pp 149-166.

26 Paz *The Double Flame*, p 25-26.

ated into nothingness.[27] An example of de-creation is poetry. Paz states that language, in the poem, recovers its pristine originality, which is mutilated by the subjugation imposed on it from everyday speech and prose. This recovering is an act of de-creation, it is an activity that brings something from imposed un-ambiguity to emancipation in ambiguity and multiplicity, from the clear and distinct to clarity, it saves the phenomenon from a *"dreary lack of subtlety."* Truth is not what matters in de-creation, rather it is making sense and emancipation, it is hope through aestheticism or conviction through faith, as were the case with Weil. De creation enchants the world, but not necessarily in a metaphysical sense. If one stops short of faith and conviction the enchantment remains aesthetic connected to hope.

A genealogical reading, with de-creative intention, of the conceptualisation of the body might lead us to Homer, in whose work there are no unified concepts of the body, rather the body is regarded as an aggregate where the word body becomes an ambiguous in-between of the body parts highlighted in each section of the text. Paul Feyerabend writes in accordance with the body in Homer:

"The epic body [. . .] differ[s] in two ways from its successors: it is an aggregate, not a whole; and it lacks a name. (This does not mean that the human body is not conceived as a unit. However, it has the unit of an aggregate, not that of a whole which transcends and modifies its parts.)

Even functions are decentralized: the knees move or relax; the arms swiftly storm from the shoulders. A collaboration of limbs that leads to a desirable result induces a special description—no standard phrase is available for it."[28]

Compare such a body with the body Michel Foucault uncovered as a result of historical cultural and political processes. *"The soul is the effect and instrument of a political anatomy; the soul is the prison of the body."*[29] Here we have the soul as a construction, but also as something that transcend and modify the body's parts, turn them in to a unified, disciplined whole, into a manner rather than a style of becom-

---

27 Weil, Simone *Gravity and Grace*, eng. transl. E. Crawford & M. von der Ruhr (London: Routledge, 2002), pp 32-39, see also Carson Anne Decreation: Petry, Essays, Opera (New York: Vintage Books, 2006), pp 155-183.

28 Feyerabend, Paul *Conquest of Abundance: a Tale of Abstraction versus the Richness of Being*, ed. B. Terpstra (Chicago: The University of Chicago Press, 1999), p 24.

29 Foucault, Michel *Discipline and Punish: The Birth of the Prison*, eng. transl. A. Sheridan (London: Penguin Books Ltd, 1991), p 30.

ing, turning it into an artefact rather than into a work of art. It is here that the discipline of contemporary dance enters the picture. The dancer's training and discipline takes him or her beyond the constructed soul's limits. He or she views these limits as thresholds through which a de-creation of the disciplined body can start, bringing it from un-ambiguity to ambiguity, uncover the different layers of violence discursive language has imprinted on the body. Such body is not brought back to some neutral state, I doubt such state exists, and therefore de-creation always starts and ends in a point of view but it provides a possibility and shows that the realm of possibilities is not exhausted.

This means that philosophy as the art of living, if it is to be able to become - through de-creation aided by poetry and contemporary dance - it must be connected to the poetic dimension of art in general. In the art of living art enters philosophy without extinguishing philosophy; they stand in a de-creative relation to each other, negotiating where one ends and the other begins in an on-going dialectic of friction. Through the art of living philosophy can be touched by poetry[30] and become aware of language's, the embodied self's and the world's status as ambiguous 'becomings' expressed through allegories, metaphors and bodily expressions; through paroles. Poetry touches philosophical language and contemporary dance provides a poetic body. Through poetry and contemporary dance philosophy enters the continuous 'becomings' of embodied minds in space and time.

This means that the art of living includes philosophy and art, here exemplified by contemporary dance and poetry, in a de-creative dialectical relationship in friction. Contemporary dance provides the poetic bodily dimension and philosophy the reflective as chiasm or intertwined embodied minds. However, there is also another dimension central for creating oneself as one's own creature directed toward the future; *dwelling.* Martin Heidegger wrote about the relationship between building, dwelling and thinking where he means that building has dwelling as its goal, but also that building itself already is dwelling.[31] Dwelling therefore ought to be connected to architecture; it is often in and through architecture we are dwelling as human beings.[32]

30 Paz *The Bow and the Lyre*, p 4.

31 Heidegger, Martin. *Poetry, Language, Thought*, eng. transl. A. Hofstadter (New York: Perennial Classics, 2001), p 145.

32 Heidegger, *Poetry, Language, Thought*, pp 143-159.

But dwelling is ambiguous since there are multifarious styles of dwelling. This is important for the art of living since it can be said that although we create architecture in which we dwell, architecture also creates us, and if dwelling is characterised as a manner both architecture(s) and selves are more liken to artefacts than to individual artworks created through the art of living. Not all architectures are dwelling places for human beings. But if building is already dwelling, no architecture ought to escape the art of living, escape its character as parole through which an embodied mind becomes a work of art. We become through dwelling in an architecture that becomes through us, hence we can become creators and creatures in one, here not only on an individual, but also on a cultural, level.

Moreover, Heidegger wrote the essay *Poetically Man Dwells*, the title of which is taken from a late poem by Hölderlin.[33] For me to dwell poetically means to dwell in ambiguity in an in-between space which enables the becoming of self-creation of embodied minds in space and time. Through dwelling poetically the world makes sense in ambiguous clarity, in all its abundance. The in-between space of poetical dwelling is what I would call *Chora*. Says Elisabeth Grosz: *"[...] chora is that which, lacking any substance or identity of its own, falls in between the ideal and the material; it is the receptacle or nurse that brings matter into being, without being material; it nurtures the idea into its material form, without being ideal."*[34] This in-between space is metaphorically like a littoral landscape, which because of its constant transformations lacks a static identity, it is continuously becoming and in fact it is *"the only place [...] where becoming, openness to futurity, outstrips the conservational impetus to retain cohesion and unity."*[35] Therefore 'chora', as a littoral landscape is the dwelling place for individuals involved in the art of living. Such individuals I have metaphorically named amphibians[36] since amphibians are perfectly adapted for an existence in the ever-changing littoral landscape. They are not bad land animals or bad marine or lacustrine animals, on the

33 Heidegger, Martin. *Poetry, Language, Thought,* pp 209-227.

34 Grosz, Elisabeth *Architecture from the Outside: Essays on Virtual and Real Space* (Cambridge Mass.: The MIT Press, 2001), p 90.

35 Grosz, *Architecture from the Outside,* p 91, on the metaphor of the littoral landscape, see Nilsson *The Amphibian Stand*, pp 80-83.

36 Nilsson, *The Amphibian Stand*, pp 77-99.

contrary, they are perfectly adapted for the in-between-ness of littoral landscapes, which because of its ever-changing character, together with their inhabitants, can be viewed as space/time 'becomings' of future. Both the amphibians and their landscapes are characterised by an openness that *"outstrips the conservational impetus to retain cohesion and unity."*

This means that we can return to a sentence I wrote above: *"Selves then are here viewed as embodied minds, and self-creation as a practice of such an embodied mind as it is moving through time and space while creating space for its own dwelling together with other dwellers."*[37] If we unpack this sentence we will find contemporary dance and poetry and philosophy as is already stated above, but also architecture as the praxis of creating space in which we *poetically dwell if we are practising the art of living.* Therefore architecture is part of this explication of the art of living, since dwelling and creation of the space in which we dwell and through which we move as embodied minds in time is as central a part of self-creation as poetry, contemporary dance and philosophy.

Therefore, my explication of the art of living has provided us with the possibilities of three amphibians, entailing that the realm of possibilities are not exhausted. Provisionally the three amphibians are Art, Philosophy and Architecture. Art is here exemplified by the *concrete forms* of contemporary dance and poetry. This entails that this are but two possibilities of expression from art as an amphibian. There are many more possibilities, for instance painting, sculpture etc. and the same goes for the other two amphibians. However, here the amphibian creature of art has as its concrete forms of expression poetry and contemporary dance. Ideally I would have to work with concrete examples like poems and particular performances, and this I will do when the amphibians are worked out more in detail, in order to provide examples in the form of parole, which is the amphibian way of expression, rather than discourse. The concrete forms of this amphibian creature of philosophy is writing, but it could also be lectures, dialogues, seminars etc., and also a combination of one or more forms, which also goes for all amphibians. Therefore when I work out the amphibians in detail my text, as in fact also goes for this text to a certain extent,

37 See above, p. ??

will be an example of parole from the standpoint of an amphibian philosopher.

What then is the concrete form of this amphibian creature of architecture? Heidegger says that building is connected to dwelling like means to an end, so in that sense the concrete form should be building, but he also says that building already is dwelling so then it should be dwelling. However, dwelling in the form of building does not really express what I am searching for here even if it is close. Rather, the concrete form of this amphibian creature of architecture is *the creation of space for dwelling* but it could also be other forms of expression like buildings, concepts, thought structures, spatial production, etc. Still, I would say that the biggest challenge for architecture, as an amphibian involved in the art of living, is the development of spaces for dwelling in the form of littoral landscapes or 'chora', and this through dialectical friction with the concrete forms of other amphibians. Like philosophy, architecture can be touched by poetry.

Moreover I would argue that when it comes to the art of living, the three amphibians are closely related, in fact each amphibian is intertwined with the other two amphibians' concrete forms, where the focused amphibian is in between. This means that this *amphibian creature of art* is intertwined with and *in between philosophical writing and the creation of space for dwelling* and thereby, through dialectic of frictions, develops *its own concrete form*, this *amphibian creature philosophy* is intertwined with the others' concrete forms and *in between poetry, contemporary dance and the creation of space for dwelling* and thereby, through dialectic of frictions develops *its own concrete form* and *this amphibian creature of architecture* is intertwined with the others' concrete forms and *in between poetry, contemporary dance and philosophical writing* and thereby, through dialectic of frictions develops *its own concrete form, which in this case is the challenge of creating space for amphibian dwelling.*

The Art form of the Amphibian per se can be labelled the *Art of Living* and that art includes at least these three amphibians. As amphibians involved in the art of living they are not about anything, they are not sciences that have predetermined subjects be they history or nature, they are not *'about'* but *'within'*. They are revolving *'within'* the art of living, creating their selves as possibilities and thereby they demonstrate that the realm of possibility is not exhausted. //

shar[illegible] displacing, [illegible]g - albe[illegible]

"The raw awareness that you have the power to change the world is more important than any other resource. Self-determination must be established on a daily basis, by acting back on the world that acts upon you – whether that means calling in sick to work on a sunny day, starting a neighborhood garden with your friends, or toppling a government. You cannot make a revolution that distributes power equally except by learning firsthand how to exercise and share power – and that exercising and sharing, on any scale, is itself the ongoing, never-concluded project of revolution. What you do today is itself the extent of that revolution, its limits and its triumph."[1]

sharing, displacing, caring: towards an ecology of contribution

alberto altés arlandis

The optimism emanating from the opening quote, which I fundamentally share, confronts a grim landscape of universal cynicism, toxic capitalism and liberal, fake ethics. Those seem to be the reigning kings of the world we live in. Or in other words, *shit-is-fucked-up-and-bullshit*. The sentence, as found in the placards of some of the Occupy protesters, can be read in different ways. On the one hand,

1 Crimeth Inc., Recipes for Disaster, 11. Quoted in Amster, Randall (2012), *Anarchism Today*, Santa Barbara, California, Praeger.

one could see it as the epitome of modern cynicism, which Sloterdijk has famously described as "*enlightened false consciousness*"[2] ; in this case, the informed consciousness that 'shit is fucked up', i.e. things are going quite bad and everything is out of control, we are not in control – no one is in control – and those in power are 'bullshitting' us while selling out to investors. There is no way out… we can't do anything but continue expressing our cynical critique and turning our back on reality to focus on our own, already difficult, survival. On the other hand, the sentence could also be understood as the necessary denunciation of an unacceptable state of things, a loud cry that signals a profound disappointment and acts as the starting point of a search for justice, one that could thrust things towards what Simon Critchley has recently called an ethics of commitment and political resistance.[3]

It is certainly an active stance that I believe we should take, and one that avoids falling on the side of active nihilism: it is not about bringing this world down, destroying it and putting a new one in its place, but rather about transforming it radically from within. We have to imagine (and make become) another future, using the imaginative space of architecture, through the direct engagement in here-and-now situations. My suggestion is that *sharing, displacing, caring* might be important and necessary ingredients of such a demanding endeavour. In what follows below, I will try to sketch out what I mean by each of those verbs and the implications of such a *performative* approach for spatial practices.

In the second version of the '*ars industrialis*' manifesto, Bernard Stiegler describes a process through which capitalism has become structurally self-destructive, or in his own terms, toxic. The speculative logics of the system in which we live have progressively shifted to a radical short-termism that manages to dissolve all notion of responsibility. A society of carelessness is produced, according to Stiegler, in a relentless process of 'dissociation' or dismantling of society.

---

2 "*Cynicism is enlightened false consciousness. It is that modernized, unhappy consciousness, on which enlightenment has labored both successfully and in vain. It has learned its lessons in enlightenment, but it has not, and probably was not able to, put them into practice. Well-off and miserable at the same time, this consciousness no longer feels affected by any critique of ideology; its falseness is already reflexively buffered.*" Sloterdijk, Peter (1987) *Critique of Cynical Reason*, Minneapolis, University of Minnesota Press. pp. 5

3 See Critchley, Simon (2008), *Infinitely Demanding: Ethics of Commitment, Politics of Resistance*, London, New York, Verso.

In his account, the consumerist model enters into a self-destructive crisis because of its inherent need to instrumentalize desire. Desire is ultimately turned into drive, which steers both the speculator's disinvestment and the consumer's practice and sense of disposability. The manifesto says: "*Like the behaviour of the speculator—who is a capitalist who no longer invests—the behaviour of the consumer has become structurally drive-based. The consumer's relation to objects of consumption is intrinsically destructive: it is founded on disposability, that is, on disinvestment. This disinvestment liberates a drive to destruction of which the consequence—insofar as it is the destruction of fidelity to the objects of desire [...]—is the spread and the systemic and destructive articulation of the drive-based behaviour of consumers as well as speculators, and such that it engenders a kind of systemic stupidity or beastliness.*"[4]

In a society in which everything becomes waste, which Stiegler calls "*a toxic and addictogenic society*", the victims/addicts can no longer take care of themselves, less even of other things or people around them. They become absolutely and chronically irresponsible.

The manifesto continues with a plea for a renewal of the genuine impulse to "*take care of the world*", and the proposed solution is referred to as an "*economy of contribution*", an articulation of a series of conditions and procedures for exchange in/through which it is possible to care for oneself and for others again, a new economy that would therefore produce "*positive externalities*" on the basis of a fundamental re-thinking of the techniques and technologies of the digital world, that should be put to work for the construction of a new "*public thing*" or power (Chose publique).[5]

Although I find Stiegler's critique and description of the process of dissociation quite useful and compelling, and I am particularly sympathetic to the notion of contribution, I disagree with his almost exclusive focus on economy and his apparent acceptance of capitalism as a given that is here to stay. I think it is useful to recall the validity of the scientific analysis of capital car-

4 See Stiegler, Bernard (2010), Ars Industrialis Manifesto, http://arsindustrialis.org/manifesto-2010, accessed 30th of July 2013.

5 See Stiegler, Bernard (2012), Interview: from Libidinal Economy to the Ecology of Spirit, in Parrhesia 14, pp. 9-15

ried out by Marx, which tells us that any fights against capitalism must be carried out in the sphere of the political. The crucial question is therefore: Can we imagine a politics that differs radically from the demands of capital? Badiou disagrees with Stiegler regarding the sites of our endeavor: "*[T]here can be no economic battle against the economy. [...] All the efforts to construct an alternative economy strike me as pure and simple abstractions, if not simply driven by the unconscious vector of capital's own reorganization. (...) [E]very proposition that directly concerns the economy can be assimilated by capital, [...] since capital is indifferent to the qualitative configuration of things.*"[6]

Global capital is not interested in the qualities of space, but sees it merely through its potentialities for surplus. Globalization has in fact generated broken territories, it continues to fragment and disintegrate spaces, places and lands. Instead, as spatial practitioners – and as inhabitants of the world– we must be (we are) particularly interested in the qualitative potentials of space and we must therefore start by inhabiting the places in which we are intervening. We have to acknowledge the specificities of the particular locations in which we happen to develop our actions. In short, we must engage actively in 'making' sites. And when I refer to 'locations', I am not thinking of them in reference to the oppositional logics of global/local, nor as a kind of multiculturalist fascination for the exotic qualities of some or other 'different-local' that has to be protected, recuperated and/or tolerated; I am thinking about them as expanded and expansive 'sites', as localized complex assemblages of intra-acting things, people, spaces, discourses and events, that change with us as we act within them. I am thinking about them as sites of encounter.[7] The economic analyses or proposals are not enough: politics requires a demand and a location.

We have to exercise and share our power in such sites of encounter. A power that relates to other powers alike and confronts those that are hegemonic. A power that challenges and *displaces* hegemony. And we *make* such sites

6 Badiou, Alain (2001), *Ethics: An Essay on the Understanding of Evil*, London, New York, Verso. pp. 105

7 See for instance, Bourriaud, Nicholas (2002), Relational Aesthetics, pp. 21, where he says that: "*In observing contemporary artistic practices, we ought to talk of 'formations' rather than 'forms'. Unlike an object that is closed in on itself by the intervention of a style and a signature, present-day art shows that form only exists in the encounter and in the dynamic relationship enjoyed by an artistic proposition with other formations, artistic or otherwise.*"

through our presence, our interests, our care and our gaze; in and through encounters, they shift and become… alive, traversed as they are by lines and relations. A multiplicity of actors acts together in these sites. Subjects develop as subjects in their commitment to the situation, as a reaction to an emerging demand. And we are, as subjects, simultaneously distributed and bounded – our minds always extended in and through the relations we have with everything and everyone else… These sites we make are therefore necessarily relational and political. This is why I prefer to imagine and think of *a relational ecology of contribution* than to entertain alternative, albeit alienated 'economies of contribution'.

Sharing and caring are closely related, we share because we care, we care through sharing. In relationship to our 'sites' and to our spatial practices, the kind of sharing that I am imagining is not so much about material things or means, but rather about a sharing of ourselves, an openness to sharing ourselves in the situation, an openness to 'openly becoming' in the situation, i.e. letting others take part in that becoming, an openness-to-being-open. All of this sharing implies that the 'sharer' in question cares about the situation. Or as Badiou will put it, he/she is 'faithful' to the situation. For in Badiou's '*ethics of truths*', someone commits him/herself to a situation on the basis of an event that will place an (ethical) demand on him/her.[8] His, is an ethics that shifts – like we are trying to do in architecture – from the nominative to the active: the subject 'becomes' in his/her fidelity to the situation; the ethical subject is formed in the process of remaining faithful to the event. *A subject that shares.*

This subject and this ethics displace, respectively, a dominant privileging of distance and objectification that is characteristic of modernity, and a moralizing, abstract universality of a liberal ethics imposed from without. She inhabits the situation, she gets close, she cares, she gets entangled in it and with things and people with which she intra-acts and develops relations of affinity.[9] And she does that with and through her body. Equipped with her

---

8 Badiou, Alain (2001), Ethics: An Essay on the Understanding of Evil, London, New York, Verso. pp. 40

9 According to Donna Haraway, affinity is precisely not identity: "*related not by blood but by choice, the appeal of one chemical nuclear group for another, avidity.*" and "*In that sense, my kinships are about keeping the lineages going, even while defamiliarizing their members and turning lines into webs, trees into esplanades, and pedigrees into affinity groups.*" HARAWAY, Donna (2004) The Haraway Reader, New York, London, Routledge. pp. 13 and 6, respectively.

ethics of commitment, she resists the science of enlightment and objectification, because "*[t]he price of objectivity is the loss of closeness. Scientists lose the capacity to behave as neighbors of the world; they think in concepts of distance, not of friendship; they seek overviews, not neighborly involvement. Over the centuries, modern science excluded everything that was incompatible with the a priori of objectifying distance and intellectual domination over the object: intuition, empathy, spirit de finesse, aesthetics, erotics. Out of all this, however, a strong current has remained effective in genuine philosophy for ages; in it, to the present day, flows the warm current of a convivial intellectuality and a libidinous closeness to the world that compensates for the objectifying drive toward the domination of things.*"[10]

Something of this libidinous closeness to the world operates and is part of the sharing and caring that I am thinking. There is warmth, intimacy and closeness. There is a becoming that embraces an internal duration but that suspends abstract time. - *We must slow down.* - And this closeness can be seen as a form of generosity; another step towards our unfolding ecology of contribution. A generosity in which what we give is our openness, our caring and our sharing; one in which the 'gift' is not what we give but an unexpected emergence that depends on what we share, on what we contribute. Or what Rosalyn Diprose has called 'corporeal generosity': "*an openness to others that not only precedes and establishes communal relations but constitutes the self as open to otherness. Primordially, generosity is not the expenditure of one's possession but the dispossession of oneself, the being-given to others that undercuts any self-contained ego*".[11] This way of thinking generosity challenges our individualistic economy of exchange: the impulse to share and the fidelity to the encounter pre-exist the situation; generosity is in Diprose's terms "*a pre-reflective, non-volitional openness*", and as such it is entangled with our sensibilities, affectivities and bodies. It precedes and exceeds the terms of what Badiou calls 'the state of the situation', or the dispositions of normative and existing, hegemonic power.[12] It signals another opening for its potential displacement.

---

10 Sloterdijk, Peter (1987) *Critique of Cynical Reason*, Minneapolis, University of Minnesota Press. pp. 140)

11 Diprose, Rosalynd (2003) *Corporeal Generosity: On Giving with Nietzsche*, New York, State University of New York Press, pp. 4

12 The knowledges, structurings, classifications, distributions and divisions that dominate a given situation on the basis of the interests of those governing the situation is what Badiou refers to as 'the state of the situation'.

These forms of generosity, sharing and caring are interested in the radical contingency of small and not so small encounters – in fact, encounters in plural and regardless of scale – and rehearse a politics of (active) listening: one that unfolds not as a passive position but precisely as a caring attention that enables engaged response and further action. This attitude is also necessary to understand the potential for radical innovation that is forming in a situation and to mobilize it in order to transform the world.

Our situation, our relational and political site, has allowed a subject to emerge through her fidelity. Her declaration of fidelity to the situation enacts her commitment: she is now an active component of the site. And she is committed to act responsibly. Her disposition to share and to care – her generosity – allows her to develop a situated knowledge which enables her to engage in responsible actions.

This situated, formed and informed interest to participate and contribute to the situation in order to transform it meaningfully puts the subject in a privileged position: one from which it is possible to push and displace the state of that situation, challenging the established powers and normative structures that define it. From such a committed position, she questions what 'is', she cares about what could be and what ought to be. An anarchic non-acceptance of the state of the situation emerges from a caring generosity that opens up the subject's self to the situation, making her responsible again.

Situations, that are generally thought and structured on the basis of descriptions and prescriptions of 'objective knowledge', as well as through binary oppositions of the either/or kind, can be therefore questioned, activated and re-thought. Illegitimate power can be located and resisted. Alternative descriptions of the situation can be given, or invented. Objective descriptions can even be suspended. Instead, conflictive and situated conversations of a more dialogical kind can be articulated, and binary oppositions displaced by more playful, inclusive and amphibian[13] *both/and/it-depends.*

For instance, where we to randomly select a site such as that of contemporary architectural theory and practice - or else, science studies… or philosophy - with their actors, structures

13 See Nilsson, Per (2009) *The Amphibian Stand: A Philosophical Essay concerning Research Processes in Fine Art*, Umeå, H:ström, pp. 80

and hegemonic powers, we would find ourselves amidst proponents of radical autonomy on the one hand, and radical contingency on the other; in-between those who advocate a return to the critical tradition, or those who claim the new religion must be projective and post-critical; those who are convinced we should operate from within, and those who think we should remain pure and purely outside; those who will fight for radical difference, and those who will cry for equality; those who might "*dry out and die on the high ground of a dogmatic certainty of absolute (linguistic) knowledge, or drown in the sea of skeptic (unjustified praxis-oriented) relativism*".[14]

Instead, I would rather choose to keep a degree of independence, autonomy and freedom while simultaneously acknowledging and caring about the contingencies of the smallest details and encounters, just as I would prefer to work from within but entertain various 'distractions' that could bring me into 'moments of outsider-ness' and perhaps an unplanned critical distance, very helpful in practices of documentation and judgment. Discourses of radical difference can be enriched and expanded through serious engagement with the notion of *the Same*; the so-called projective practices in architecture run the risk of devolving into "*the merely pragmatic, and to the merely decorative, with astonishing speed*"[15], unless they develop alternative or parallel models of critical assessment and engagement, and furthermore, both critical and projective are to remain extraneous and incidental unless they embrace the embodied and active registers of the performative, expanding their knowledges, fields of practice and abilities to make/sense. It is possible to imagine '*amphibian creatures*'[16] whose practical and situated knowledge can not only adapt to the liminal landscapes that emerge in and around these combinations, but are formed and developed precisely in the multiplicities of these encounters.

This amphibian creature, like our situated and faithful subject, creates herself through her movement/practice, along the lines of relations and through '*littoral landscapes*'[17], and in the unex-

14 Nilsson, Per (2009) Ibid, pp. 80

15 Baird, George (2004) Criticality and Its Discontents, in Harvard Design Magazine 21.

16 Nilsson, Per (2009) Ibid, pp. 80

17 Nilsson, Per (2009) Ibid, pp. 81

pected energies of encounters, gifts, and events. Nevertheless, she has to create herself with others. While she inhabits the situation, she dwells. She necessarily co-exists.

"*Self and Other complement and complete one another. There is no Absolute Category, no Ego, no Society – but only a chaotically complex web of relation – and the 'Strange Attractor', attraction itself, which evokes resonances and patterns in the flow of becoming.*"[18]

A tension emerges here between self-creation and dwelling, between an individual process of becoming and a necessarily collective co-existence or dwelling-together-with-others. An ecology of contribution might be a non-oppositional, amphibian way of managing such a tension, something that we could think through contemporary developments within anarchism pointing towards existential or ontological anarchy, as the creative construction of an entire art of living, or the deployment of poetic imagination in everyday life: "*[A] condition of free creativity generated through motility and revolt, can only be conceived and realised by the poetic imagination and, as far as words are concerned, can only find expression in poetic language.*"[19]

The 'contributors' participate in their ecology on the basis of their individual and faithful commitment to a situation, one in which they are genuinely interested. They contribute as part of their own subjective development and only in as long as they continue to be interested. *Contributing as becoming.* Yet, contributing is also a part of something else that emerges out of the interplays of all contributions. This something else cannot be fully determined a priori, nor can it be fully controlled. It is born out of the relations and free-flowing contributions, and it exceeds the powers, expectations and possibilities of those who contribute. This something else is only possible through the real time articulation of the contributions, displacements and care shared by the subjects that take part.

It is not an individual that forces others to adapt, nor a collective that forces the individual into forms of co-habitation, but an ever-shifting balance based on sharing, displacing and caring in which contribution is the active register. *Contribution as performative.*

---

18 Bey, Hakim (1994), 'Ontological anarchy in a nutshell' in Immediatism, Edinburgh: AK Press, pp. 3

19 Moore, John (2004), Lived Poetry: Stirner, Anarchy, Subjectivity and the Art of Living, in Purkis, Jonathan (2004) Changing Anarchism: Anarchist Theory and Practice in a Global Age, Manchester University Press. pp. 57

Besides being performative, I believe that contribution is necessarily fragile. Even more, it must endure its fragility. There is something fragile about the fact that it all depends on the individual contributions, something that cannot be guaranteed. Yet, this lack of guarantee, this fragility, can only be dealt with or eliminated through the setting up and deployment of various mechanisms of power and control. It is only in its fragile uncertainty that contribution remains a free-flowing ecology. Fragility is its power. A different power.

A power that resists and challenges traditional, managed and administered power, by means of distributed, emergent and partial ownerships, contributions and dispositions – by means of a resilient fidelity that is capable of locating and resisting the diverse forms of corruption and wear that can threaten the continuity of an 'evental' site.

An ethics of encounter is not a universal ethics, a totality or a frozen set of moral principles that steers our behavior, but a passion for reality, a fidelity to the encounter as a situation, as a site, as an event. The ethical demand raised is precisely to stick to the encounter, to care about the meeting. To endure.

As I have started to sketch here, such an ethics could emerge from the articulation of sharing, displacing and caring; respectively understood as a sharing of oneself in the situation and with others; as an ability and a force that pushes the state of things an questions what 'is' by focusing on what could be and what ought to be; and as a fidelity to the situation, a persistence and a willingness to stay put and to care about the things that matter. Imagining such an emergence might seem again too multiple a desire, but all the terms are necessary if difficult or dangerous. We must embrace the logics of *both/and/in-different-ways* to become simultaneously 'of-the-world' and critical; situated, grounded and in constant movement: "*So, I think my problem, and "our' problem, is how to have simultaneously an account of radical historical contingency for all knowledge claims and knowing subjects, a critical practice for recognizing our own "semiotic technologies" for making meanings, and a no-nonsense commitment to faithful accounts of a "real" world, one that can be partially shared and that is friendly to earthwide projects of finite freedom, adequate material abundance, modest meaning in suffering, and limited happiness.*"[20]

---

20 Haraway, Donna (1988). "*Situated Knowledges: The Science Question in Feminism and the Privilege of Partial Perspective*", in Feminist Studies Vol. 14, No. 3. pp. 579

Enduring fidelity, enduring the encounter, enduring fragility. Or in other words, a special kind of stubborn persistence: “*[...] it will be I, it will be the silence, where I am, I don’t know, I’ll never know, in the silence you don’t know, you must go on, I can’t go on, I’will go on.*”[21] //

21 Beckett, Samuel (1959) *The Unnamable* London, 2010: Faber and Faber, pp. 154

contributors

contributors

Editors

Alberto Altés Arlandis is a registered architect, a researcher and a Lecturer at Umeå School of Architecture. He studied architecture in Valladolid, Barcelona and Delft, and is currently working on a PhD dissertation entitled "*Dissenting City Narratives: Interplays of Space, Film and Politics*". His work interrogates the loss of critical and utopian impetus in architecture and explores the possibilities of the moving image as an apparatus of spatial critique and encounter. Together with Oren Lieberman he directs the "*Laboratory of Immediate Architectural Intervention*" at Umeå School of Architecture exploring and making architecture as a relational, political, social and ethical practice that unfolds in the making of the world in/through intraventions.

Oren Lieberman is Professor of Architecture and Dean of the Faculty of Art and Design at the Arts University Bournemouth and a Guest Professor at Umeå School of Architecture, where, with Alberto Altés, he coordinates the "*Laboratory of Immediate Architectural Intervention*". He has a BA in philosophy and psychology, and a MArch from SCI-ARC. His work focuses on performative practices which entangle knowledge, methodologies and techniques from various disciplines, including architecture, performance, geography, anthropology, and sociology. He is interested in how architecture's processes of relational/contingent production participate in the construction of political practices and the establishment of the 'common'.

Guest Contributors

Francesco Apuzzo was born in Naples, (Italy) in 1972, he studied Architecture in Berlin (TU Berlin) where he graduated with a Diploma (Masters) in 2003. He was awarded the DCI Prize for Best Diplom Thesis. He has been in practicing partnership with Axel Timm since 2004 and a member of raumlaborberlin since 2005.

Karin Berggren is an architect and researcher. She studied architecture in Barcelona and Göteborg, and graduated from the master's program 'Design for Sustainable Development' at Chalmers School of Architecture. Her master's thesis resulted in a book entitled '*Stories, Images and Architectures: Real and Fictional Account of the Fabrication of the Swedish Suburbs*' dealing with the problems around the media image of stigmatized Swedish suburbs. She is currently involved in research related to housing segregation and the developments in Swedish post-war mass housing areas.

Antonio Collados Alcaide is Doctor of Fine Arts at the University of Granada (2012) with a PhD on collaborative art practices and critical spatiality. Researcher and Professor in the Department of Sculpture at the University of Granada. He is the co-founder of 'Aulabierta', and other independent cultural initiatives in the city of Granada such as 'TRN-Transborder Artistic Laboratory'. He coordinates with Javier Rodrigo the cultural-research project 'Transducers'. He has edited and contributed to numerous publications and national and international research projects about cultural policy, artistic practice and collaborative artistic and educational processes in public space.

Hélène Frichot, PhD, is a researcher and teacher in Critical Studies in Architecture at the School of Architecture and the Built Environment, KTH, Stockholm. She has co-curated the Architecture+Philosophy public lecture series in Melbourne, Australia since 2005. Between 2004-2011 she held an academic position in the School of Architecture and Design, RMIT University. Her research examines the transdisciplinary field between architecture and philosophy (while her first discipline is architecture, she holds a PhD in philosophy from the University of Sydney, 2004). Hélène's published research has ranged widely from commentary on the ethico-aesthetics of contemporary digital architecture operating within the new biotechnological paradigm, to the role of emerging participatory and relational practices in the arts, including critical, creative, and feminist spatial practices. She considers architecture-writing to be her mode of practice.

Susan Kelly, PhD, is a Lecturer in Fine Art at Goldsmiths College, London. Her research looks at relationships between art and micropolitics, rhetoric and practices of organisation in situations where questions are asked and answers are given. She makes performances, public time-based work, installations and videos, she writes and publishes and convenes events and performative investigations. She works both independently and collectively with the Micropolitics Research Group and the Carrot Workers Collective among others. Over the last nine years she has shown her work in Belfast, New York, Toronto, Helsinki, Prague, Dublin, St Petersburg, Krasnoyarsk, Tallin, Zagreb, and elsewhere.

Peter Kjaer is a Danish architect. He was the rector in Aarhus School of Architecture from 1998 to 2005, where he was later the Head of the Department from 2006 to 2009. More recently he has been part of the founding and development of Umeå School of Architecture, where he has also been the rector from 2008 to 2013, positioning the school where it is today. He is also a member of the steering board of "aarhus arkitekterne" and AHO. Presently he is the artistic director of "Open_Architecture".

Per Nilsson is a philosopher, Associate Professor and Vice-Dean at the Academy of Fine Arts, Umeå University, Sweden. He obtained his PhD in Philosophy in 2001 at the department of Philosophy at Umeå University. In 2009 he published "The Amphibian Stand: A Philosophical Essay Concerning Research Processes in Fine Art" (Umeå: h:ström Text-Kultur, 2009) a book in which he starts developing some of the concepts that he is still using in his ongoing research and work on the Philosophies of Art. Since 2012 he leads the research project "Amphibian Decreations in Choreography and Philosophy", which he develops together with the choreographer Björn Säfsten and the dancers Anja Arquist and Sophie Augot.

Javier Rodrigo Montero is an art educator and researcher. Coordinator of the cultural and pedagogical project *'Transductores'* in all its different international venues: Granada, Medellín, Quit. He has lectured and coordinated workshops in different universities, cultural centers and MA's internationally (Spain, Costa Rica, Brazil, Ecuador, Colombia, EEUU). Editor and writer of '*Desacuerdos6*', '*Dialogical practices*' and the two volumes of 'Transductores', as well as author of various articles and book chapters on cultural practices, collective pedagogies and political interventions. He is also a community worker in several projects about youth action research, critical mediation in museums and collective production. Partner with institutions like Museo Nacional Reina Sofia, MACBA, Fundació Pilar i Joan Miro, etc, Javier likes biking, slow food and overall slower politics and education.

Aida Sánchez de Serdio Martín is lecturer at the Fine Arts Faculty of the University of Barcelona. Her fields of specialisation are Visual Culture, Collaborative Art Practices, Arts Education, and Cultural Politics. She is coordinator and lecturer of the MA in Visual Arts and Education of the University of Barcelona. She is also member of the research group *'Esbrina, Contemporary Subjectivities and Learning Environments'* at the University of Barcelona. Besides her work at the University she has collaborated with several cultural institutions and organizations such as *La Virreina Centre de la Imatge*, *Transducers*, or *Artibarri*.

Axel Timm was born in Hannover in 1973, he studied Architecture in Berlin (TU Berlin), where he graduated with a Diploma (Masters) in 2004. From 2003 to 2005 he was a member of the board of *Kunstfabrik am Flutgraben e.V.* Since 2005 he has been head of "Autotrans Ltd.", a society for artistic production and studio administration. During the period 2010-2011 he taught at the FH Dortmund as Guest Professor. He has been in practicing partnership with Francesco Apuzzo since 2004 and a member of raumlaborberlin since 2005.

Roemer van Toorn is Theory and Media Professor at the Umeå School of Architecture, Sweden. From 1993 till 2010 he was in charge of the History and Theory program, and was Head of publications at the Berlage Institute (NL). He was guest lecturer at the Delft School of Design (NL), while at the same time pursuing a career as international lecturer. He has been the editor of the annual publication Architecture in the Netherlands, as well as an advisor of the magazines *Volume, Hunch, Domus* and *Abitare*. As author and photographer he contributes to many publications. In 1994 he published '*The Invisible in Architecture*' in collaboration with Ole Bouman. His photography has been exhibited in Winnipeg, Los Angeles and was part of the exhibition '*Cities on the Move*' curated by Hou Hanru and Hans-Ulrich Obrist. Forthcoming is his photobook '*The Society of The And*', which includes his own texts and articles by Stefano Boeri and Bart Lootsma. www.roemervantoorn.com

contributors

LiAi Directors
Oren Lieberman, Alberto Altés Arlandis

LiAi Part-Time Faculty
Sepideh Karami, Miguel Angel Rosique Valverde, Esther Escribano Rivera

LiAi Guest Faculty
Isaac Marrero-Guillamón (Birkbeck, London), Israel Casanovas (ETSAV, Barcelona), Roger Tudó and Claudi Aguiló (HARQUITECTES and dataAE, Barcelona), Susan Kelly (Goldsmiths, London), Joan Vila-Puig and Elvira Pujol (Sitesize, Barcelona), Aida Sánchez de Serdio (UB, Barcelona), Per Nilsson (Konsthögskolan Umeå), Javier Rodrigo (Transducers, Spain), Francesco Apuzzo and Axel Timm (Raumlabor, Berlin), Linda Stoian Cassens (Swiss Architecture Museum), Roland Spolander (Konsthögskolan Umeå), Jon Goodbun (University of Westminster, UK), Tim Ingold (University of Aberdeen), Jeremy Till (Central Saint Martins, London, UK, Roemer van Toorn (UMA, Umeå)

LiAi Students

Kimberley Beauprez, Veronica Gerini, Erika Henriksson, Maria Hudl, Paula Idun, Christina Kousgaard Martin Livian, Johan Marklund, Anna Misharina, Olga Oreshkina, Febe Roels, Kirstine Skyum, Audingas Sumskas, Sofia Sjölin, Tobias Westerlund.

image credits

p. 018: *"Agbar Tower across a site in the heart of Poblenou's 22@"*- LiAi Fieldtrip / Photo: Alberto Altés
p. 022: *"Kids playing in the streets of Istanbul's Tarlabasi"*- LiAi Fieldtrip / Photo: Alberto Altés
p. 027: *"A displaced building 'parked' in central Umeå"*- LiAi In Our Own Backyard / Photo: Erika Henriksson
p. 028: "*Flyttblock:* Elevated Encounter" B&W- LiAi In Our Own Backyard / Photo: LiAi Files
p. 034: *"Flyttblock: Fire and Projection 1"* - LiAi In Our Own Backyard / Photo: Axel Timn & FrancescoApuzzo
p. 042: *"Pushing Together"*- LiAi Workshop with Sitesize / Photo: Alberto Altés
p. 046: "*Flyttblock:* Digging it Out" - LiAi In Our Own Backyard / Photo: Alberto Altés
p. 050: "*Flyttblock:* Carrying" - LiAi Workshop with raumlabor / Photo: Olga Oreshkina
p. 051: "*Flyttblock:* Three in the Fog" - LiAi In Our Own Backyard / Photo: Olga Oreshkina
p. 052: "*Flyttblock:* Celebrating the First One" - LiAi Workshop with raumlabor / Photo: Olga Oreshkina
p. 053: "*Flyttblock:* Balcony Encounter" Color - LiAi Workshop with raumlabor / Photo: LiAi Files
p. 054: "*Flyttblock:* Drawings" - LiAi Workshop with raumlabor / Drawings: Olga Oreshkina
p. 055: "*Flyttblock:* People Taking Them" - Spring in Umeå / Photo: Alberto Altés
p. 056: "*Flyttblock:* LiAi Exhibition at Bildmuseet" - LiAi Year 1 / Photo: Alberto Altés

p. 057: From left to right and from top to bottom:
"Flyttblock 2.0 on the ground" - LiAi Warm-Up Workshop / Photo: Alberto Altés
"Flyttblock 2.0 Reconstituted" - LiAi Warm-Up Workshop / Photo: Alberto Altés
"Flyttblock Winter Square" - Umeå Art Campus / Photo: Anna Misharina
"Flyttblock Transported" - LiAi In Our Own Backyard / Photo: Alberto Altés
"Flyttblock: On the Road" - LiAi In Our Own Backyard / Photo: Christina Kousgaard
"Flyttblock: Transported through the Snow" - LiAi In Our Own Backyard / Photo: Olga Oreshkina
"Flyttblock 2.0 Building Performance" - LiAi Exhibition at Bildmuseet / Photo: Alberto Altés
"Small *Flyttblock Under Construction*" - LiAi Exhibition at Bildmuseet / Photo: Alberto Altés
"Flyttblock Roundtable" - LiAi Exhibition at Bildmuseet / Photo: Alberto Altés

p. 058: "*Flyttblock:* Three by the River" - LiAi In Our Own Backyard / Photo: Olga Oreshkina
p. 060: "*Flyttblock:* Third One Carried" - LiAi Workshop with raumlabor / Photo: Olga Oreshkina
p. 062: *"Flyttblock: Projection and Talks"* - LiAi In Our Own Backyard / Photo: Axel Timn & FrancescoApuzzo
p. 064: *"Imminent Evictions: Istanbul's Fikirtepe-Kadiköy"*- LiAi Fieldtrip / Photo: Alberto Altés

p. 078 - 207: Work produced at the LiAi / Photos by the authors of the work unless otherwise stated

image credits

p. 208 - 209: *"Flyttblock 2.0 Building Performance"* - LiAi Exhibition at Bildmuseet / Photo: Alberto Altés
p. 210: *"Flyttblock 2.0 Under Construction"* - LiAi Exhibition at Bildmuseet / Photo: Alberto Altés
p. 211: *"LiAi Exhibition Space"* - LiAi Exhibition at Bildmuseet / Photo: Alberto Altés
p. 212: *"Walter Unterrainer at one of the LiAi Roundtables"* - LiAi Exhibition at Bildmuseet / Photo: Alberto Altés
p. 213: *"Lida Dances on Red"* - LiAi Exhibition at Bildmuseet / Photo: Alberto Altés
p. 214-215: *"LiAi Roundtable Discussion"* - LiAi Exhibition at Bildmuseet / Photos: LiAi Files
p. 216-217: *"Fair City Project Explorations"* - LiAi In Our Own Backyard / Photos: LiAi Students
p. 218-221: *"Fair City Project/Pavilion Drawings"* - LiAi In Our Own Backyard / Drawings: LiAi Students

p. 222: From left to right and from top to bottom:
"Fair City Project Exhibition at Umeå School of Architecture: CLT Panels" - LiAi / Photo: Alberto Altés
"Fair City Project Workshop with Roger Tudó and Claudi Aguiló" - LiAi / Photo: Alberto Altés
"Fair City Project Exhibition at Umeå School of Architecture: Hanging Prints" - LiAi / Photo: Alberto Altés

p. 223: From left to right and from top to bottom:
"Fair City Project Exhibition at Umeå School of Architecture: 1:20 Model 1" - LiAi / Photo: Alberto Altés
"Fair City Project Exhibition at Umeå School of Architecture: 1:20 Model 2" - LiAi / Photo: Alberto Altés
"Fair City Project Exhibition at Umeå School of Architecture: 1:20 Model 3" - LiAi / Photo: Alberto Altés

p. 224: *"Performance on the Snow: Making 1"* - UMA/LiAi Lecture Series / Photo: Tobias Westerlund
p. 225: *"Performance on the Snow: Making 2"* - UMA/LiAi Lecture Series / Photo: Tobias Westerlund

p. 228: *"Can Batlló-Barcelona"* - LiAi Fieldtrip / Photo: Alberto Altés
p. 239: *"SuccessCarrot=Fuck Everyone Else"* - Fund Our Future Demo / Photo: CarrotWorkers' Collective
p. 242: *"Umeå Under Construction"* - LiAi In Our Own Backyard / Photo: Olga Oreshkina
p. 245: *"Pedagogical Camp at MDE11: Enseñar y Aprender"* - Medellín, Colombia / Photo: Transductores
p. 250: *"At the Edge of the River"* - LiAi Workshop with Aida Sánchez de Serdio / Photo: Erika Henriksson
p. 253: *"Postcards"* - LiAi Workshop with Aida Sánchez de Serdio / Photo: Maria Hudl & Febe Roels
p. 255: *"Texts"* - LiAi Workshop with Aida Sánchez de Serdio / Photo: Maria Hudl & Febe Roels
p. 258: *"After the Fire"* - Around Tahrir Square, Cairo / Photo: Alberto Altés
p. 272: *"Rolling Forward"* - Manshiyat Naser, Mokattam, Cairo / Photo: Alberto Altés

This page intentionally left blank

!